I0198515

The Poetry and Prose of Wang Wei
Volume I

Library of Chinese Humanities

The Poetry and Prose of Wang Wei

Volume I

Translated by Paul Rouzer

Volume edited by Christopher M. B. Nugent

De Gruyter

This book was prepared with the support of the Andrew W. Mellon Foundation.

ISBN 978-1-5015-1600-9
e-ISBN (PDF) 978-1-5015-1602-3
e-ISBN (EPUB) 978-1-5015-0759-5
ISSN 2199-966X

Library of Congress Control Number: 2020930402

Bibliografische Information published by the Deutsche Nationalbibliothek
The Deutsche Nationalbibliothek lists this publication in the Deutsche Nationalbibliografie; detailed bibliographic data are available in the Internet at http://dnb.dnb.de.

Typesetting: Meta Systems Publishing & Printservices GmbH, Wustermark
Printing and binding: CPI books GmbH, Leck

www.degruyter.com

Table of Contents

Juan 3: Old-style poems (王右丞集卷之三 古詩)

Juan 4: Old style poems (王右丞集卷之四 古詩)

Juan 5: Old style poems (王右丞集卷之五 古詩)

Juan 6: Old style poems (王右丞集卷之六 古詩)

Juan 7: Recent style poems (王右丞集卷之七 近體詩)

Juan 8: Recent style poems (王右丞集卷之八 近體詩)

Juan 9: Recent style poems (王右丞集卷之九 近體詩)

Juan 10: Recent style poems (王右丞集卷之十 近體詩)

Introduction

Wang Wei (701–61) is one of a very small group of Chinese poets whose fame can be said to be truly international. Along with Li Bo 李白 (701–62), Du Fu 杜甫 (713–70), and Tao Qian 陶潛 (365–427), he defines what Chinese poetry essentially is to readers around the world. Moreover, his verse has come to epitomize in global terms (for better or ill) what a Chinese representation of nature looks like – often a reclusive gentleman sitting in a thatched hut nestled in a mountain nook or a pine grove, playing his zither, reading his books, and observing the beauties of the season pass before him. For many, his poems seem precise visualizations of traditional Chinese landscape painting. No wonder, then, that critics within China and without are quick to connect his verse to his paintings (though few if any of his artworks survive in anything other than copies). And rarely do people fail to quote the prominent literatus Su Shi's 蘇軾 (1037–1101) comment on him: "When you savor a poem by Wang Wei, there is a painting within; and when you behold a painting by Wang Wei, there is a poem within."[1] Yet there is a good bit more to Wang Wei than this picturesque quality, even if most selections of his verse tend to downplay his considerable poetic range. This complete translation should help to broaden our vision of who Wang Wei was exactly, and the scope of his talents.

Active during the so-called "High Tang" (roughly the reign of Emperor Xuanzong 玄宗, 712–756), Wang Wei helped define the art of poetry during its cultural high water mark, along with his great contemporaries Li Bo and Du Fu. One could argue that his work was more pervasively influential than that of either Li or Du: unlike Li, Wang was not an eccentric with a powerful poetic persona stamped on almost every line he wrote; and, unlike Du, Wang was immediately successful while still alive and was widely read from the 730s on. This meant that Wang was perceived as a more imitable model for the poetry of social interaction. For every poet who aspired to the greatness of Li or Du, there

1 味摩詰之詩。詩中有畫。觀摩詰之畫。畫中有詩。 From a painting colophon, "Written on a painting by Wang Wei: 'Misty Rain on Lantian'" 書摩詰藍天煙雨.

https://doi.org/10.1515/9781501516023-203

were a thousand literati who wanted to write competent poems to commemorate moments of their lives spent with friends or to impress their superiors. Wang Wei helped provide them a template. This can be seen already in the decades after the death of Xuanzong; during the Dali 大曆 era (766–780), poets like Qian Qi 錢起 and Liu Changqing 劉長卿 perfected Wang Wei's regulated verse and turned it into a general style. Jia Dao 賈島 refined it further, giving it some late-Tang tweaks; and with that, the model for mass-produced quatrains and octets of East Asian poetry over the next millennium was created.

This is not to say that Wang Wei's work is bland or mediocre. Critics recognized from the beginning that he was a master poet; and that while the general poetic rhetoric of his work was imitable, he wielded that rhetoric with a skill that was unsurpassed. Most traditional poetic criticism in China occurs in the form of "poetry talks" (*shihua* 詩話), collections of comments from prominent literati. They have tended to pair Wang Wei with other High Tang contemporaries, usually Meng Haoran 孟浩然 (691–740) and Wei Yingwu 韋應物 (737?–ca. 792), and have attempted to capture his style in distinctive descriptive phrases. They did not always view him uncritically, especially during the Song, but Wang was always one of the touchstones for what High Tang poetry (and poetry in general) was supposed to do. By the Ming, when the preference for High Tang style was largely dictating critical tastes, his place as a canonical master was assured. One trait that continued to make him a source of admiration was his ability to break the tendency of other great Tang poets to favor one particular genre over another; critics acknowledged that he could produce examples of very high quality in every available form: long *yuefu* ballads, short *yuefu* quatrains, epigrammatic quatrains, regulated verse poems in seven or five lines, old-style epistle poems, and elegant *pailü*. Of course, the fact that he could do so also made him a little problematic: he could compose great *yuefu* comparable with Li Bo's, though still not quite as masterful as his; similarly, his regulated verse could compete with Du Fu's while never surpassing him. And the fact that he was so seemingly chimeric and adaptable perhaps made him a little suspect among those late imperial and modern readers who held self-expression as the most important aspect of poetics.

In more recent times we have seen the gradual development of a sort of conceptual canon of Wang Wei poems that has proved influential among modern readers. The outsized impact of the eighteenth-century anthology *Three Hundred Tang Poems* (*Tang shi san bai shou* 唐詩三百首) on modern pedagogy helped set that taste: Wang is represented by twenty-nine poems there (in comparison, Li Bo has twenty-seven – though many of them quite long – and Du Fu has thirty-six).[2] Though a dozen or so other poems are often added to this "canon," depending on individual preferences, we have here the Wang Wei verses that most readers educated in the East Asian literary tradition know. This canon has been affected in turn by certain concerns and issues connected to the globalization of literature. The popularity of English romantic-era poetry among twentieth-century Chinese intellectuals helped create the category of "nature poetry" in the Chinese context, and Wang Wei was seen as an exemplar of that cross-cultural genre. Meanwhile in the United States the countercultural tendencies that produced American Buddhism wanted to see Wang Wei as a Zen poet who concealed transcendent wisdom within his imagery. The fact that many of the canonical Wang Wei poems came relatively free of cultural baggage (historical and literary allusions, culture-specific concerns and rhetoric) also helped with this Western popularity, especially among poet-translators. As a result, he is one of the most frequently translated of Chinese poets.

Obtaining a deeper understanding of Wang Wei – one that transcends the impressions provided by the anthology pieces – requires a reading of all 371 poems that can be reliably attributed to him. Hence the advantage of having a complete translation. What do we learn about Wang Wei from doing this? In the comments that follow, I make some suggestions that may prove useful in reading him in a more comprehensive way.

The complete poet

Much of the scholarship on Wang Wei is focused on relating his poetry to his life; so the first question we might ask is: does reading the com-

2 Here is a list of Wang's poems anthologized in The *Three Hundred*: 3.5, 3.7, 3.11, 3.23, 4.7, 5.10, 6.5, 6.7, 6.8, 7.12, 7.16, 7.18, 7.19, 7.23, 7.34, 8.19, 8.29, 10.1, 10.5, 10.9, 10.14, 13.14, 13.26, 13.31, 13.43, 14.14, 14.19, 15.16, 15.36 (of doubtful attribution).

plete poems provide a biographical framework for understanding the poet's development and aesthetic preoccupations? Unfortunately, reliable biographical detail is scarce, and the handful of significant moments in his life that are available to us can be summarized briefly. Wang Wei was born in 701, a member of the powerful Wang clan of Taiyuan, though his immediate forbears were only moderately successful office-holders. He soon gained a reputation for precocity and befriended princes of the royal blood while still a teenager. He passed the *jinshi* examination in 721, and this initiated his official career. Over the course of his life, he held increasingly important (but not major) offices until his death in 761. During those forty years, a number of events stand out:

1. In 721, shortly after earning the *jinshi* degree, he offended his superiors (for reasons that are not entirely clear) and was exiled to a minor post in Jizhou in Shandong. There he remained until 726.
2. He eventually received the patronage of the chief minister Zhang Jiuling 張九齡; after Zhang fell from power in 737, Wang received the support of Zhang's enemy Li Linfu 李林甫 as well. In 737, Wang was sent as an Investigating Censor to assist the military governor Cui Xiyi 崔希逸 on the northwestern frontier at Liangzhou 涼州. He returned to the capital of Chang'an after Cui's death the following year.
3. When he was appointed Palace Censor in 740, he was sent to the south to supervise official selections in the provinces. This resulted in a year of traveling.
4. Sometime in the 740s he acquired an estate at Wangchuan 輞川 (Wang Stream) at Lantian 藍田 in the Zhongnan mountain range south of the capital. The estate provided a rural retreat for the poet, and he probably divided his time between retirement there and his court duties in the capital.
5. When the An Lushan rebellion broke out, Wang Wei was captured by rebel troops in 756. When Wang faked an illness in order to avoid being pressed into the rebel administration, An Lushan sent him as a prisoner to Luoyang. Eventually Wang took up a post under duress. When he was captured in turn by the loyalists in 757, he was imprisoned once more and threatened with punishment; but the intercession of his younger brother Wang Jin 縉 and the surfacing of two poems he claimed to have written during the

rebel occupation that suggested his continuing loyalty to the emperor led to his pardon. He resumed official office and was promoted several times before his death, eventually achieving the office of Assistant Director of the Right (右丞 *youcheng*) in the Department of State Affairs. As a result, he is often referred to in later times as Wang Youcheng.

6. After his death, the emperor Daizong 代宗 (r. 762–779) expressed his admiration for Wang Wei and requested his brother, Wang Jin (then serving as Chief Minister) to submit a copy of his works. Jin told him probably only one of ten poems still survived; he then made inquiries among Wang's friends and associates and compiled the first collection of his work. He submitted it to the emperor, who then deposited it in the imperial library.

These specific events allow for the dating of a certain fraction of Wang Wei's surviving poems. Beyond that, scholars can determine date of composition in many cases through other clues connected to the various offices held by Wang Wei and by the friends and associates mentioned in his verse. Nonetheless, a systematic chronological ordering of Wang Wei's poetry is still largely speculative, and many poems cannot be dated at all. Consequently, we cannot create a coherent "literary biography" of the poet in which life events can help serve as a frame for discussing stylistic developments in the poetry – a strategy that tends to dominate Du Fu scholarship, for example. But even if we had more biographical detail, it is doubtful that Wang Wei's corpus would permit such a reading. Unlike Du Fu, Wang Wei spent most of his life as a courtier in the capital, and his verse does not convey the same sense of confession and revelation that is found in Du. In fact, Wang Wei might be termed the last great "medieval" poet of the Chinese tradition. The speaking self in his verse consists of a matrix of social contexts and relationships; who Wang Wei "is" in any particular poem is largely a product of whom he is addressing and the situation in which he is composing. He would not have seen this variability as hypocritical, or as the mere projection of an assumed persona, however: any temporarily held position would be perfectly valid for the moment. This may help explain why he was one of the most versatile poets of the Tang, equally comfortable writing paeans to the emperor, Confucian critiques of policy, celebrations of the rural recluse, descriptions of Daoist Transcendents, and militaristic frontier ballads. Though evidence suggests that he was most concerned with Buddhist principles (more on this below), he certainly felt no discomfort entering into other modes of life experience. This variety is particularly evident when we read all of the poetry, not just the group of nature poems that tend to attract modern attention and which gives us the illusion of a coherent poetic personality in the modern sense.

In fact, this social aspect needs to be placed at the center of any discussion. When we divide his poetry up by thematic categories, as modern critics often do ("nature poetry," "Buddhist poetry," "court poetry," "reclusion poetry," etc.), we tend to ignore the fact that Wang wrote with an immediate audience in mind and that almost every verse was meant to ornament a social occasion of some sort, from the highly formal to the intimate. He does not use the social moment as an excuse to express himself and his intellectual and aesthetic concerns; rather, he deploys these concerns in ways to ornament the poem and make it more effective as a form of communication that assists in the maintenance of public and private relationships.

The most attractive aspect of this sociality is the way that it commemorates and celebrates friendship. Most famously, there was the poet's close relationship with Pei Di (about whom we know little other than what these shared texts tell us).[3] But there are many friends in Wang Wei's verse, and when he speaks to these friends, he relies on a wide variety of themes, tropes, and rhetorical devices:

Happy that Zu Three has come to spend the night

Before my gate, a guest from Luoyang
Dismounts and brushes off his traveling clothes.
An old friend's carriage does not come in vain,
Though in the course of my life I've often shut my door.
Strollers return to their secluded lanes,
And accumulated snow bears the lingering sunlight.

---

3 Compositions that reference Pei Di or are authored by him in this collection: 2.9; 2.28; 7.16; 7.29; 7.31a; 7.32a; 9.5; 10.11; 10.16; 10.16a; 11.24b; 11.24c; 13.1; 13.1a; 13.3; 13.10–29; 13.33a; 13.41; 14.17c; 14.26; 18.6.

You're a bosom friend from our earliest years –
So where else could your lofty carriage find refuge? (7.13)

The Wang Wei touch here is the sensitive, "painterly" evocation of bucolic calm in the third couplet. But it is placed here not out of a desire to portray Nature as such but rather as an evocation of mood, a background to the pleasure of two friends sharing an evening together.

One could write a good bit about the way that shared experiences and comradeship are expressed in Wang Wei's verse – writing as he did to a male elite with an education and career goals in common, he could easily articulate their concerns in a variety of modes. Perhaps one largely ignored mode is humor; there are a substantial number of poems that indulge in gentle satire. In "Presented to an Official from Wu," for example, he sympathizes with (but also teases) an official from southeast China put off by the climate and cuisine of Chang'an:

The Chang'an guest-house is boiling hot
With no tea-infused congee to mitigate the heat.
In vain you wave your white fan – this is the Truth of Suffering;
You wish to take your blue book bag and head back home.
The shipment of salted carp from your river home doesn't arrive;
How could you tolerate the noodle soup of these Qin people?
"I'd rather let myself wander free,
Go shrimping in straw sandals on a Fuchun River islet." (6.17)

To ignore this social aspect of Wang Wei's verse and to treat him as a "serious poet" in the modern sense – an artist struggling to capture the nature of the self and the world in order to fulfill some internalized compulsion – results in a thorough misreading.

The social aspect of Wang's verse also accounts for his taste for sophisticated parallelism that he inherited from the court poetry tradition of the Southern Dynasties and the Early Tang. This dominates not merely his poetry but most of his prose as well (which is written in the highly formal and euphuistic style of the time). Parallelism is perhaps the chief vehicle for wit in medieval Chinese literature, and that is a quality that emerges only when there is a cultivated community available to appreciate it. Though this is a difficult quality to appreciate now (and its beauty is often lost in translation), paying sympathetic attention to it has its rewards. For example, in writing of a country excursion with the Prince of Qi early in his writing career, the poet delicately evokes the event:

By the time our enthusiasm is satisfied, the singing birds have changed;
As we sit there long, falling blossoms grow many.
The path swerves, makes our silver candles turn back;
The forest opens, dispersing our jade bridle pendants. (7.2.3–6)

The party-goers themselves seem so wrapped in their pleasures that they only notice the passage of time when Nature reminds them (with the transition of birds and the increase of fallen blossoms). As the excursion wends its way back to the city, he imagines a trail of lights as the only indication of the curving country paths; and the change from forest to plain is indicated by a dispersal of the sound of the bridle pendants over a wider space. In both couplets, he subtly suggests that Nature is controlling the event – warning the party-goers when it is time to go home, and laying out the path they have to follow on their way. He concludes with a surprisingly original couplet, in which raucous entertainers pile up in front of the closed city gates waiting for dawn:

By curfew law the city gates have yet to open;
On the road in front our musicians and singers throng. (7.2.7–8)

The use of elegant parallelism is even more evident in the formal poetry he wrote for imperial occasions. In a poem on the emperor's patronage of the worthy, Wang writes:

He pulls back the tassels from his crown to let his four pupils see keenly;
He leans over the rail, stooping to humble himself thrice to worthies. (11.6.5–6)

Xuanzong, possessed of the sage-emperor Yao's double pupils, releases these keen minister-seeking organs as he brushes aside the crown-tassels of office; and when he sees such worthy men, he abases himself for the sake of his empire, just like Liu Bei, who visited Zhuge Liang three times before the latter agreed to enter his service. Wisdom and humility are combined within the parallel structure, hanging together partly through the symmetrical deployment of numbers (four and three). Appreciation of lines like these is an acquired taste, but they display a profound mastery of style.

Other ways in which sociality influences Wang's verse have also been largely ignored. Note, for example, the famous Wang Stream Collection (13.10–19). While these elegant nature quatrains are often held up as the epitome of Wang's interest in capturing the workings of Nature, few critics lay stress on the social context for their production: Wang Wei and his friend Pei Di are wandering Wang's estate, giving names to the most picturesque sites, and exchanging poems that attempt to capture the essential feel of each. It is a combination of tourism, literary gamesmanship, and territorial mapping.[4] If we ignore this playfulness (and if we read the poems deprived of the matching Pei Di verses), then we miss much of their pleasure, and we end by fetishizing certain of them through decontextualization, as has happened with "Deer Fence" (13.14) or "Lodge in Bamboo" (13.26). For example, we might notice the interactions occurring in two of the lesser-known poems of the collection, 13.22, "Gold-Dust Creek":

Daily drink from Gold-dust Creek
And at the least you'll live for over a thousand years.
Then on emerald phoenix, with patterned wyverns hovering,
With feathered standards you'll come to the Jade Emperor's court.
(Wang Wei)

The eddy trembles and does not flow on,
So that it seems like you could pluck the gold and jade-green.
In the dawn, when it is filled with white blossoms,
I go alone to the task of fetching our morning water. (Pei Di)

We cannot actually be sure which one was written first (we tend to assume that Pei is always responding to Wang, but we have no proof of this). But simply juxtaposing these two quatrains brings out the

4 Ding Xiang Warner (2005) is one of the few scholars who has written about the cycle's social dimensions.

inherent humor of both. Wang Wei engages in a Daoist fantasy, imagining that the gold-enriched waters can be used for an elixir of immortality that will turn its drinker into a Transcendent; but underlying that second couplet is the common substitution of Daoist tropes for the secular court of Xuanzong, so there is a secondary hint at the continuing thematic tension between service and reclusion – the ideal reclusive activity (becoming a Transcendent) brings the individual back into public service. Pei Di deflates this facetious resplendence by relocating the inhabitant in the modest world of the present and not in the world of future goals and fantasies: he goes to fetch water. The repetition of the word *chao/zhao* 朝 here accentuates these two opposing views of reclusion in a particularly clever way: "morning" and "attending [morning] court."

Another social aspect that becomes evident on a complete reading is the disproportionate number of "seeing off" poems (usually but not exclusively marked by *song* 送): out of 371 poems, no fewer than 71 fit this category.[5] These span many different levels of formality – from the *yuefu* generality and simplicity of 3.23, to the personal affection of 3.20 and 8.11, to the complex rhetoric of 3.18 and 12.3 (with its lengthy parallel-prose preface). All of Wang Wei's concerns emerge in these poems in one place or another: reclusion, government service, Daoist Transcendents, even Buddhist detachment. But one can detect certain recurring rhetorical strategies as well: historical tourism, for example, in which the poet evokes the famous sites his recipient will encounter on his journey; consolation and sorrow, depending on the reason for separation; and recurring allusions to the biographies of Confucian officials throughout the centuries. To divide this body of verse among certain modern thematic categories and ignore the social occasions that inspired it is to ignore the way the poet could deploy his poetic tools to fit the circumstances – possibly the skill that he himself valued the most as a courtier.

5 This is made more obvious in the Zhao Diancheng edition, which tends to follow the ordering of earlier Ming editions that place all the "seeing off" poems together – see especially *juan* 3, 4, and 8. It is difficult to be sure why there should be so many. Perhaps it has something to do with the conditions of the collection's initial compilation by Wang Wei's brother Wang Jin.

Wang Wei and Buddhism

The presence of Buddhist ideas and allusions in Wang Wei's work deserves special attention and discussion. Many scholars in China, Japan, and the West have claimed that there is an underlying Buddhist metaphysical perspective in Wang that manifests itself in the way he deploys images (especially nature images). There is also a recurring argument that his poetry shows a serious engagement with the intellectual concerns of the Chan (Zen) movement. Unfortunately, much of this discussion is rooted in two misconceptions.

First, recent scholarship from Buddhologists (John McRae, Bernard Faure, and others) has clarified the state of the Chan movement during the first half of the eighth century.[6] Later accounts in traditional Chan historiography dating from the Song era tend to portray the Chan movement – especially the more radical "southern" school – as a fully formed manifestation of classic Chan from its earliest days, with its use of paradox, of radical intellectualism, and hostility to ritual and to the religious establishment. But Chan as Wang Wei would have known it was nothing like this; it was still largely defined by a group of monks who placed meditation in the center of their practice and who received court and aristocratic patronage. It was by no means seen as anti-establishment. Wang Wei's mother studied with Puji, a disciple of Shenxiu, who exemplified in many ways this urban and courtly Chan. And though Wang Wei was asked by Shenxiu's opponent Shenhui to write a stele inscription for the so-called founder of Southern Chan, Huineng (25.1), there is nothing in his piece that suggests that he viewed Huineng in the way that the later lineage accounts saw him. It should also be pointed out that later Chan literature, though often formally innovative in its use of the vernacular language and creation of new religious literary genres, usually employed a vocabulary derived from a sutra literature well-known to the educated Chinese believer. It is hardly surprising in such a case that Wang Wei would use philosophical Buddhist terms also employed by Chan texts. If Wang Wei's Buddhist allu-

6 See especially McRae's two books: *The Northern School and the Formation of Early Ch'an Buddhism* (University of Hawai'i Press, 1987); and *Seeing Through Zen: Encounter, Transformation, and Genealogy in Chinese Chan Buddhism* (University of California Press, 2004).

sions show a fondness for paradox and humor, for example, he is not borrowing this from Chan, but more probably from his favorite Buddhist text, the *Vimalakīrti Sutra* – which derives much of its terminology from the rhetoric on non-duality found in the *prajñāpāramitā* literature.[7] The sutra's literary qualities, as well as its central conceit – that a lay believer with a secular life can understand Buddhist enlightenment better than the Buddha's own disciples – would be particularly attractive to the poet as well. But other sutras make their mark on his writing also: in particular, the *Lotus Sutra*, the *Nirvana Sutra*, the Pure Land Sutras, and occasionally the *Huayan Sutra*. These were all texts that an educated believer would be familiar with to a greater or lesser extent. The Wang Wei commentator Chen Tiemin also makes a strong case that Daoguang, whom Wang Wei names as his own teacher in his stele inscription (25.2), was most likely a Huayan practitioner from Wutai (the center of the Huayan movement). I suspect that Wang, like most lay believers, was not terribly interested in sectarian differences.[8]

The second misconception that tends to occur in the literature on Wang Wei and Buddhism is the modern tendency to see Buddhism not as an actual religion with its rituals, devotions, and forms of practice but rather as a sort of psychological affect or as a cluster of philosophical tenets. It is assumed that as a well-read "intellectual," the poet would mainly engage with Buddhism in terms of its ontology, and this would be reflected in subtle ways in his Nature poetry – especially in images that show a preoccupation with emptiness, impermanence, or seemingly epiphanic insights into the cosmos. Unfortunately, this sort of interpretation is largely unprovable. While it is not unlikely that some of these ideas influenced the way that Wang Wei wrote, showing conclusively that he would not have derived the same language and use of imagery from the Chinese poetic tradition as it was practiced in the early eighth century is a difficult task.[9]

---

7 The importance of this sutra for Wang Wei cannot be underestimated. He chose his polite name (Mojie 摩詰) so that it would combine with his personal name (Wei) to spell out the Chinese rendering of Vimalakīrti (Weimojie 維摩詰).

8 The case against Wang Wei's poetry as Chan-influenced is ably made by Yang Jingqing (2007).

9 Owen (1981) and Chou (1982) both tend to see Wang's use of imagery as having roots in a strictly literary tradition.

There is an irony here that when critics address this issue they tend to ignore the poetry that Wang Wei wrote that explicitly addresses his Buddhist interests. Again, this may reflect modern prejudices: that Buddhism should be psychological and aesthetic, and not doctrinal; and looking at poems where he openly *says* what he believes, rather than interpreting Buddhist profundity in the movement of a cloud or a stream, may seem unsatisfying. Perhaps even less attractive to many modern critics are the times in which Wang Wei displays his devotion to Buddhist ritual and to traditional forms of piety.[10] But it is hard to deny that this was a very important aspect of his belief. This is evident enough in poems addressed to monks, or poems visiting temples; but it is most strongly displayed in the prose that he wrote for fellow believers, especially in some of his memorials and eulogies (*juan* 19 and 20). One might argue that the devotion he expresses in such pieces is merely catering to the tastes of his recipients and does not express his own perspective. But ultimately it is equally likely that he was simply devout, and saw ritual, prayer, and other forms of practice as just as valid as intellectual speculation.

It may also seem a little intimidating when Wang Wei employs Buddhist jargon, and this may explain why critics have preferred to look at the descriptive poems for Buddhist influence, rather than the poems and prose where he is explicitly articulating his Buddhist world view. I have done my best to translate these passages clearly, but I admit that many lines are open to interpretation. However, regardless of their precise meaning, they tend to revolve around the poet's concern with the concept of non-duality and the way it is articulated in *prajñāpāramitā* texts and in the Vimalakīrti Sutra.

In these passages, Wang Wei tends to express his main position in this way: whenever we attempt to understand and express the difference between our world of suffering (samsara) and the realm of enlightenment or absolute reality (nirvana or *bhūtatathatā*), we are doomed to failure, because our language is inherently limited by samsaric values.

10 This probably also influences the desire to see Wang as a Chan poet – since there is an assumption among many modern intellectuals and academics that Chan is rational and opposed to ritual and "superstition" – a position that has been largely debunked by recent Buddhological scholarship.

Moreover, one of the chief characteristics of samsara that dooms us to suffering is our tendency to think in oppositional categories, and that one such oppositional category is the very placing of samsara and nirvana in opposition. A similar paradox results if we think in terms of the category *śunyatā* or "emptiness": if we assert that all phenomena are essentially "empty" – that is, that they have no inherent existence in themselves – then we run the risk of creating the conceptual categories of "empty" and "not empty," which would not be valid if we hope to truly comprehend actual, true reality. So "emptiness" is not really "empty" (unless we are thinking of the *category* "emptiness" that we use to designate it as such in order to talk about it; *that* really *is* "empty").

However (and this is important for Wang Wei's role as a poet and as a courtier), we should not give up on language in order to attain some deeper wisdom, because it is a basic tool in the samsaric world. We *can* use language, not to express adequately the true non-dualistic nature of ultimate reality, but to constantly question and undermine our excessive dependence on duality. If we realize that every time we make an assertion about ultimate reality we must simultaneously acknowledge that assertion's limitations, we are engaged in a fruitful exploration of the problem, even if we can only ultimately experience that reality in a way that transcends language. There is some resemblance here to the *via negativa* in Christian theology.

Wang Wei uses *prajñāpāramitā* techniques to make this point, but he also relies on Daoist rhetoric, especially when the *Laozi*, the *Zhuangzi*, and other texts question the ability of language to express the nature of reality. This can be frustrating to read, because it often means that the poet says (in highly rhetorical and parallelistic fashion) that something is simultaneously true and not-true. However, he can deploy this philosophical insight in ways that have concrete relevance to real-life situations. For example, in 19.10, "Preface to a poem: 'Flowering herbs at the lodging of Master Daoguang at Jianfu Monastery,'" he begins:

> The mind is lodged in the midst of Being and Nonbeing, and the eye is bounded by *rūpa* [sensuous appearance] on the one hand and Emptiness on the other. All is illusory, and detachment from them is illusory as well. The Fully Realized Person does not cast aside illusion, but he does go beyond the limits of Being and Nonbeing, of *rūpa* and Emptiness. For that reason his eye may reside

> in the dust while his mind never once shares in that condition. His mind is not in the world, and his body never becomes an object; for identifying oneself as an object causes the Self to be attached through limitless realms, and this is dangerous indeed.

Here we have a typical attempt to undermine dualistic tendencies. The purpose of this rhetoric is more practical, however: he wants to explain why a monk is fond of his herb garden: "His Reverence follows the movements of yin and yang, and acts in company with the passions. At the twin tree's place of practice he turns all the flowers into a form of Buddhist activity."

Analysis of non-duality is perhaps most important for the poet when he uses it to resolve the ever-present tension between government service and retirement – which had a long history in Chinese philosophy and literature, and was a major preoccupation of his own. In 3.14 he provides a meal for monks of a local monastery, then argues that he does not need to withdraw from public service to practice:

Already awakened to the joy of Stillness,
I have more than enough leisure for this life.
A desire to retire – why must it be serious?
For both self and world are truly empty.

He makes this argument in a much more detailed way in his "Letter to Layman Wei" (18.7) – introducing a general critique of Chinese reclusion in the process:

> A lofty one of old said, "Xu You hung his gourd from a tree; but because the wind blew through it, he disliked it and tossed it aside. When he heard that Yao had abdicated, he came to the river and washed out his ears." But the ears are not the place to block sounds, nor do sounds have traces that stain the ear; rather, if one despises things on the outside, one is polluted within; and a dislike for external things springs up from within the Self. Someone like this cannot attain the status of a truly open-hearted man. How is this truly entering the gate of the Buddhist path? And when it came to Xi Kang, he as well has said, "When a deer is captured, it will toss its head wildly to throw off its bonds, and will long more and more

> for its tall forest trees and will pine for its lush grasses." "Tossing its head wildly to throw off its bonds" – how is that any different from lowering one's head and accepting the restrictions of office? "Tall forest trees and lush grasses" – how is that any different from the gates leading to government office? When discriminating views arise, then the true nature is obscured; when sensuous phenomena intervene, then our ability to apply wisdom weakens. How could this be a viewpoint that allows for the sole existence of a vision that sees all things as equally empty, so that emptiness pervades all things and brings illumination to all? This is also something that you know.

In other words, from a non-dualistic perspective, being a hermit is the same as being in office – an ideal position to take for a devout courtier and an admirer of Vimalakīrti.

Recurring clusters of allusions

In the translations that follow, I have attempted to footnote allusions to the extent that it makes the poems comprehensible – it would take too much space to explore every way in which Wang echoes or plays with the phrasing of an old text or is engaged in dialogue with the literary past. However, it may help the reader here to make some generalizations about what texts and what historical references occur most often, beyond the Buddhist concerns mentioned above.

Textual allusions: Though Wang was probably familiar with the full range of Chinese literature up to his own time, he tends to allude to the same small group of texts over and over again. Most evident are allusions to *The Analects*, the *Zuo zhuan*, the *Shijing*, and the *Zhuangzi*. The *Yijing* and the *Liezi* show up occasionally as well, but not nearly as often.

Historical allusions: these tend to fall into four general categories:

1) *Han era topography and administration*: Tang era palaces, institutions, bureaucratic titles and (often) place names are replaced with their Han equivalents. This perhaps should not even be termed allusion; it is more a form of elegant substitution. In particular, the use of Han era palace names is meant to glorify the Tang court by

comparing it (especially) to the reign of Emperor Wu. Very little Confucian criticism of Emperor Wu's excesses is ever suggested.

2) *The Xiongnu wars*: any frontier poetry inevitably alludes to the history of conflict with the Xiongnu during the Western Han, especially during the reign of Emperor Wu. The great generals of the time (Huo Qubing, Wei Qing, Li Ling, Li Guangli, etc.) are regularly evoked. The degree to which the foreign policy conflicts of Xuanzong's reign are being seen through the lenses of a distant and idealized past (though common enough in Tang verse) is quite striking.
3) *Eastern Jin and Southern dynasties eccentrics*: Not surprisingly, Wang draws on the anecdotal literature of this period (usually found in the *Shishuo xinyu*): Xie An, Wang Xizhi, Shi Chong, Huiyuan, and others are mentioned fairly often.
4) *Tales of Daoist Transcendents*: While Wang deploys the technical language of the Daoist faith, he leans toward the anecdotal when addressing poems to Daoist friends and acquaintances. This suggests that he is sympathetic to Daoism and broadly familiar with it, but not at the level of an initiate.

Conventions of translation and editions

Some translation conventions: Daoist *xian* 仙 are translated as "Transcendents." The Yangtze is translated as "the Jiang." When poem titles refer to the recipient's age rank within his extended family, this is rendered as a cardinal number rather than an ordinal one (e.g., "Zu Yong Three"). Official titles are translated for the most part using Charles O. Hucker, *A Dictionary of Official Titles in Imperial China* (Stanford University Press, 1985).

The edition translated follows the basic order and text of the Zhao Diancheng 趙殿成 edition of 1733. This is by far the best known. It follows the structure of Ming editions in organizing the poems by metrical genre. In this case, *Juan* 1 consists of "old style verse" of irregular and 4-syllable lines; *Juan* 2–5 consist of old-style verse in five-syllable lines; *juan* 6 consists of old-style verse in seven-syllable lines; *juan* 7–9 consist of five-syllable regulated octets; *juan* 10 consists of seven-syllable regulated octets; *juan* 11–12 consist of five-syllable *pailü*; *juan* 13 consists of five-syllable quatrains; *juan* 14 consists of six-syllable and seven-syllable quatrains; and *juan* 15 consists of a supplement of poems of doubtful provenance. There is a tendency to group poems by occasional subgenre within these groups (e.g., all the parting poems are placed together). The prose collection is also arranged by genre. There is no attempt to order things chronologically (not surprising, since the majority of Wang's poems and much of the prose cannot be dated with certainty).

Zhao decided to include all of the poems available to him that had been attributed to Wang Wei, even if he himself was convinced that they were not by him. I have decided to be completist as well and translate all of them, noting when evidence suggests a different author. Poems likely misattributed by Zhao that are not in *juan* 15 include: 3.22; 4.14–15; 4.24; 8.8; 12.8. The most striking example of misattribution is the group of thirty poems likely composed by Wang Ya that have been included in many (but not all) early editions; their inclusion seems to stem originally from Guo Maoqian's attribution of them to Wang Wei in the *Yuefu shi ji*.

Zhao also includes matching or answering poems by other poets, and I have translated most of those as well, since I believe that seeing the compositional context of a poem when possible increases our understanding; this is especially true of the famous Wang Stream Collection, where the inclusion of the Pei Di poems is essential. The only exceptions are a number of "blue sparrow" poems (6.3) and some long imitations of Wang by Chu Guangxi (to 5.4–5.9 and 5.20) that Zhao has included, but which I find insufficiently engaged with the Wang Wei texts to warrant their translation.

In selecting what prose to translate I have tried to pick the pieces a modern reader would find most interesting. I have tended to favor those with Buddhist content, since this gives us a better context for understanding the poet's engagement with the faith in its entirety. Even in his letters Wang tends to write in a florid style with frequent use of parallelism. I was tempted to translate all of the prose as verse, but I decided eventually that that would detract from the narrative coherence of each piece.

Readers should also take note that one of his best prose pieces, the preface bidding farewell to Abe no Nakamaro, is here placed with the poem it prefaces and not with the prose (12.3).

I have reluctantly decided not to translate the discourse on landscape (*Shanshui lun*), in spite of its fame: scholars have known for a very long time that it is not by Wang Wei, and it deserves the attention of an art historian. Besides, we already have an excellent translation of it by Susan Bush and Hsiao-yen Shih.[11]

As with the works any great Tang poet, Wang Wei's collection has a large variety of variant readings, and I have included the important ones in a section at the end.[12] Not surprisingly, the poems that were famous from early on often have the widest variety of variants. The amount of variation within the textual lines of the Wang Wei collection itself is fairly reasonable, but there is a good bit of difference when the collection text is collated with the early compendia (*Wenyuan yinghua, Yuefu shiji, Tang wen cui*, etc.). I have largely kept to the Zhao edition, but have often accepted the practical emendations suggested by Chen Tiemin (1997). The *Quan Tang shi* text also has a surprising number of unique variants, suggesting that its editors relied on earlier editions of the collection no longer extant.

11 *Early Chinese Texts on Painting* (Cambridge: Harvard University Press, 1985), 173–76.

12 To prevent too large a selection, I have only included actual surviving edition variants. I have omitted variants listed as such in pre-modern editions that do not cite a source (usually marked only by *yi zuo* 一作).

The Poetry and Prose of Wang Wei

王右丞集卷之一 古詩

1.1

奉和聖製天長節賜宰臣歌應制

太陽升兮照萬方，
開閶闔兮臨玉堂。
儼冕旒兮垂衣裳，
金天淨兮麗三光。
彤庭曙兮延八荒，
德合天兮禮神遍。
靈芝生兮慶雲見，
唐堯后兮稷禼臣。
匝宇宙兮華胥人，
盡九服兮皆四鄰。
乾降瑞兮坤獻珍。

1 Sagely composition: a poem composed by the emperor. Festival of Heaven Longevity was the name established in 748 for the celebration of the emperor's birthday on the fifth day of the eighth month.
2 To let the robe drape down means to rule virtuously through non-action, a Daoist ideal.
3 Sky of Metal is the sky of autumn; the Three Lights are the sun, the moon, and the stars.
4 Crimson Court was a Han era palace; here used as a general term for the imperial palaces. Eight Wilds is a general term for the full breadth of the empire.
5 An auspicious fungus that appears in response to virtue.

https://doi.org/10.1515/9781501516023-001

Juan 1: Old style poems

1.1

Respectfully harmonizing to the sagely composition on the Festival of Heaven Longevity presented to his high ministers: at imperial command[1]

The Great Yang rises   and shines on a myriad sites;
They open the palace gate   and He looks down from His jade hall;
He sets right His crown's tassels,   lets His robes drape down;[2]
The metal sky is clear   and makes lovely the Three Lights.[3]
It is dawn in the Crimson Court;   the light extends to the Eight Wilds.[4]
His virtue harmonizes with the Heavens   as he sacrifices to spirits everywhere.
The numinous polypore has arisen   and felicitous clouds have appeared;[5]
Lord Yao of Tang,   the ministers Ji and Qi:[6]
All of them circuit the cosmos;   they are men of Huaxu.[7]
Every part of the Nine Feudatories: neighbors in every four direction:[8]
And Heaven lets descend its auspicious signs   and Earth presents its treasure.[9]

6 Tang Yao is the ancient sage emperor Yao. Ji was the ancestor of the Zhou people and served Yao as a minister of agriculture; Qi was the ancestor of the Shang people and served Yao's successor Shun as a minister of works. Here Wang Wei is referring to the emperor and his ministers.

7 In the *Liezi*, the Yellow Emperor dreams of a Daoist utopia called Huaxu; when he wakes up, he strives to put what he dreamt into practice in the empire.

8 Nine Feudatories was a way of classifying the various states that owed allegiance to the house of Zhou, from closest to most remote (barbarian lands).

9 Perhaps a reference to the numinous polypores and felicitous clouds mentioned in the seventh line.

1.2

登樓歌

聊上君兮高樓，
飛甍鱗次兮在下。
俯十二兮通衢，
綠槐參差兮車馬。
卻瞻兮龍首，
前眺兮宜春。
王畿鬱兮千里，
山河壯兮咸秦。
舍人下兮青宮，
據胡牀兮書空。
執戟疲于下位，
老夫好隱兮牆東。
亦幸有張伯英草聖兮龍騰虬躍，
擺長雲兮捩迴風。
琥珀酒兮彫胡飯，
君不御兮日將晚。
秋風兮吹衣，
夕鳥兮爭返。
孤砧發兮東城，
林薄暮兮蟬聲遠。

1.2

Song: Climbing a Tower

I shall climb your   lofty tower, sir
The flying eaves overlap like fish scales   below me
I look down upon twelve   open avenues,
Mid the sophoras' uneven rows   are carts and horses.
I turn and look up   at Dragon Head Hill,[1]
Gaze afar in front   at Yichun Palace.[2]
The king's realm is densely forested   for a thousand li;
Hills and rivers grand   in Qin's Xianyang.[3]
The secretary comes down   from the Crown Prince's Palace,
Props himself on a folding stool   he writes in the air.
Fatigued from grasping his halberd   in his lowly place,
The old man cherishes reclusion   to the east of the wall.[4]
Fortunately we have Zhang Boying, the sage of grass calligraphy here,
with his galloping dragons and leaping wyverns.[5]
He parts the long clouds   and twists the whirlwind.
Amber ale   and cooked wild rice –
If you won't make use of them   it will soon be too late.
An autumn wind   blows our robes,
Evening birds   hurry each other home.
Solitary fulling blocks sound   by the eastern city wall,
The forest turns to dusk   cicada's sound distant.

1 A mountain in Shaanxi, south of the Wei 渭 River not far from Chang'an.

2 Detached palace of the Qin era; in the Tang it was located in the southeast corner of Qujiang 曲江 Park.

3 Xianyang was the capital of the Qin dynasty; here it is a poetic substitution for nearby Chang'an.

4 When the Eastern Han official Wang Jungong 王君公 encountered political turmoil, rather than fleeing into the country (like his friends), he chose to stay in the city and hide among cattle merchants. An expression of the time described him as "Wang Jungong, who fled from the world east of the wall." "East of the wall" then became a cliché for reclusion.

5 Zhang Boying is Zhang Yin 諲, a drinking companion of Wang Wei's, good at calligraphy and painting. See also 2.23–2.25.

時不可兮再得，
君何為兮偃蹇。

1.3

雙黃鵠歌送別（時為節度判官。在涼州作。）

天路來兮雙黃鵠，
雲上飛兮水上宿。
撫翼和鳴整羽族，
不得已。
忽分飛，
家在玉京朝紫微。
主人臨水送將歸，
悲笳嘹唳垂舞衣。
賓欲散兮復相依，
幾往返兮極浦。
尚徘徊兮落暉，
岸上火兮相迎。
將夜入兮邊城，
鞍馬歸兮佳人散，
悵離憂兮獨含情。

The season will not   come again,
Why do you, sir,   stand there waiting?

1.3

Song: A Pair of Brown Swans (seeing you off) (At the time, serving as Administrative Assistant to the Military Commissioner, written in Liangzhou)[1]

On Heaven's Road coming   a pair of brown swans,
Flying above the clouds   roosting on the waters.
They beat their wings, cry in harmony, preen their feathers.
Being discontented,
They part in sudden flight;
One heads home to Jade Capital Mountain, the other goes to court in the Purple Tenuity.[2]
The host on the bank sees you off, about to return;
Grieving reed pipes are shrill and sharp, dancing robes hang down.
Guests about to disperse   yet they still linger together,
Soon to return   to the farther shore.
Yet still they hesitate   amid the setting radiance,
Fires on the riverbank   welcome us.
As it turns to night you enter   the frontier town,
Your saddled horse returns,   the fine guests disperse.
I hate this sadness of parting   yet I keep my feelings to myself.

---

1 Composed when serving Cui Xiyi 崔希逸 in Hexi on the northwest frontier, ca. 737–738.

2 Jade Capital Mountain – in Daoist lore, a habitation of Immortals. Purple Tenuity: a constellation of fifteen stars around the pole star, and site of the divine ruler of the cosmos in Daoism.

1.4

贈徐中書望終南山歌

晚下兮紫微，
悵塵事兮多違。
駐馬兮雙樹，
望青山兮不歸。

1.5–1.6

送友人歸山歌二首

1.

山寂寂兮無人，
又蒼蒼兮多木。
群龍兮滿朝，
君何為兮空谷。
文寡和兮思深，
道難知兮行獨。
悅石上兮流泉，
與松間兮草屋。
入雲中兮養雞，

1.4

Song: Gazing toward Zhongnan Mountain, presented to Vice Director Xu of the Secretariat

In the evening I depart   from the Department of Purple Tenuity,[1]
Despairing that worldly matters   have mostly turned contrary.
I halt my horse   by a *sal* tree;[2]
Gaze toward green mountains   I will not return.

1.5–1.6

Two songs: seeing off a friend on his return to the hills

1.

How lonely the mountains   no one there,
And deepest green   with many trees.
Flocks of dragons   fill the court;[3]
What are you doing here   in this empty valley?
Your writings resonate with few   you deeply brood;
The way is hard   you walk alone.
You delight in streams   flowing over the stones,
You enjoy your thatched hut   amid the pines.
You enter into the clouds   raise chickens;[4]

---

1 Here the term is used as a poetic substitution for the Secretariat (*zhongshu sheng* 中書省).

2 Shorea robusta, the sal or or *śala* tree: the tree under which the Buddha's mother gave birth to him. Also by some accounts the tree where the Buddha achieved *parinirvaṇa*. Sometimes used as a poetic substitution for a Buddhist monastery.

3 Many virtuous men are serving the emperor.

4 Probably an allusion to a Daoist Transcendent who lived over a hundred years and raised over a thousand chickens, to each of whom he assigned a name. Each would come to him when he called its name.

上山頭兮抱犢。
神與棗兮如瓜，
虎賣杏兮收穀。
愧不才兮妨賢，
嫌既老兮貪祿。
誓解印兮相從，
何詹尹兮可卜。

2.

山中人兮欲歸，
雲冥冥兮雨霏霏。
水驚波兮翠菅靡，
白鷺忽兮翻飛。
君不可兮褰衣，
山萬重兮一雲。
混天地兮不分，
樹晻曖兮氛氳。
猿不見兮空聞，
忽山西兮夕陽。
見東皋兮遠村，
平蕪綠兮千里。
眇惆悵兮思君。

You ascend the mountains with the calf you possess.[1]
The spirits will give you dates as big as melons;[2]
You'll sell apricots with your tigers and store your grain.[3]
I am ashamed I am talentless and block the progress of the worthy;
Hate that I have now grown old and yet still greedy for salary.
I swear I'll untie my seal of office and follow you away;
What need for divination from Zhan Yin?[4]

2.

The man of the mountains wants to return;
The clouds are dark and murky, the rain falls in gusts.
The water in startled waves, the green thatch scattered;
White egrets abruptly flutter in the wind.
My lord, you cannot hoist your robe to cross;
Hills in myriad layers, a single cloud.
Heaven and earth confounded, cannot be distinguished;
Trees dim and gloomy, dense and full.
Gibbons cannot be seen but their cries are heard in the air;
Sudden, to the west of the hills, the evening sun.
Look to the eastern riverside fields the distant villages;
Level grasslands green for a thousand li.
My distant gaze disconsolate; I long for my lord.

1 Reference to "Possess Calf Mountain" in Shandong, so named because a recluse cultivated crops there, with only a single calf to help him.

2 The Han wizard Li Shaojun 李少君 claimed that he met the immortal Master Anqi 安期, who ate dates the size of melons.

3 A certain Dong Feng 董奉 lived at Mt. Lu 廬, where he treated patients. He had them plant apricot trees in payment. When this formed a forest, he set up a storehouse and asked people to pay for his apricots with grain. Anyone who cheated was pursued by five tigers.

4 In "Divination," (*Bu ju* 卜居), a short piece in the Han anthology *Chu ci*, Qu Yuan after years of exile begs the diviner Zhan Yin to tell him what he should do. Confronted with Qu Yuan's moral dilemma, Zhan Yin surrenders his milfoil stalks and tells him that divination would be of no help to him.

1.7–1.8

魚山神女祠歌

1.

迎神曲

坎坎擊鼓，
魚山之下。
吹洞簫，
望極浦。
女巫進，
紛屢舞。
陳瑤席，
湛清酤。
風淒淒兮夜雨。
神之來兮不來。
使我心兮苦復苦。

2.

送神曲

紛進拜兮堂前，
目眷眷兮瓊筵。
來不語兮意不傳，

1.7–1.8

Songs: The shrine of the goddess of Fish Mountain[1]

1.

Welcoming the Goddess

Bang bang the drums are struck,
At the foot of Fish Mountain.
They blow the bamboo flutes,
4 Gaze to the farther shore.
The shamanka approaches,
In a profusion of many dances.
Roll out the precious offering mats!
8 Pour out the crystal ale!
The wind is cold and dismal   at night it rains.
Does the goddess come or not?
This makes our hearts bitter beyond bitter.

2.

Bidding the Goddess Farewell

In a flurry they come forward to bow   before the hall,
Eyes that gaze with yearning   on the garnet mat.
She comes without speaking   does not convey her thoughts,

1 In Jizhou; poems were composed when Wang Wei was serving there (721–726).

作暮雨兮愁空山。
悲急管，思繁絃，
靈之駕兮儼欲旋。
倏雲收兮雨歇，
山青青兮水潺湲。

1.9

白黿渦（雜言走筆）

南山之瀑水兮，
激石瀉瀑似雷驚。
人相對兮不聞語聲，
翻渦跳沫兮蒼苔濕。
蘚老且厚，
春草為之不生。
獸不敢驚動，
鳥不敢飛鳴。
白黿渦濤戲瀨兮，
委身以縱橫。
主人之仁兮，
不網不釣，
得遂性以生成。

She makes the rain at dusk   turns the empty hills doleful.
With grief the swift flutes are played; brooding, the intricate strings.
Her numinous carriage   solemnly begins to turn.
Swiftly the clouds pull away   and the rain ceases;
How green are the hills   and the water flows on and on.

1.9

White Turtle Eddy (Irregular lines, written on the spur of the moment)

That waterfall at Zhongnan Mountain:
It spurts from the rock with an angry roar   like thunder startling.
When people face it   they cannot hear themselves speak;
Upending eddies, leaping foam   it soaks the gray-green moss.
The lichen grows old and thick there,
And spring grasses do not grow because of it,
And beasts do not dare to leap in its presence,
And birds do not dare to fly or cry.
White Turtle Eddy's billows and playful rapids,
Give themselves over to flying this way and that.
The ruler's benevolence:
No nets, no hooks,
Able to follow your nature in birth and growth.

1.10

酬諸公見過（時官出在輞川莊。）

嗟予未喪，
哀此孤生。
屏居藍田，
薄地躬畊。
歲晏輸稅，
以奉粢盛。
晨往東皋，
草露未晞。
暮看煙火，
負擔來歸。
我聞有客，
足掃荊扉。
簞食伊何，
副瓜抓棗。
仰廁群賢，
皤然一老。
媿無莞簟，
班荊席藁。
汎汎登陂，
折彼荷花。

1.10

Reply to several gentlemen who came to visit (at the time I was out of office and living on my Wangchuan estate)

Alas! My mourning has not ended,
And I lament this solitary life.
Living as a recluse in Lantian,
I do my own plowing on my barren land.
At the end of the year I pay my tax,
Offering grain to fill the ruler's sacrificial vessels.
At dawn I go to the eastern riverbank fields,
When the dew on the grass has not yet dried.
At dusk, when I see the smoky fires,
Carrying my burdens I come back home.
When I heard that guests had come,
I swept everything within my scrap-wood door.
What food is in my rice basket?
Split melons, and dates I've pulled off the tree.
Humbly I mingle with this group of worthies,
A single white-haired old man.
Ashamed I have not rugs woven of fine *guan* leaves,[1]
I spread orchid-tree branches on the floor and use straw for mats.
Then drifting along as we sail out on the lake,
We pluck the reed flowers.

---

1 Skimmia japonica, an evergreen shrub whose leaves were woven to make mats.

靜觀素鮪，
俯映白沙。
山鳥群飛，
日隱輕霞。
登車上馬，
倏忽雨散。
雀噪荒村，
雞鳴空館。
還復幽獨，
重欷累歎。

In the stillness we watch the white sturgeon,
Set off below against the white sand.
Mountain birds fly in their flocks,
The sun is hidden in the light clouds of sunset.
Then we climb our carriages, mount our horses,
And all of a sudden the rain disperses.
Sparrows are raucous in the rustic village,
And roosters crow in the empty lodge.
Then I return once more, secluded alone,
Sobbing and sighing again and again.

王右丞集卷之二 古詩

2.1–2.5

扶南曲歌詞五首

1.

翠羽流蘇帳，
春眠曙不開。
羞從面色起，
嬌逐語聲來。
早向昭陽殿，
君王中使催。

2.

堂上青絃動，
堂前綺席陳。
齊歌盧女曲，
雙舞洛陽人。
傾國徒相看，
寧知心所親。

https://doi.org/10.1515/9781501516023-002

Juan 2: Old style poems

2.1–2.5

Five Lyrics for the Funan Melody

1.

Tasseled curtains with kingfisher feathers
Stay unopened at dawn as they sleep in spring.
Shy to rise because of their complexions;
Too frail to come to the sound of voices.
Early at the Zhaoming Palace
Eunuch envoys of their lord bid them hasten.[1]

2.

Up in the hall the blue strings twang,
While before the hall the intricate mats are spread.
A song of Qi – a ballad from Lady Lu;
Paired dancers, girls from Luoyang.[2]
But he only watches these kingdom-toppling beauties;
Who can know whom his heart holds dear?

---

1 Zhaoming Palace: a women's quarters in Han times; used since then as a general term for the quarters of imperial favorites.

2 Lady Lu was a court lady from the time of Emperor Wu 武 of the Wei 魏 (Cao Cao 曹操). She was famous for her musical talents. One piece in her repertoire was a melody from Qi called "The Pheasants Fly at Dawn." Women from Luoyang were famous in popular verse for their beauty.

3.

香氣傳空滿，
妝華影箔通。
歌聞天仗外，
舞出御樓中。
日暮歸何處，
花間長樂宮。

4.

宮女還金屋，
將眠復畏明。
入春輕衣好，
半夜薄妝成。
拂曙朝前殿，
玉墀多珮聲。

5.

朝日照綺窗，
佳人坐臨鏡。
散黛恨猶輕，
插釵嫌未正。
同心勿遽遊，
幸待春妝竟。

3.

A fragrant scent pervades the air,
And light from their makeup shines through the screen.
Their songs are heard beyond the celestial guard,[1]
While their dances issue forth from imperial pavilions.
Whither do they return at dusk?
To Changle Palace amid the flowers.[2]

4.

Palace ladies return to their gilded chambers,
Where they will sleep, afraid once more of the dawn.
As they move into spring, lighter robes are welcome;
At midnight, they apply a light layer of makeup.
As dawn breaks, they assemble at the front palace:
On jade stairs, the frequent chime of their jade pendants.

5.

The morning sun shines on their intricate windows;
Lovely ladies sit facing the mirror.
They spread eye-black, irked that it is yet too thin;
Insert hairpins, annoyed that they're still askew.
Dear companions, don't be in a hurry to go out with them!
I hope you will wait until their spring makeup is done.

---

1 That is, beyond the palace (where the imperial guard is stationed).
2 Changle Palace: A Han era palace hall dating from the reign of Gaozu 高祖.

2.6

從軍行

吹角動行人，
喧喧行人起。
笳悲馬嘶亂，
爭渡金河水。
日暮沙漠垂，
戰聲烟塵裏。
盡係名王頸，
歸來報天子。

2.7

隴西行

十里一走馬，
五里一揚鞭。
都護軍書至，
匈奴圍酒泉。
關山正飛雪，
烽戍斷無烟。

2.6

Ballad: With the Army

They blow the horns to put the troops on the move;
In a clamor the men begin to stir.
The nomad flutes are shrill, a chaotic whinnying of horses;
They vie to cross the waters of the Jin.[1]
The sun turns to evening at the edge of the desert;
The sounds of battle rise from smoke and dust.
We will halter the necks of all their great kings,
Bring them back and requite the Son of Heaven.

2.7

Ballad of Longxi[2]

Every ten li he drives his steed;
Every five li he brandishes his whip.
A military dispatch from the Protector-General arrives:
The Xiongnu are besieging Jiuquan.[3]
Flying snow just now over mountains and passes;
The beacon-fire posts have been cut off – no smoke rises.[4]

---

1 Literally, the Metal River, frequently mentioned as a frontier river in poetry. It is likely identical to the modern Hei He ("Black River") that flows through western Gansu.

2 Longxi: in Gansu.

3 In western Gansu.

4 The poem may be suggesting that the blizzard has prevented the lighting of beacon fires, resulting in the need of the post horse messenger in lines 1–4.

2.8

早春行

紫梅發初徧，
黃鳥歌猶澀。
誰家折楊女，
弄春如不及。
愛水看妝坐，
羞人映花立。
香畏風吹散，
衣愁露霑濕。
玉閨青門裏，
日落香車入。
游衍益相思，
含啼向綵帷。
憶君長入夢，
歸晚更生疑。
不及紅簷燕，
雙棲綠草時。

2.8

Ballad: Early Spring[1]

Purple plum blossom begins to bloom everywhere;
Yellow orioles' song yet halting and rough.
Girls from some household break willow branches,
4 They can't be restrained in their delight of spring.
Cherishing the water, they sit and attend to their makeup;
Shy of others, they stand hidden in flowers.
They fear that the wind will blow away the fragrance,
8 And grieve that the dew dampens their dresses.
Through blue gates into a jade bedroom
The scented carriage enters when the sun sets.
She had gone out to take pleasure, but longed for him even more,
12 Now suppressing her sobs within the colored silk bedcurtains.
When she longs for him, she always sees him in dreams;
Having returned late, she again thinks he is there.
Better to be swallows in the crimson rafters,
16 Who can nest in pairs in the season of green grass.

---

1 The poem falls into two erotic vignettes. The first part (lines 1–8) describes girls out enjoying a spring outing; the second part (lines 9–16) describes a wife separated from her husband who returns to her lonely bedroom after going out to enjoy the weather.

2.9

贈裴迪

不相見，
不相見來久。
日日泉水頭，
4 常憶同攜手。
攜手本同心，
復歎忽分衿。
相憶今如此，
8 相思深不深。

2.10

瓜園詩（并序）

維瓜園高齋。俯視南山形勝。二三時輩。同賦是詩。兼命詞英數公。同用園字為韻。韻任多少。時太子司議郎薛璩發此題。遂同諸公云。

余適欲鋤瓜，
倚鋤聽叩門。
鳴騶導驄馬，

2.9

Presented to Pei Di

I haven't seen you,
I haven't seen you for so long!
Daily, by the waters of the stream
I always reminisce how we held hands,
We held hands, sharing the same mind.
I sigh again and again, now we're parted.
For my memories of you to be like this now,
Is my longing for you deep or not?

2.10

The Melon Patch (with preface)

From the lofty study by my melon patch I can look down upon the splendid scenery of Zhongnan Mountain. Two or three men of the age have composed poems on this subject. I also requested various prominent men with literary skill to write poems with as many lines as they like, using *yuan* (garden) as the rhyme. At that time, the Remonstrance Secretary of the Crown Prince, Xue Qu, wrote on this topic. I composed this poem, following these gentlemen.

I was just going out to hoe my melons,
When, leaning on my hoe, I heard a knock at the gate.
Shouting grooms were leading piebald steeds,

常從夾朱軒。
窮巷正傳呼，
故人儻相存。
攜手追涼風，
放心望乾坤。
藹藹帝王州，
宮觀一何繁。
林端出綺道，
殿頂搖華幡。
素懷在青山，
若值白雲屯。
回風城西雨，
返景原上村。
前酌盈尊酒，
往往聞清言。
黃鸝囀深木，
朱槿照中園。
猶羨松下客，
石上聞清猿。

And constant attendants flanked vermilion carriages.
Orders were transmitted in this humble lane;
Perhaps old friends have come to visit?
Hand in hand we sought out the cooling breeze,
Light of heart, we gazed out over Heaven and Earth.
And the rich, populous Imperial lands –
How manifold its palaces and watchtowers!
An intricate pattern of roads emerges from the edge of the woods,
And from the palace roofs the splendid pennons stir.
Always my affections lie in green hills,
And now I meet with a gathering of white clouds.
A gust of wind, rain west of the city,
Sunset glow on the villages of the plain.
I imbibe before them, fill up the ale cups,
Again and again I hear enlightened conversation.
Yellow orioles warble in the deep wood,
Vermilion rose-mallow flowers shine in my garden.
Still, I envy sojourners under the pines,[1]
Where amid stones they hear the clear calls of the gibbon.

1 I.e., more serious recluses than Wang Wei.

2.11

同盧拾遺韋給事東山別業二十韻給事首春休沐維已陪遊及乎是行亦預聞命會無車馬不果斯諾

託身侍雲陛，
昧旦趨華軒。
遂陪鵷鴻侶，
霄漢同飛翻。
君子垂惠顧，
期我于田園。
側聞景龍際，
親降南面尊。
萬乘駐山外，
順風祈一言。
高陽多夔龍，
荊山積璵璠。
盛德啟前烈，
大賢鍾後昆。

2.11

Matching Reminder Lu and Supervising Secretary Wei:[1] "East Mountain Villa" in 20 rhymes. I had already accompanied the Supervising Secretary on a day off in the first month of spring to this villa. Having been given another invitation, it happened that I had no carriage at my disposal and so was unable to fulfill my promise.

I committed myself to attending on the cloud stairs,
Before dawn hurrying off to splendid balustrades.
I accompanied my companions among the ranks of phoenixes
and herons,
Soaring together among the River of Stars.[2]
You, a true gentleman, extended your kind regard,
Invited me to your fields and gardens.
I've heard it said that in the Jinglong era,[3]
This was a personal gift of the honored south-facing one.[4]
When His myriad carriages halted beyond the hills,
With submissive air He implored words of instruction.
Gaoyang had many Kuis and Longs,[5]
Jing Mountain had amassed many ornamental jades.[6]
Your family's flourishing virtue produced men of high achievement,
And great worthiness is concentrated in their successors:

1 Wei Heng 韋恆, son of the prominent minister Wei Sili 嗣立, owner of the East Mountain Estate located at Mount Li 驪 (east of the capital, and location of the hot springs often visited by the emperor). This poem is mostly a paean to the Wei family.

2 Poetic descriptions of attending at court.

3 707–710.

4 I.e., the emperor. He granted Wei Sili (Wei Heng's father) the estate and the title "Duke of Easy Wandering" (*Xiaoyao gong* 逍遙公) in 709.

5 Gaoyang was a name for the ancient mythical sage emperor Zhuan Xu 顓頊. Kui and Long were both ministers of the ancient sage emperor Shun. This is saying that a wise ruler has wise ministers.

6 Jing Mountain was famous for its jade (and produced the fine jade that the craftsman Bian He 卞和 discovered during the Warring States period). Jade here stands for eminent men whose talents are recognized by the court.

侍郎文昌宮，
給事東掖垣。
謁帝俱來下，
冠蓋盈邱樊。
閨風首邦族，
庭訓延鄉村。
采地包山河，
樹井竟川原。
巖端迴綺檻，
谷口開朱門。
階下群峰首，
雲中瀑水源。
鳴玉滿春山，
列筵先朝暾。
會舞何颯踏，
擊鐘彌朝昏。
是時陽和節，
清晝猶未暄。
藹藹樹色深，
嚶嚶鳥聲繁。
顧已負宿諾，
延頸慙芳蓀。
蹇步守窮巷，

The Vice Minister at the Department of State Affairs,[1]
And you, Supervising Secretary, at the Eastern Annex office.[2]
Emperors inquiring after you all come down here,
And officials' caps and carriages crowd your hills and fences.
The customs of your family lead state and clan;
Your father's instructions reach to the countryside.
Your fief embraces hills and rivers,
Your streams and plains reach to arboreal hamlets.
At cliff-edge curve your carved railings,
At valley mouth open your vermilion gates.
A herd of crags throngs at the foot of your stairs,
A spring drops in waterfalls among the clouds.
Tinkling jade pendants fill the spring hills,
Arrayed banquet mats precede the dawn light.
How numerous the assembled dances!
The ringing of bells spans dawn to dusk.
At this time, the season of the second month,
The daylight is clear but not yet warm.
How lush, the depth of the trees' colors;
And profuse the twittering of birdsong.
But I've already betrayed my earlier promise;
I crane my neck toward you, ashamed before your fragrant virtue.[3]
With lame steps I keep to my humble lane,

1 Reference to Wei Heng's brother Wei Ji 濟, Vice Director of the Board of Revenue. "Wenchang Palace" was the name Empress Wu gave to the Department of State Affairs (*shangshu sheng* 尚書省).
2 Eastern Annex: another term for the Chancellory (*menxia sheng* 門下省).
3 Literally, "fragrant sweet-flag," a *Chu ci* image of moral virtue.

高駕難攀援。
素是獨往客，
脫冠情彌敦。

2.12

和使君五郎西樓望遠思歸

高樓望所思，
目極情未畢。
枕上見千里，
牕中窺萬室。
悠悠長路人，
曖曖遠郊日。
惆悵極浦外，
迢遞孤烟出。
能賦屬上才，
思歸同下秩。
故鄉不可見，
雲水空如一。

Impossible to climb into lofty carriages.
All along I've been one who walks alone;
I remove cap of office, my feelings ever more sincere.

2.12

Harmonizing with the Emissary Fifth Gentleman: Gazing afar from the western tower and longing to go home[1]

In the high tower, gazing toward what I long for,
My vision ends but my feelings don't cease.
From my pillow I can see a thousand li;
4 In my window I peer out at ten thousand homes.
With endless longing, the man on the long road;
Dark and gloomy, the sun in distant outlands.
Melancholy, beyond the farther shore,
8 In the distance solitary smoke emerges.
You, who can compose, belong to the higher talents;
But you long to go home, the same as this low-ranking one.
We cannot see our homeland here;
12 Water and clouds are empty, seem all as one.

---

1 Composed while serving in Jizhou in Shandong. "Emissary" here is another term for governor.

2.13

酬黎居士淅川作（曇壁上人院走筆成）

儂家真箇去，
公定隨儂否。
著處是蓮花，
無心變楊柳。
松龕藏藥裹，
石唇安茶臼。
氣味當共知，
那能不攜手。

2.14

奉寄韋太守陟

荒城自蕭索，
萬里山河空。
天高秋日迥，
嘹唳聞歸鴻。
寒塘映衰草，
高館落疏桐。
臨此歲方晏，
顧景詠悲翁。

2.13

Replying to Layman Li, written in Xichuan (Written on the spur of the moment at the cloister of His Reverence Tanbi)[1]

I'm truly going to retire –
Are you really going to follow me?
Everywhere there are lotus flowers,
4 A state of mindlessness transforms into a willow-bearing
Avalokiteśvara.[2]
Medicine pouches are stored in the pine-tree shrine;
A tea mortar sits at the edge of the rocks.
The flavor of this we should both get to know;
8 Why can't you go off hand in hand with me?

2.14

Respectfully sent to Governor Wei Zhi

The overgrown town is bleak and dreary;
For ten thousand li hills and rivers are empty.
The sky is high; the autumn sun is distant;
4 A sonorous cry – I hear the homing geese.
The chilly pool reflects the withered grass;
By the high lodge the sparse paulownias shed their leaves.
As I face all this – the year coming to its end,
8 I look back on my shadow, chant "Grieving Old Man."[3]

---

1 "Layman" (*jushi*) is the Chinese rendering of the Sanskrit *kulapati*, a devout lay householder. It can also be applied to retired gentlemen in general.
2 This couplet suggests that the cloister resembles the Pure Land. The bodhisattva Avalokiteśvara (who often attended upon Amida in the Pure Land) is often shown holding a vase with a willow branch.
3 A *yuefu* song title. The original describes longing for absent loved ones.

故人不可見，
寂寞平林東。

2.15

林園即事寄舍弟紞

寓目一蕭散，
消憂冀俄頃。
青草肅澄陂，
4 白雲移翠嶺。
後浦通河渭，
前山包鄢郢。
松含風裏聲，
8 花對池中影。
地多齊后癘，
人帶荊州癭。
徒思赤筆書，
12 詎有丹砂井。
心悲常欲絕，
髮亂不能整。
青簟日何長，
16 閑門晝方靜。
頹思茅簷下，
彌傷好風景。

My old friend I cannot see –
Sad and lonely east of the woods on the plain.

2.15

Things encountered in my garden in the woods: sent to my younger brother Dan

Casting my eyes about – suddenly I feel free and easy;
I hope for an instant to dissipate my worries.
Green grass is peaceful by the limpid pond,
White clouds move over the bright-blue ridge.
The inlet behind me connects with the Yellow River and the Wei,
While the hills in front embrace Yan and Ying.[1]
The pines enclose the sound in the wind;
Flowers face their reflections in the pool.
The land here is full of the Lord of Qi's ague,
And people bear the goiters of Jingzhou.[2]
In vain I long for writings from the Transcendents' red brush;
How can I obtain a cinnabar well?[3]
My heart grieves – always inconsolable.
My hair all tangled – I cannot put it straight.
How long the days seem on my summer mats!
Daylight is quiet by my idle gate.
I would vanquish this brooding under my thatched eaves,
But the fine scene just makes me more disconsolate.

1 This couplet suggests how far-ranging the poet's vision seems to be. On the one hand, the stream nearby flows into the Yellow River valley basin, while the hills he observes stretch into a range that extends all the way to Chu (Hubei).

2 This couplet draws upon literary allusions to comment on local ailments. The *Yanzi chun qiu* mentions Duke Jing of Qi 齊景公 suffering from an ague that lasted a year; while the Jin 晉 dynasty scholar and general Du Yu 杜預 (who commanded the area of Jingzhou) suffered from goiters.

3 The fourth-century Daoist alchemist Ge Hong 葛洪 tells of a village of people of unusually extended longevity; it was discovered that their wells were dug in a bed of cinnabar, which was leaking into the water supply.

2.16

贈從弟司庫員外絿

少年識事淺，
強學干名利。
徒聞躍馬年，
苦無出人智。
即事豈徒言，
累官非不試。
既寡遂性歡，
恐招負時累。
清冬見遠山，
積雪凝蒼翠。
皓然出東林，
發我遺世意。
惠連素清賞，
夙語塵外事。
欲緩攜手期，
流年一何駛。

2.16

Presented to my cousin Qiu, Vice Director of the Bureau of Provisions

When I was young I was shallow in my understanding;
I forced myself to study, toiling for fame and profit.
I would only hear of "spurring horse" years,[1]
And I hated that I hadn't preeminent intelligence.
Hardly vain to say that I took up my tasks;
And I was tested indeed in my successive offices.
Though seldom had I the joy of following my nature –
I was afraid I would invite the predicament of failing the age.
Now in the clear winter weather I see the far hills;
Piled-up snow freezes their verdant green.
And exhilarated I emerge from the eastern wood,
Expressing my wishes to escape from the world.
Huilian has always been pure and lofty;[2]
For long we have discussed affairs beyond the dust.
I wish we could prolong the time when we hold hands;
But how rapidly the flowing years pass!

1 Cai Ze 蔡澤 (Warring States era) expressed his desire to attain the pleasures of the nobility in the life that remained to him, including that of "spurring horses and driving them fast."

2 Wang compares his relationship to Qiu to that between the prominent fifth-century poet Xie Lingyun 謝靈運 and his cousin the talented Xie Huilian 惠連.

2.17

座上走筆贈薛璩慕容損

希世無高節，
絕跡有卑棲。
君徒視人文，
吾固和天倪。
緬然萬物始，
及與群物齊。
分地依后稷，
用天信重黎。
春風何豫人，
令我思東谿。
草色有佳意，
花枝稍含蕙。
更待風景好，
與君藉萋萋。

2.17

Written ex tempore from my seat and presented to Xue Qu and Murong Sun

Among those who aspire to the world's approval there are none of lofty virtue;
But there are low-ranking ones among those who remove their traces.[1]
You gentlemen vainly look into human patterns,
While I assuredly harmonize with the distinctions of Heaven.
Remote is the origin of the ten thousand things,
And yet it is the same with the mass of things themselves.[2]
I rely on Hou Ji to define the divisions of the land;
In the use of the seasons I trust Zhong and Li.[3]
How the spring breeze delights me –
It makes me think of Eastern Stream.[4]
The color of the grass has a splendid demeanor,
Flowered branches gradually put forth shoots.
I continue to wait for the scenery to improve,
So that I can sit together with you on the verdant green.

1 Remove traces: become recluses.

2 Wang Wei is making the Daoist claim that being and non-being have the same source.

3 Allusions to the development of civilization in Chinese myth. The ancient sage-god Hou Ji invented the division of land for the purpose of clarifying its agricultural purposes. The ancient mythical emperor Zhuan Xu appointed the minister Zhong to oversee the heavens, and the minister Li to oversee the earth. Wang is poetically expressing his desire to be a farmer.

4 Eastern Stream flowed out of Mount Song in Henan (where Wang Wei once briefly lived as a recluse).

2.18

贈李頎

聞君餌丹砂，
甚有好顏色。
不知從今去，
幾時生羽翼。
王母翳華芝，
望爾崑崙側。
文螭從赤豹，
萬里方一息。
悲哉世上人，
甘此羶腥食。

2.19

贈劉藍田

籬中犬迎吠，
出屋候柴扉。
歲晏輸井稅，
山村人夜歸。
晚田始家食，
餘布成我衣。
詎肯無公事，
煩君問是非。

2.18

Presented to Li Qi

I heard that you've taken the cinnabar pill,
And that it's greatly improved your complexion,
Though I don't know when, starting from today,
You will grow your wings.
The Queen Mother conceals herself under her canopy,
And looks to you from the side of Kunlun Mountain.[1]
You'll ride mottled wyverns with red leopard attendants,
Resting only once after ten thousand li.
Alas! These people in the world
Who find sweet all the food that stinks of meat.

2.19

Presented to Liu of Lantian

In the hedges a dog welcomes them, barking;
We come out of the house and wait by the scrap-wood door.
Since the year is late, they're remitting their field taxes,
Returning at night to their mountain village.
"We only have provisions when the late crop comes in;
Our own clothing comes from what's left after taxes.
It's not that we want exemption from our public duties;
But we'd trouble you, Sir, to inquire what's wrong and what's right."

1 The Daoist divinity the Queen Mother of the West (*Xi wangmu* 西王母) dwells at the semi-mythical Kunlun Mountain.

2.20

贈房盧氏琯

達人無不可，
忘己愛蒼生。
豈復小千室，
絃歌在兩楹。
浮人日已歸，
但坐事農耕。
桑榆鬱相望，
邑里多雞鳴。
秋山一何淨，
蒼翠臨寒城。
視事兼偃臥，
對書不簪纓。
蕭條人吏疎，
鳥雀下空庭。
鄙夫心所向，
晚節異平生。
將從海嶽居，
守靜解天刑。
或可累安邑，
茅茨君試營。

2.20

Presented to Fang Guan of Lushi[1]

There is nothing impossible for a man of penetration;
He forgets his own self, cherishes the common people.
How could he consider petty a thousand households?
Rather, he has music performed in his main hall.[2]
Vagrants daily are returning home,
Only to take up farm and plow;
Mulberries and elms face each other in lush growth,
And roosters crow often in borough and hamlet.
How pure are the autumn hills!
Their verdant green overlooks the cold city.
In seeing to office or lying at rest,
You have book at hand, do not don official hairpin or sash.
Your office is desolate, clerks are few;
Sparrows have descended in the empty court.[3]
The direction my humble mind has taken
In recent season is different from customary –
I would go off to lakes and peaks to dwell,
Preserve quiescence, released from Heaven's punishments.[4]
Perhaps I might burden your peaceful borough –
Might you consider erecting a thatched roof for me?

---

1 Written early in Fang Guan's career, some time before 733. Fang Guan went on to have an uneven but largely successful career, and is most famous in Chinese literature as a patron of Du Fu. Lushi was a town on the Luo River, east-southeast of Luoyang, in modern Henan.

2 Literally, "strings and singing between the two columns." "Two columns" refers to the two central supports of a building and in early ritual texts refers to the main public space of a house where important rituals would be performed. The passage alludes to *Analects* 17.4, in which Confucius's disciple Ziyou 子游 has music performed in his modest district of Wucheng 武城.

3 These four lines suggest that Fang Guan rules by Daoist principles, with the result that he has largely eliminated needless court cases.

4 From *Zhuangzi*, chapter 5: Heaven's punishments are the social obligations and expectations placed on one.

2.21

贈祖三詠（濟州官舍作）

蠨蛸挂虛牖，
蟋蟀鳴前除。
歲晏涼風至，
君子復何如。
高館闃無人，
離居不可道。
閑門寂已閉，
落日照秋草。
雖有近音信，
千里阻河關。
中復客汝潁，
去年歸舊山。
結交二十載，
不得一日展。
貧病子既深，
契闊余不淺。
仲秋雖未歸，
暮秋以為期。
良會詎幾日，
終自長相思。

2.21

Presented to Zu Yong Three (composed at the official lodge in Jizhou)[1]

Long-legged spiders hang webs in the window;
Crickets cry on the front stairs.
At the end of the year a cool breeze comes;
And how are things with you, sir?
The high office is quiet – no one here;
But I cannot talk of becoming a hermit yet.
The idle gates are lonely and closed already;
The setting sun shines on the autumn grass.
Though there has been news recently,
A thousand miles are blocked by rivers and passes.[2]
Moreover, you're living as a sojourner on the Ru and Ying Rivers;[3]
And last year you returned to your former hills.
We've been bound in friendship for twenty years,
And haven't been comfortable for even one day.
You're already quite poor and sick,
And my toil and efforts have not been light.
Though you have yet to return at mid-autumn,
Let's agree to meet later in the season.
A fine reunion can't be many days off –
That will bring my longing to an end.

---

1 Written while Wang Wei was stationed in Jizhou, probably in 724 (Zu Yong won the *jinshi* degree the following year). Jizhou was located on the south bank of the Yellow River in Shandong.

2 That is, though he does get news occasionally, the path it must take from the capital is long and arduous.

3 Both rivers in the Luoyang region.

2.22

春夜竹亭贈錢少府歸藍田

夜靜羣動息，
時聞隔林犬。
却憶山中時，
人家澗西遠。
羨君明發去，
采蕨輕軒冕。

2.22a

錢起：酬王維春夜竹亭曾別

山月隨客來，
主人興不淺。
今宵竹林下，
誰覺花源遠。
惆悵曙鶯啼，
孤雲還絕巘。

2.22

Presented to District Defender Qian Qi at a bamboo pavilion on a spring night upon his return to Lantian

The night is still – all stirrings have ceased;
We hear now and then a dog barking beyond the grove.
I recall my own time in the mountains,
4 When our house was far to the west of the stream.
I envy you, departing at dawn;
You'll pluck bracken, scorn the cap and carriage of office.[1]

2.22a

Qian Qi: Answering Wang Wei: "Presented at parting at a bamboo pavilion on a spring night"

The mountain moon comes, following the guest;
The host's excitement is not small.
This evening, under the bamboo grove,
4 Who feels that the Peach Blossom Stream is far away?[2]
We feel disheartened when the dawn orioles cry;
A solitary cloud returns to steep hilltops.

1 Picking bracken is associated with the early Zhou recluses Bo Yi 伯夷 and Shu Qi 叔齊, who preferred to live on weeds in the mountains rather than associate themselves with the Zhou state. They starved to death. "Picking bracken" often is poetic image for high-minded reclusion. This poem (written shortly before Wang Wei's death) shows him fondly recalling his life of reclusion at Lantian, and he suggests to Qian that the district will allow him to be a recluse while still serving in office.

2 Tao Qian 陶潛 (365–427) composed a fable about a woodcutter who discovers an rural paradise hidden in a mountain valley when he travels up a stream covered with peach blossoms. After visiting for a while, he becomes homesick and returns home, only to find that he cannot retrace his steps. Wang Wei mentions the story obsessively in his poetry, and rewrites the story in the *yuefu* ballad style (6.7).

2.23–2.25

戲贈張五弟諲三首（時在常樂東園。走筆成。）

1.

吾弟東山時，
心尚一何遠。
日高猶自臥，
鐘動始能飯。
領上髮未梳，
牀頭書不卷。
清川與悠悠，
空林對偃蹇。
青苔石上淨，
細草松下軟。
窗外鳥聲閑，
階前虎心善。
徒然萬慮多，
澹爾太虛緬。
一知與物平，
自顧為人淺。
對君忽自得，
浮念不煩遣。

2.23–2.25

Playfully sent to younger brother Zhang Yin Five: three poems (At the time I was at East Garden in Changle and composed these ex tempore)[1]

1.

My little brother, when you lived at East Mountain,[2]
How far reaching the things you revered!
When the sun was high you were still in bed,
Only able to eat after bells had sounded.[3]
Your hair still uncombed over your collar;
Unrolled books covered your couch.
You shared the unhurried mood of the clear streams;
Reclined at leisure facing the empty woods.
The green moss was pure on the stones;
Slender grass soft under the pine trees.
Birdsong was idle beyond the window;
The hearts of tigers turned benevolent before the stairs.
In vain did myriad worries multiply;
You were tranquil, far off in the Ultimate Void.
Once you realized your equality with things,
You could observe yourself, hold your status as human as unimportant.
When I faced you, I suddenly felt contented
And baseless conceptions could not distract me.

---

1 Zhang Yin: See note to 1.2.13. Wang calls him "little brother" here out of affection. The two of them lived in retirement together on Mt. Song near Luoyang during the 730s. Changle was a ward of Chang'an.

2 The fourth-century statesman Xie An 謝安 lived for a time in reclusion on East Mountain, outside of the capital of Jiankang. Wang Wei often uses "East Mountain" as a poetic term for a recluse's dwelling.

3 Probably the monastic bells ringing the noon hour (after which monks were not allowed to eat).

2.

張弟五車書，
讀書仍隱居。
染翰過草聖，
賦詩輕子虛。
閉門二室下，
隱居十年餘。
宛是野人野，
時從漁父漁。
秋風日蕭索，
五柳高且疎。
望此去人世，
渡水向吾廬。
歲晏同攜手，
只應君與予。

2.

Little brother Zhang, with your five cartloads of books –[1]
You read your books, yet still lived as a recluse.
When you dipped your brush, you surpassed the grass-style sage;[2]
In composing verse you could hold "Sir Fantasy" at naught.[3]
You closed your gate at the foot of the Two Houses,[4]
Where you lived in reclusion for over ten years –
As if you were wilder than the rustics,
At the time following the old fishermen in their fishing.
Daily the autumn wind grew more desolate;
The five willows were tall and sparse.[5]
Seeing from afar how you had left the world of men,
I forded the waters and headed toward my own hut.
At year's end we held hands together;
There was only you and me.

---

1 A cliché for a book-obsessed scholar. Chapter 33 of the *Zhuangzi* uses the term to describe the erudite sophist Hui Shi 惠施.

2 Reference to Eastern Han calligrapher Zhang Zhi 張芝.

3 The Han poet Sima Xiangru 司馬相如 presented his "Sir Fantasy" rhapsody to Emperor Wu and thence gained preferment at court.

4 The two peaks of Mt. Song (Taishi and Shaoshi, "Big House" and "Little House").

5 A reference to Tao Qian's veiled autobiography, "An Account of Master Five Willows." The subject of the account planted five willow trees in front of his house and took his name from them.

3.

設罝守毚兔，
垂釣伺遊鱗。
此是安口腹，
非關慕隱淪。
吾生好清靜，
蔬食去情塵。
今子方豪蕩，
思為鼎食人。
我家南山下，
動息自遺身。
入鳥不相亂，
見獸皆相親。
雲霞成伴侶，
虛白侍衣巾。
何事須夫子，
邀予谷口真。

3.

You set snares for the cunning hare;
You dropped your line, waiting for the roaming fish scales.
These are things that satisfy mouth and belly;
They have nothing to do with a recluse's true aspirations.
All my life I've admired the pure and quiet;
A vegetarian, I've cast off the dust of passions.
Nowadays you've grown bold and unconstrained,
And you think to become a member of the nobility.[1]
My home is at the foot of Mount Zhongnan;
And I forget the Self whether in public or private.
I can live with the birds without disturbing them;
I can watch the beasts and become their intimates.
The rosy dawn clouds I've made my companions,
And daylight attends upon me when I dress.
For what reason must you, Sir,
Seek out me, the True Man of Gukou?[2]

1 Literally, "eating from tripods." The possession of tripods is a poetic idiom for members of the nobility.

2 Zheng Zizhen 鄭子真 (or Zheng Pu 樸) of Gukou, a famous Eastern Han recluse.

2.26

至滑州隔河望黎陽憶丁三寓

隔河見桑柘，
藹藹黎陽川。
望望行漸遠，
孤峰沒雲烟。
故人不可見，
河水復悠然。
賴有政聲遠，
時聞行路傳。

2.27

秋夜獨坐懷內弟崔興宗

夜靜群動息，
螅蛄聲悠悠。
庭槐北風響，
日夕方高秋。
思子整羽翮，
及時當雲浮。
吾生將白首，
歲晏思滄洲。

2.26

Arriving at Huazhou, I gaze toward Liyang on the other side of the Yellow River and remember Ding Yu Three[1]

I can see mulberry and cudrania on the far shore,
Growing thick by the Liyang stream.
Gazing on and on, I travel farther away;
The solitary peak is sunk in clouds and mist.
I cannot see my old friends;
The Yellow River's waters continue to flow far away.
Luckily your reputation in office reaches far,
So I hear news of you sometimes on the road.

2.27

Sitting alone on an autumn night and remembering my cousin Cui Xingzong

The night is silent; all living things rest.
The sound of the mole crickets drags on.
The north wind echoes in the courtyard sophoras;
In the evening, the high sky of autumn.
I think of you, off preening your pinions;
Very soon you should be drifting in the clouds.[2]
While I am turning gray-headed in my life;
At the end of my years, I think of blue river islets.[3]

1 Probably composed while the poet was traveling to his post in Jizhou, 721. Huazhou is on the southern bank of the Yellow River, about halfway between Luoyang and Jizhou.

2 Soon you will be appointed to office.

3 A standard term for a recluse's habitation.

高足在旦暮，
肯為南畝儔。

2.28

贈裴十迪

風景日夕佳，
與君賦新詩。
澹然望遠空，
如意方支頤。
春風動百草，
蘭蕙生我籬。
曖曖日暖閨，
田家來致詞。
欣欣春還皋，
澹澹水生陂。
桃李雖未開，
荑萼滿其枝。
請君理還策，
敢告將農時。

Soon enough you'll be riding a high-stepping horse –
How could you then be my companion on southern acres?

2.28

Presented to Pei Di Ten

The scenery is splendid towards dusk;
I'm composing new poems with you.
Tranquil, I gaze toward the distant sky,
Propping my chin on my back-scratching staff.
The spring breeze moves all the plants;
Thoroughwort and melillot grow in my hedge.
With mellow light the sun warms the inner rooms;
Farmers come to bring me word.
Flourishing, spring returns to the riverside fields;
The rolling waters rise within the lakes.
Though peach and plum have not yet blossomed,
Shoots and buds fill the branches.
Direct your traveling staff homeward!
I inform you that the farming season begins.

2.29

華嶽

西嶽出浮雲，
積翠在太清。
連天凝黛色，
百里遙青冥。
白日為之寒，
森沉華陰城。
昔聞乾坤閉，
造化生巨靈。
右足踏方止，
左手推削成。
天地忽開拆，
大河注東溟。
遂為西峙嶽，
雄雄鎮秦京。
大君包覆載，
至德被羣生。
上帝佇昭告，
金天思奉迎。
人祇望幸久，
何獨禪云亭。

2.29

The Hua Marchmount[1]

The western marchmount rises from floating clouds,
Massed kingfisher-green in the clear void.
Its congealed blue-black hues are linked to the sky;
For a hundred li it stretches into black obscurity.
It makes the white sun turn cold,
And makes gloomy the town of Huayin.
I once heard that when sky and earth were sealed,
Creation gave birth to the Great Spirit;
With his right foot he trod on Fangzhi,
And with his left hand he shoved and scraped.
Then suddenly Heaven and Earth were torn open,
And the great Yellow River surged to the eastern main.
Then Hua became a marchmount facing west,
Mighty and steadfast, guarding the Qin capital.
The great ruler embraces the sky above and the earth below,
His perfect virtue covers all living things.
God above awaits his shining declaration,
The metal spirit intends to make his greeting.[2]
Men and earth gods have long hoped for his coming;
So why alone offer sacrifice at the peaks of Tai?[3]

---

1 The westernmost of the five sacred mountains (marchmounts) of China; Hua is located near the capital of Chang'an.

2 The god of Mount Hua (metal being the presiding element in the west).

3 Yun and Ting in the text (minor peaks of Mount Tai) are used here as a substitute for the *feng* and *shan* 封禪 sacrifices carried out at Mount Tai 泰, traditionally a prerogative of the emperor since Han times.

王右丞集卷之三 古詩

3.1

胡居士臥病遺米因贈

了觀四大因，
根性何所有。
妄計苟不生，
是身孰休咎。
色聲何謂客，
陰界復誰守。
徒言蓮花目，
豈惡楊枝肘。
既飽香積飯，
不醉聲聞酒。
有無斷常見，
生滅幻夢受。
即病即實相，
趨空定狂走。
無有一法真，

https://doi.org/10.1515/9781501516023-003

Juan 3: Old-style poems

3.1

Sent to Layman Hu with some rice as he lay sick[1]

If one observes completely the Four Great Elements,[2]
Then what does essential nature possess?
If reckless conceptions do not arise,
Then what will this Self have of good fortune or bad?
How then can you call phenomena the objects of perception?
Who then keeps the six *skandha* and eighteen *dhātu*?[3]
If you should only speak of the Buddha's lotus-flower eyes,
Then why dislike the tumor growing from your elbow?[4]
Already full of fragrant rice,[5]
You do not get drunk on *śrāvaka* wine.[6]
Being and Non-Being are views tied to interruption and constancy,
"Arising" and "ending": receiving an illusion or dream.
Now that you are sick, you are close to real appearance,
Directed toward Emptiness, you bring wild flight to an end.
Not a single dharma is real,

---

1 See note to 2.13.

2 The four elements that make up all matter (including one's physical form): earth, water, fire, and wind.

3 *Skandha* – the six psychological processes that result in the illusory conception of a Self. *Dhātu*: the six senses, their objects of perception, and the six forms of consciousness that arise when the first two categories are combined. If one can realize the illusory nature of the Self, then both that Self and its objects of perception will disappear.

4 *Zhuangzi*, chapter 18: When a tumor sprung up from Huajie Shu's 滑介叔 elbow, he calmly explained to his friend Zhili Shu 支離叔 that it was just a natural part of transformation, like life and death. Wang Wei is suggesting that excessive attention to and veneration of the Buddha distracts from one's own self-cultivation.

5 In chapter 10 of the *Vimalakīrti Sutra*, Vimalakīrti feeds the assembly at his house by creating a bodhisattva who travels to another Buddha world and brings back fragrant rice.

6 In Mahayana Buddhism, *śrāvakas* are the inferior "voice-hearers" who are content to achieve enlightenment merely through listening to the preaching of the Buddha.

無有一法垢。
居士素通達，
隨宜善抖擻。
牀上無氈臥，
鎘中有粥否。
齋時不乞食，
定應空漱口。
聊持數斗米，
且救浮生取。

3.2–3.3

與胡居士皆病寄此詩兼示學人二首

1.

一興微塵念，
橫有朝露身。
如是觀陰界，
何方置我人。
礙有固為主，
趣空寧捨賓。
洗心詎懸解，
悟道正迷津。
因愛果生病，

Not a single dharma is impure.
You sir, have long been perceptive;
Following what is suitable, you are good at the *dhūtas*.[1]
You have no carpet on your couch for you to lie on;
Does your pot have any gruel at all?
At fasting time you do not beg for food;
It must be useless for you to rinse your mouth!
For the time being, take these several pecks of rice
That will allow you to preserve your floating life for a while.

3.2–3.3

Having fallen sick with Layman Hu, I sent these poems to him and also showed them to some fellow students

1.

Once you give rise to thoughts of the trivial, dusty world,
You suddenly possess a body as fragile as the morning dew.
And if you look at the *skandha* and the *dhatu* that way,[2]
Nothing prevents you from creating Self and Other.
Obstructed by Being, you definitely create the Subjective;
Even if you incline towards Emptiness, how can you cast off
the Objective?
How can you untie your bonds, even if you cleanse the mind?
Though you awaken to the Way, you still are lost on the path.
Because of desire, in the end you become ill;

---

1 Forms of ascetic practice.
2 See note to 3.1.6.

從貪始覺貧。
色聲非彼妄，
浮幻即吾真。
四達竟何遣，
萬殊安可塵。
胡生但高枕，
寂寞與誰鄰。
戰勝不謀食，
理齊甘負薪。
子若未始異，
詎論疏與親。

2.

浮空徒漫漫，
汎有定悠悠。
無乘及乘者，
所謂智人舟。
詎捨貧病域，
不疲生死流。
無煩君喻馬，
任以我為牛。

1 Boats are common metaphors for methods to achieve enlightenment.

In the course of craving, you become aware that you're poor.
Sensory perceptions are not false because of others;
12 Floating illusions are the reality of the Self.
What must be rejected on the comprehensive path?
How can myriad phenomena bring any pollution?
You, Master Hu, simply rest aloft,
16 In remote stillness – and who is your neighbor?
Conquering your own will, you make no plans for your meals;
Making all principles equal, you're content to haul firewood.
You have kept yourself apart from the beginning,
20 Then why talk about whether people are close to you or remote?

2.

Ephemeral Emptiness is pointlessly boundless,
Drifting Being is decidedly remote.
The non-vehicle which is a vehicle –
4 That is what we call the boat of the Wise.[1]
If you cast aside the realms of poverty and illness,
If you do not grow fatigued in the current of life and death,
Then there will be no need for you to imagine yourself a horse;[2]
8 Feel free then to consider me an ox.[3]

---

2 The *Nirvana Sutra*, chapter 40: The Buddha compares the Three Vehicles (bodhisattvas, pratyekabuddhas, and śrāvakas) to three horses owned by the king: a strong, well-trained horse, a weak, badly trained horse, and an aged horse. The king will of course prefer to ride the first one.

3 *Zhuangzi*, chapter 13: Laozi tells Shicheng Qi 士成綺 that he has freed himself from "clever wisdom," so was utterly indifferent whether Shicheng were to call him an ox or a horse. This couplet means that a person who has transcended concerns about poverty, illness, or death will no longer be caught up in false distinctions.

植福祠迦葉，
求仁笑孔丘。
何津不鼓棹，
何路不摧輈。
念此聞思者，
胡為多阻修。
空虛花聚散，
煩惱樹稀稠。
滅想成無記，
生心坐有求。
降吳復歸蜀，
不到莫相尤。

3.4

藍田山石門精舍

落日山水好，
漾舟信歸風。
玩奇不覺遠，

1 Mahākāśyapa was a disciple of the Buddha's famous for his ascetic practice and his commitment to poverty. Embracing his way of life will enable one to transcend the comparatively petty concerns of Confucianism (Kong Qiu is the personal name of Confucius).

2 Serious practice is difficult and painful.

Establishing roots of good fortune, pray to Mahākāśyapa,
And laugh at Kong Qiu when you seek benevolence.[1]
What ford does not require you to ply your oars?
What road does not break your cart shafts?[2]
Recall those who are wise through learning and thinking –
Why are they still obstructed when they practice?
Illusory specks gather and scatter;
The forest of *kleśa* grows sparse or thick.[3]
If you annihilate thought, then things remain too neutral;
But if the mind arises, then that leads to desire.
Surrender to Wu or return to Shu?[4]
If you don't reach your goal, then don't blame me.

3.4

Stone Gate Monastery at Lantian Mountain[5]

Hills and waters are fine in the setting sun;
A bobbing boat is entrusted to the homebound breeze.
Enjoying the marvelous, not noticing how far it was,

3 *Kleśa* are the various delusions, afflictions, and passions that compel one to continue to generate karma and remain trapped in the world of samsara.

4 During the Three Kingdoms period, the Shu general Huang Quan 黄權 was cut off from Shu after a military defeat inflicted by Wu. He felt he had no option but to defect to Wei, stating that he could neither return to Shu in shame nor surrender to Wu.

5 Wang Wei models this monastery visit on Tao Qian's famous "Account of Peach Blossom Stream." See note to 2.22a.4.

因以緣源窮。
遙愛雲木秀，
初疑路不同。
安知清流轉，
偶與前山通。
捨舟理輕策，
果然愜所適。
老僧四五人，
逍遙蔭松柏。
朝梵林未曙，
夜禪山更寂。
道心及牧童，
世事問樵客。
暝宿長林下，
焚香臥瑤席。
澗芳襲人衣，
山月映石壁。
再尋畏迷誤，
明發更登歷。
笑謝桃源人，
花紅復來覿。

In this way I reached to the source of the creek.
I loved from afar the splendor of these cloudlike trees,
But began to suspect that the road wouldn't reach them.
How could I know that the clear current would turn,
And by chance would meet up with the hills in front?
I left boat behind, took light staff in hand;
As it turned out, I found pleasure in the place I reached.
Old monks, four or five of them,
Sauntered freely, taking shade under pines and cypress.
Morning sutra chanting, before the forest turns to dawn;
Evening meditation, when the hills are even more quiet.
Minds focused on the Way reach to the herd boys;
They ask woodcutters about worldly affairs.
At dusk I spend the night under tall trees,
Burn incense, lie down on precious mats.
The stream is fragrant – the scent invades our robes;
The mountain moon shines on the stone walls.
If I search for this again, I afraid I'll go astray;
At dawn I set out and continue my climbing.
With a smile I bid farewell to the Peach Blossom folk:
When flowers bloom red I'll come again to see them.

3.5

青溪

言入黃花川，
每逐青溪水。
隨山將萬轉，
趣途無百里。
聲喧亂石中，
色靜深松裏。
漾漾汎菱荇，
澄澄映葭葦。
我心素已閒，
清川澹如此。
請留盤石上，
垂釣將已矣。

3.6

崔濮陽兄季重前山興（山西去亦對維門）

秋色有佳興，
況君池上閒。
悠悠西林下，
自識門前山。

3.5

Green Creek

Whenever you enter the stream of yellow flowers,
You must always go along the waters of Green Creek.
It follows the mountain, taking a myriad turns,
4 Though its rushing course is less than a hundred li.
It makes raucous noise through the jumbled rocks,
And its color is calm amid the deep pine trees.
Its rolling current floats caltrop and water-fringe;
8 Pellucid, it reflects the reeds.
My mind has long been at rest;
And this clear stream is tranquil in the same way.
Please let me remain on a flat rock,
12 And come to my end, just dangling a hook.

3.6

I am inspired by the mountains in front of the house of my cousin Cui Jizhong of Puyang (having left Shanxi, he is living opposite me)[1]

The autumn colors have a splendid appeal,
Even more so by the calm of your pool.
Remote and dim, below the western wood,
4 I can make out the hills before your gate.

1 Puyang: on the southern bank of the Yellow River in Shandong.

千里橫黛色，
數峰出雲間。
嵯峨對秦國，
8 合沓藏荊關。
殘雨斜日照，
夕嵐飛鳥還。
故人今尚爾，
12 歎息此頹顏。

3.7

終南別業

中歲頗好道，
晚家南山陲。
興來每獨往，
4 勝事空自知。
行到水窮處，
坐看雲起時。
偶然值林叟，
8 談笑無還期。

For a thousand li they spread their blue-black color,
Several peaks rising from the midst of the clouds.
Jutting and looming, they face the land of Qin;
In rising layers they hide away the Jing pass.
The setting sun shines in the lingering rain;
Flying birds return through the evening mountain mist.
An old friend is now just the same as he was;
He sighs for my features grown haggard with age.

3.7

My villa at Mt. Zhongnan

In middle age I grow rather fond of the Way;
My late home is in a corner of Mt. Zhongnan.
When the mood comes, I always go out alone;
I myself know, emptily, of these splendid things.[1]
I walk to where the waters begin,
I sit and watch when the clouds arise.
By chance I meet an old man of the woods;
We chat and laugh, no time we have to go home.

---

1 The adverbial use of *kong* ("empty") in this line evades reasonable translation. It suggests that the poet is both conscious of the splendor of the scene but that it is also part of *śunyatā*, the essentially "unreal" nature of our reality.

3.8

李處士山居

君子盈天階，
小人甘自免。
方隨鍊金客，
林上家絕巘。
背嶺花未開，
入雲樹深淺。
清晝猶自眠，
山鳥時一囀。

3.9

韋侍郎山居

幸忝君子顧，
遂陪塵外蹤。
閑花滿巖谷，
瀑水映杉松。
啼鳥忽臨澗，
歸雲時抱峰。
良游盛簪紱，
繼跡多夔龍。

3.8

Recluse Li's mountain residence

Gentlemen fill the stairs of Heaven;
But this petty man is content to excuse himself.
Just now, I'm following a smelter of gold[1]
To his house above the wood, on a steep precipice.
With their backs to the ridge, the flowers have yet to open;
As they enter the clouds, the trees are both dense and thin.
In clear daylight, you still slumber away,
While a mountain bird utters a single trill from time to time.

3.9

Vice Director Wei's mountain residence[2]

I, unworthy, have the good fortune to attract the attention of gentlemen;
And so I have accompanied them on paths beyond the dust.
Wildflowers fill the cliff valleys;
Waterfalls shine among the cypress and pine.
Twittering birds suddenly appear at the edge of the creek;
Homing clouds from time to time embrace the peak.
This fine outing is replete with official hatpins and sashes;
Many Kuis and Longs among the succession of followers.[3]

1 I.e., a Daoist alchemist (describing Recluse Li).
2 See note to 2.11. The Vice Director is Wei Heng's younger brother, Wei Ji.
3 See note to 2.11.11.

詎枉青門道，
故聞長樂鐘。
清晨去朝謁，
12 車馬何從容。

3.10

丁寓田家有贈

君心尚棲隱，
久欲傍歸路。
在朝每為言，
4 解印果成趣。
晨雞鳴鄰里，
羣動從所務。
農夫行餉田，
8 閨婦起縫素。
開軒御衣服，
散帙理章句。
時吟招隱詩，
12 或製閒居賦。
新晴望郊郭，
日映桑榆暮。
陰盡小苑城，

How could the road from Blue Gate take us out of our way?
All along we can hear the bells of Changle Palace.[1]
In the clear dawn we go off to attend court;
How leisurely move our carriages and horses!

3.10

I have a poem to present for Ding Yu's farm estate

Your mind is still set on living in reclusion;
For long you have wished to pursue a road back home.
Every time we spoke at court,
It turned out you were inclined to untie your seal of office.
Roosters at dawn crow in the neighboring village;
All living things take up their chosen tasks.
Farmers go by, bringing meals into the fields;
Wives in their chambers rise to sew their plain-silks.
You open a window, straighten your clothes,
Pull off your scroll wraps, put in order your commentaries.
Sometimes you'll chant "Summoning the Recluse,"
Or you'll compose a rhapsody on living at leisure.[2]
In the recent clear weather you gaze out over the outskirts,
The sun shines on mulberry and elm at dusk.
The shadows it casts end at the walls of the small garden,

---

1 The eminence of the officials going on the outing is like moving the court from the palace to the country. Blue Gate (originally a Han name) indicates one of Chang'an's eastern gates, the gate that officials would have to pass through on the way to Wei's country estate at Mount Li. For Changle, see note to 2.3.6.

2 "Summoning the Recluse": A subgenre of pre-Tang poems. The *Wen xuan* has noted examples by Zuo Si 左思 and Lu Ji 陸機. Pan Yue 潘岳 composed a "Rhapsody on Living at Leisure."

微明渭川樹。
揆予宅閭井，
幽賞何由屢。
道存終不忘，
迹異難相遇。
此時惜離別，
再來芳菲度。

3.11

渭川田家

斜光照墟落，
窮巷牛羊歸。
野老念牧童，
倚杖候荊扉。
雉雊麥苗秀，
蠶眠桑葉稀。
田夫荷鋤至，
相見語依依。
即此羨閒逸，
悵然歌式微。

16 And its faint glow lights the trees by the Wei River.[1]
When I appraise my own residence in the city ward,
How can I appreciate seclusion there very often?
The path of friendship, we'll never forget it;
20 But on different tracks, it's difficult to meet up.
This time I regret that we have to part;
When I come next time, I'll pass the fragrant season with you.

3.11

A farmhouse on the Wei River

Slanting sunlight shines on the village;
Cows and sheep return to the lowly lanes.
An old rustic thinks of the cowherd lads,
4 And leaning on his staff he waits by his scrap-wood door.
Pheasants call; the wheat is in ear;
The silkworms sleep; the mulberry leaves are few.
Farmhands arrive, bearing hoes on shoulders;
8 When they meet, their speech is gentle and calm.
When I meet this, I envy this leisure and freedom,
And I sadly sing "Shi wei."[2]

1 This indicates that Ding's retreat is within sight of Chang'an. Small garden: a palace garden; some commentators suggest that it is a garden in the Qujiang Park to the southeast of the city.

2 *Shijing* 36: "How few we are! / Why don't we return? / Were it not for the reason of our lord, / Why would we be in the middle of the dew?" Here Wang Wei merely wants to evoke the desire to abandon office and return to the country.

3.12

春中田園作

屋上春鳩鳴，
村邊杏花白。
持斧伐遠揚，
荷鋤覘泉脈。
歸燕識故巢，
舊人看新曆。
臨觴忽不御，
惆悵遠行客。

3.13

過李揖宅

閒門秋草色，
終日無車馬。
客來深巷中，
犬吠寒林下。
散髮時未簪，
道書行尚把。
與我同心人，
樂道安貧者。

3.12

Written in fields and gardens in mid-spring

From the rooftops the spring doves cry;
By the village the apricot flowers are white.
They take their axes, lop off high branches;[1]
With hoes on shoulders, they look for underground streams.
Returning swallows recognize their former nests,
While the same old people consult the new calendar.
Goblet before me, I suddenly put it away;
A disheartened traveler who has traveled far.

3.13

Visiting the homestead of Li Yi

By the idle gate, the color of autumn grass;
No carriages or horses the entire day.
A guest comes into the remote lanes;
A dog barks below the chilly woods.
He's let his hair down – he's not wearing official hatpins at present.
When he goes out he still has Daoist books in hand.
A man who shares the same mind with me,
Delights in the Way, is at peace with poverty.

1 There is an allusion to *Shijing* 154, which describes the harvest of mulberry leaves for the silkworms and the pruning of the mulberry trees.

一罷宜城酌，
還歸洛陽社。

3.14

飯覆釜山僧

晚知清淨理，
日與人羣疎。
將候遠山僧，
先期掃敝廬。
果從雲峰裏，
顧我蓬蒿居。
藉草飯松屑，
焚香看道書。
燃燈晝欲盡，
鳴磬夜方初。
已悟寂為樂，
此生閒有餘。
思歸何必深，
身世猶空虛。

Once I'm done imbibing his ale from Yicheng,[1]
I'll go home again to my hamlet outside of Luoyang.

3.14

Feeding the monks of Fufu Mountain[2]

In old age I understand principle of purity;
Daily I grow apart from the crowd.
I will wait for these monks from the distant hills,
Sweeping my shabby hut before their appointed coming.
As expected, they come from their cloudy peak
To visit me in my overgrown dwelling.
Sitting on the grass, they dine on pine nuts;
Burning incense, they look through books on the Way.
The lamps are lit as day draws to an end;
The temple chimes are struck at the beginning of the night.
Already awakened to the joy of Stillness,
I have more than enough leisure for this life.
A desire to retire – why must it be serious?
For both self and world are truly empty.

1 A district mentioned from early times as a producer of fine ale.

2 Possibly the Fufu Mountain located in the Tang district of Guozhou 虢州, near where the modern provinces of Shanxi, Shaanxi, and Henan meet.

3.15

謁璿上人（并序）

上人外人內天。不定不亂。捨法而淵泊。無心而雲動。色空無得。不物物也。默語無際。不言言也。故吾徒得神交焉。玄關大啟。德海羣泳。時雨既降。春物具美。序于詩者。人百其言。

少年不足言，
識道年已長。
事往安可悔，
4 餘生幸能養。
誓從斷葷血，
不復嬰世網。
浮名寄纓珮，
8 空性無羈鞅。
夙從大導師，
焚香此瞻仰。
頹然居一室，
12 覆載紛萬象。
高柳早鶯啼，

3.15

Visiting His Reverence Xuan (with preface)[1]

His Reverence is a man in appearance, but harbors the celestial within. He is neither settled nor undisciplined; he has cast aside all dharmas and he is profound and serene. He moves as the clouds, without motive. He has no obtaining of either the sensual or of Emptiness; this is because he does not regard things as things. He has no boundaries on his silence or on his speech, because he does not treat words as words. Consequently, we are able to obtain a spiritual communion with him. The mysterious gate of his Dharma is open wide, and multitudes may swim in his sea of merit. Since a timely rain has fallen, the spring scenery is lovely. What I have written in this preface others could expand on a hundredfold.

My youth is not worth speaking of;
And I am old enough now to recognize the Way.
These things have passed – how can I regret them?
4 For with luck I can nourish my remaining years.
I swear I will accordingly abstain from garlic and meat,
And will no longer entangle myself in the world's net.
Fleeting fame is lodged in the ribbons and pendants of office,
8 While a nature of Emptiness has no bridle or harness.
Long have I followed you as the Great Guide,
Burning incense and paying you due reverence.
You remain in one room,[2]
12 While all above and below teem with a myriad forms.
Early orioles twitter in the tall willow trees,

1 Composed ca. 741. Xuan was a monk associated with the contemporary Chan movement, and a disciple of Puji 普寂.

2 Like Vimalakīrti, who preached from his sickroom to untold millions of followers.

長廊春雨響。
牀下阮家屐，
牕前筇竹杖。
方將見身雲，
陋彼示天壤。
一心在法要，
願以無生獎。

3.16

送魏郡李太守赴任

與君伯氏別，
又欲與君離。
君行無幾日，
當復隔山陂。
蒼茫秦川盡，
日落桃林塞。
獨臥臨關門，
黃河向天外。
前經洛陽陌，

1 *Shishuo xinyu* 6.15 compares Ruan Fu's 阮孚 fascination with clogs to Zu Yue's 祖約 obsession with money. Ruan Fu's hobby is seen as by far the better obsession.

2 A special form of bamboo used for staffs, found on Mount Qiong in Shu.

Spring rain echoes in the long gallery.
At the foot of your couch a pair of Ruan family clogs;[1]
Before your window, a Mount Qiong bamboo cane.[2]
Just now I behold your cloud of incarnations,
Displaying to the humble the Heaven's-Soil manifestation.[3]
Your entire mind lies with the Dharma's essentials;
And you vow to reward me with non-birth.

3.16

Seeing off Governor Li of Wei Commandery on the way to his office[4]

I've parted with your elder brother,
And now I'm about to separate from you.
In your travels, before many days,
You should be cut off from me by mountain slopes.
Boundless expanse to the end of the Qin plain;
The sun sets on the peach-wood borderland.[5]
Alone you lie at the gate to the pass;
The Yellow River flows beyond the sky.
Previously you frequented the streets of Luoyang,

---

3 *Zhuangzi*, chapter 7: Liezi astonishes the physiognomist Jixian 季咸 by deliberately displaying to him more and more powerful features. The second set of features he shows is "Heaven's Soil," a manifestation beyond names and realities, fame and profit. Here Wang Wei combines the Daoist text with a Buddhist interpretation of a bodhisattva's different incarnations that serve as a skillful means.

4 Governor Li most likely here is Li Xian 峴, an imperial scion. He and his brother Li Huan 峘 had been exiled to provincial posts with the rise of Yang Guozhong 楊國重. Li Huan is the elder brother mentioned in the first line. Wei Commandery was on the north bank of the He in Hebei, across the river from Shandong.

5 The Qin plain: a term for the capital area. Peach-wood borderland: a term for the area east of Tong 潼 Pass (through which Li Xian must pass on the way to his commandery). Wang Wei emphasizes their separation by contrasting where he is and where Li will be.

宛洛故人稀。
故人離別盡，
淇上轉驂騑。
企予悲送遠，
惆悵睢陽路。
古木官渡平，
秋城鄴宮故。
想君行縣日，
其出從如雲。
遙思魏公子，
復憶李將軍。

3.17

送康太守

城下滄江水，
江邊黃鶴樓。
朱欄將粉堞，
江水映悠悠。

---

1 Wan and Luo refer to Luoyang and the city of Nanyang in Wan County – both substantial cities in the Eastern Han. In poetry, the two are often linked together to indicate urban spaces.

2 A river that flows into the Yellow River slightly west of Wei Commandery.

3 Wang Wei here alludes to Li Xian's brother, Li Huan, who was sent to govern the district of Suiyang, located on the other side of the Yellow River and some distance further south (in Shandong).

At Wan and Luo, when friends were few.[1]
Friends – you've bid them all farewell;
You'll turn the course of your team at the Qi River.[2]
Craning to gaze afar, you grieve for the one you've sent off,
Disconsolate on the Suiyang Road.[3]
Old trees – the Guandu Terrace is leveled;
Autumn town – the Ye Palace now a relic.[4]
I imagine days when you tour your districts,
Bringing an entourage with you like trailing clouds.
You'll think of the Prince of Wei so long ago,
And you'll remember General Li.[5]

3.17

Seeing off Prefect Kang[6]

Below the city walls, the gray-blue river waters;
Beside the river, Yellow Crane Tower:
Its vermilion railings and white parapets,
And the glitter of the river that stretches far away.

---

4 These are both structures that date from the Wei dynasty, when the Cao family ruled from the city of Ye (near Weizhou, which Li Xian has been sent to govern). Guandu was also the site of a famous battle in which Cao Cao decisively defeated his rival warlord Yuan Shao 袁紹.

5 If Wang Wei is continuing to allude to Wei history and the rise of Cao Cao, then the Prince of Wei probably refers to Cao Pi 丕 (still an imperial prince during Cao's rise at Ye), and General Li refers to Li Dian 典, one of Cao Cao's most valiant and capable commanders.

6 Probably written ca. 740, during Wang Wei's tour of the south. Xiakou was in the central Jiang valley, where the modern city of Wuhan is located. Other sites mentioned in this poem are in the same area.

鐃吹發夏口，
使君居上頭。
郭門隱楓岸，
候吏趨蘆洲。
何異臨川郡，
還來康樂侯。

3.18

送陸員外

郎署有伊人，
居然古人風。
天子顧河北，
詔書隸征東。
拜手辭上官，
緩步出南宮。
九河平原外，
七國薊門中。
陰風悲枯桑，
古塞多飛蓬。
萬里不見虜，
蕭條胡地空。

Bells and flutes emerge from Xiakou,
And the emissary is at the vanguard.
The outer gates are concealed by the maple-tree banks;
Welcoming messengers hurry to Reed Islet.
How is this different from when the Duke of Kangle
Came once again to Linchuan Commandery?[1]

3.18

Seeing off Vice Director Lu

This man is among the Court Gentlemen,
Yet he clearly possesses the manner of the men of old.
The Son of Heaven attends upon matters in Hebei,
And has issued an edict attaching you to the Military Commissioner.[2]
With prostrations you took leave of your high office;
With measured gait you departed the Department of State Affairs,
To go beyond the Nine Rivers and Pingyuan,[3]
Mid the seven lands at Jimen.[4]
A northern wind grieves in the withered mulberries;
Many drifting tumbleweeds at the ancient frontier.
For a myriad li no outlanders are seen;
In desolation the northern lands are empty.

1 Kang is being compared to the poet Xie Lingyun when he took up his post as governor of Linchuan (near Fuzhou in modern Jiangxi).
2 Zhengdong ("expedition against the east") here probably a version of Andong 安東 ("pacifier of the east"), likely a name for the Military Commissioner of Hebei (the frontier region around modern Hebei and Liaoning).
3 Pingyuan – in Shandong. The Nine Rivers is unclear but seems to be referring generally to the area of modern Hebei.
4 Archaic designations of the Youzhou 幽州 area (around modern Beijing).

無為費中國，
更欲邀奇功。
遲遲前相送，
16 握手嗟異同。
行當封侯歸，
肯訪南山翁。

3.19

送宇文太守赴宣城

寥落雲外山，
迢遙舟中賞。
鐃吹發西江，
4 秋空多清響。
地迥古城蕪，
月明寒潮廣。
時賽敬亭神，
8 復解罟師網。
何處寄想思，
南風吹五兩。

No use to waste the resources of the empire
In a further striving for extraordinary merit.
With hesitant steps I come forward to see you off;
We clasp hands, lament that we dissent from others.[1]
When you return to be enfeoffed,
Will you consent to visit this old man of Zhongnan Mountain?

3.19

Seeing off Prefect Yuwen on his way to Xuancheng[2]

Fading away, the hills beyond the clouds;
When you've gone afar, you delight in them from your boat.
Bells and pipes come forth on the Jiang as it flows from the west;
Their clear echoes multiply in the autumn sky.
Land stretches far; the old city covered in weeds;
The moon is bright, the chill current is broad.
At times you'll offer thanks to the gods of Jingting,[3]
And once more untie the fishermen's nets.[4]
Where can I lodge my thoughts of you,
Now that the southern breeze blows the vane on the mast?

1 I.e., with our opinion that military action is ill-advised.

2 Likely composed during Wang Wei's tour of the south (ca. 740). Xuancheng was located west of Taihu, in modern Anhui. It was noted in literature from poems composed by Xie Tiao 謝朓, who served there as a magistrate.

3 The god of Jingting Mountain north of Xuancheng. When Xie Tiao was prefect there he also composed verses about sacrificing to the god.

4 Tang, the founder of the Shang dynasty, once instructed fishermen to open part of their nets, so that those fish that were destined not to be caught would be able to escape.

3.20

送綦毋校書棄官還江東

明時久不達，
棄置與君同。
天命無怨色，
人生有素風。
念君拂衣去，
四海將安窮。
秋天萬里淨，
日暮澄江空。
清夜何悠悠，
扣舷明月中。
和光魚鳥際，
澹爾蒹葭叢。
無庸客昭世，
衰鬢日如蓬。
頑疎暗人事，
僻陋遠天聰。
微物縱可採，
其誰為至公。
余亦從此去，
歸耕為老農。

3.20

Seeing off Editor Qiwu after he resigned his post on his return to Jiangdong[1]

Long unsuccessful in an enlightened era,
I have been cast aside, the same as you.
Yet you have no resentment toward Heaven's decrees;
Your entire life you've had an air of purity.
I think of you as you brush off your robe and depart –
Throughout the wide world, contented with poverty.
The autumn sky is clean for a myriad li;
At dusk the pellucid river is empty.
How relaxed is this clear night;
You tap on the side of the boat in the bright moonlight.
You'll blend in amid the fish and birds;
Be tranquil in a thicket of reeds.
Nothing to do, a sojourner in a brilliant age,
Your graying temples grow more tangled each day.
Stubborn and careless, ignorant of men's affairs,
Remote and lowly, you'll be far from the Divine Hearing.[2]
Even if insignificant men might be chosen,
Who is there who would come to you?
I too will depart from now,
Return to plow, become an old farmer.

1 Jiangdong: probably Qianzhou 虔州, in southeastern Jiangxi.
2 I.e., the emperor's awareness.

3.21

送六舅歸陸渾

伯舅吏淮泗，
卓魯方喟然。
悠哉自不競，
退耕東皋田。
條桑臘月下，
種杏春風前。
酌醴賦歸去，
共知陶令賢。

3.22

邱為： 留別王維

歸鞍白雲外，
繚繞出前山。
今日又明日，
自知心不閒。
親勞簪組送，
欲趁鶯花還。
一步一迴首，
遲遲向近關。

3.21

Seeing off Sixth Uncle on his return to Luhun[1]

When my esteemed uncle was sent to the Huai and Si,
Zhuo and Lu would have sighed in admiration.[2]
But your thoughts were remote, you did not vie with others;
You're retiring to your plow in the fields on the east bank.
You'll prune mulberry branches under the twelfth-month moon,
Plant apricot trees before the spring breeze.
Ladling ale, you'll compose a rhapsody on "going home" –
Both of us know the wisdom of Magistrate Tao.[3]

3.22

Qiu Wei: Taking leave of Wang Wei[4]

My returning saddle beyond the white clouds
Winds round and about, emerging from the hills in front.
Today it is clear once more:
I myself know that my mind is restless.
You've personally bothered to see off this official
Who wishes to return in the season of orioles and flowers.
Turning my head back with every step,
I reluctantly head toward the nearest pass.

---

1 Luhun: southeast of Luoyang, near the Shandong border. The Huai River flowed nearby, as well as the Si, one of its tributaries.

2 Two magistrates from the Eastern Han, Zhuo Mao 卓茂 and Lu Gong 魯恭, known for their benevolence and competence.

3 An allusion to Tao Qian, who composed a rhapsody on returning to his farm.

4 This is probably not a Wang Wei poem, but a poem by Qiu Wei (later editors may have taken the identification of the author as part of the title). It is probably a response to Wang Wei's poem 8.9.

3.23

送別

下馬飲君酒，
問君何所之。
君言不得意，
4 歸臥南山陲。
但去莫復問，
白雲無盡時。

3.23

Farewell

I dismount, give you ale to drink,
Ask you where you are going.
You tell me that things have not gone as you had wished;
4 And you are returning to recline at the side of Zhongnan Mountain.
Just go then – I will ask nothing more –
In this time when the white clouds have no end.

王右丞集卷之四 古詩

4.1

送張五歸山

送君盡惆悵，
復送何人歸。
幾日同攜手，
一朝先拂衣。
東山有茅屋，
幸為掃荊扉。
當亦謝官去，
豈令心事違。

4.2

淇上別趙仙舟

相逢方一笑，
相送還成泣。
祖帳已傷離，
荒城復愁入。
天寒遠山淨，
日暮長河急。

Juan 4: Old style poems

4.1

Seeing off Zhang Five, who is returning to the hills[1]

Seeing you off completely disheartens me –
For whom am I sending home once more?
For several days we've held hands together,
And then suddenly you're brushing off your robe to leave.
There is a thatched dwelling on East Mountain;[2]
I hope you'll sweep around the thorn-wood door there.
I really should resign my post and go –
Why let the heart run contrary to things?

4.2

On the Qi River, parting with Zhao Xianzhou

When we met, barely time for a smile;
Now I see you off, and it has turned to tears.
Already heart-broken over separation at the farewell banquet,
I will be melancholy again when I enter the desolate town.
The sky is cold, the distant hills are pure;
At twilight the long river is surging.

1 Probably Zhang Yin (see 1.2.13 and 2.23–25).

2 See note to 2.23.1.

解纜君已遙，
望君猶佇立。

4.3

送縉雲苗太守

手疏謝明主，
腰章為長吏。
方從會稽邸，
更發汝南騎。
按節下松陽，
清江響鐃吹。
露冕見三吳，
方知百城貴。

4.4

送從弟蕃遊淮南

讀書復騎射，
帶劍遊淮陰。
淮陰少年輩，

1 Jinyun: in Guazhou 括州, in modern Zhejiang.

You untie the cable and already you are far off;
I gaze off to you, still standing here.

4.3

Seeing off Miao, Prefect of Jinyun[1]

You personally drafted a memorial thanking your enlightened lord;
With seal of office at your waist, you have become a high-ranking official.
Just now, coming from the Guiji magistrate's hostel,
You set out again with Runan riders.[2]
You will halt your whip when you descend on Songyang;[3]
On the clear river the bells and pipes will echo.
You will display your ceremonial cap in the three Wu districts;
Then will you know the value of controlling a hundred towns.[4]

4.4

Seeing off my cousin Fan, who is traveling to Huainan

You read books but also ride and shoot;
With sword at your belt, you travel south of the Huai.
All the young men south of the Huai

---

2 Allusion to two Han era anecdotes. Zhu Maichen 朱買臣 was appointed magistrate to Guiji 會稽, and was awaiting his official seal of office while staying in the capital hostel reserved for prefects; he astonished others by the modesty of his behavior. When Han Chong 韓崇 departed for his post in Runan 汝南, the emperor presented him with a gift of carriages, horses, swords, and leather belts.

3 A town about forty kilometers west of Jinyun.

4 "Hundred towns": poetic substitution for a governor's district.

千里遠相尋。
高義難自隱，
明時寧陸沈。
島夷九州外，
泉館三山深。
席帆聊問罪，
卉服盡成擒。
歸來見天子，
拜爵賜黃金。
忽思鱸魚膾，
復有滄洲心。
天寒蒹葭渚，
日落雲夢林。
江城下楓葉，
淮上聞秋砧。
送歸青門外，
車馬去駸駸。
惆悵新豐樹，
空餘天際禽。

From a thousand li away will seek you out.
With your lofty sense of justice, you could not become a recluse;
Why conceal yourself in an enlightened age?
The island barbarians, beyond the Nine Provinces
Are deep in their water lodges at the Three Mountains.[1]
Setting sail, you intended to call them to account,
Captured all of them in their clothes of plaited straw.
You returned, had an audience with the Son of Heaven;
He enfeoffed you, gifted you with gold.
But now you long for the minced sea-bass of home,[2]
And have a mind bent on living on a blue islet.[3]
The weather is cold on the bank of reeds and rushes;
The sun sets on Cloud-Dream forest.[4]
Maple leaves fall on the river city;
On the Huai you hear the autumn fulling blocks.
I see you on your return trip out the Blue Gate;[5]
How swiftly our carriages and horses go!
I am disconsolate among the trees of Xinfeng,
Where there are only birds at the edge of the sky.

---

1 Allusive description of the Tungusic Mohe 靺鞨 from Manchuria, who were carrying out pirate raids on the Chinese coast at this time. They are often described as "mermen" (living in water lodges), living near the Three Immortal Isles in the eastern sea.

2 Zhang Han 張翰 was a statesman from Wu who served the Eastern Jin. While in Luoyang, he began to long for the minced sea-bass of home, and so surrendered his office.

3 Standard poetic cliché for a recluse's residence.

4 Refers to the large marshland of Chu known as "Cloud-Dream," part of which extends into the Huainan area.

5 See note to 3.9.10.

4.5

送權二

高人不可友，
清論復何深。
一見如舊識，
一言知道心。
明時當薄宦，
解薜去中林。
芳草空隱處，
白雲餘故岑。
韓侯久攜手，
河嶽共幽尋。
悵別千餘里，
臨堂鳴素琴。

4.5

Seeing off Quan Two

It is not right for a lofty man to have friends –
But how profound our unsullied discourses have been!
I saw you once and you were like an old acquaintance;
One word with you and I knew your heart committed to the Way.
In an enlightened time you should accept even a lowly post,
So you took off your hermit weeds and left your forest.
Now only fragrant grass grows in your place of reclusion,
And white clouds remain on your former summit.
I held hands long with the Marquis of Han[1]
When together we sought the secluded among rivers and peaks.
Despondent that we will be parted by a thousand li,
In the hall I make my plain zither resound.

1 *Shijing* 261 mentions the Marquis of Han leaving the court and then sacrificing to the god of the road. Similarly, Quan is leaving the court and having a farewell banquet with Wang.

4.6

送高道弟耽歸臨淮作（坐上成）

少年客淮泗，
落拓居下邳。
遨游向燕趙，
結客過臨淄。
山東諸侯國，
迎送紛交馳。
自爾厭游俠，
閉戶方垂帷。
深明戴家禮，
頗學毛公詩。
備知經濟道，
高臥陶唐時。
聖主詔天下，
賢人不得遺。
公吏奉纁組，
安車去茅茨。
君王蒼龍闕，
九門十二逵。
群公朝謁罷，
冠劍下丹墀。

4.6

Seeing off Gao Dao's younger brother Dan on his return to Linhuai (composed at the banquet)[1]

As a youth you wandered about the Huai and Si valleys,
Living free and easy in Xiapi.[2]
You roamed at your pleasure in Yan and Zhao,
Made friends with nobles' retainers when you visited Linzi.[3]
In all the feudal lords' states to the east of the mountains,
Numerous greetings and partings came and went in succession.
After this you grew tired of being a wandering knight-errant;
You closed your door and lowered your curtains.[4]
You deeply comprehended the Dai Family's Rites,
And studied rather well the Mao Masters' Poetry.[5]
You prepared to learn the Way of governing,
Reclining at ease in an age of Yao.
Our sagely ruler issued a decree through the empire,
One that worthy men could not neglect.
Officials presented you with the pink sash of honor,
And a carriage with seats departed your thatched cottage.[6]
The ruler's Gray Dragon Watchtower,
The nine palace gates and the twelve avenues –
After the assembled gentlemen had ended their court audience,
You descended the cinnabar stairs with an official's cap and sword.

1 Linhuai: more commonly known during the Tang as Sizhou 泗州, in modern Jiangsu.
2 Xiapi: A town in Linhuai district.
3 The old capital of the state of Qi.
4 Implies dedication to study.
5 The Dai brothers produced two versions of the classic *Liji*; the Mao family produced the standard early commentary on the *Shijing*.
6 Alludes to the efforts Emperor Guangwu 光武 of the Han made to persuade Yan Guang 嚴光 to join his government.

野鶴終踉蹌，
威鳳徒參差。
或問理人術，
但致還山詞。
天書降北闕，
賜帛歸東菑。
都門謝親故，
行路日逶遲。
孤帆萬里外，
淼漫將何之。
江天海陵郡，
雲日淮南祠。
杳冥滄洲上，
蕩漭無人知。
緯蕭或賣藥，
出處安能期。

But you, a crane of the wilds, fell out of step in the end,
An awesome phoenix, only with bedraggled wings.
If someone asked you about the techniques of governing men,
24 You could only present words about returning to the hills.
An imperial proclamation came down from the northern towers,
Gifting you with silk and sending you back to your eastern fields.
At the capital gates you bid farewell to relatives and friends;
28 On the road you will daily drift further away.
Your solitary sail beyond a myriad li –
Over the vastness of the water – where are you going?
River and sky at Hailing Commandery,[1]
32 Cloud and sun at the Huainan river shrine.
Vast and distant, above the blue islet,[2]
In the river's breadth no one will know you.
Weaving southernwood or selling herbs –[3]
36 How can one set times for activity or rest?

1 A Wei-era name for an area further south of Linhuai.
2 See note to 4.4.14.
3 Classic recluse behavior.

4.7

送綦毋潛落第還鄉

聖代無隱者，
英靈盡來歸。
遂令東山客，
不得顧采薇。
既至君門遠，
孰云吾道非。
江淮度寒食，
京洛縫春衣。
置酒臨長道，
同心與我違。
行當浮桂棹，
未幾拂荊扉。
遠樹帶行客，
孤城當落暉。
吾謀適不用，
勿謂知音稀。

4.7

Seeing off Qiwu Qian as he returns home after failing the examinations

There are no recluses in an age of sages;
Talented men have all come to give allegiance at court.
This made the sojourner of East Mountain[1]
Give up the task of picking bracken.[2]
After you arrived, the lord's gate was far away;
But who can claim that our Way is wrong?
You'll pass Cold Food Festival on the Jiang and Huai,[3]
Sew your spring clothes in Luoyang.
Holding a banquet before the long road,
A sympathetic friend turns away from me.
You will let drift your oars made from cinnamon wood,
In no time at all will brush off your thorn-wood door.
Distant trees will flank the traveler,
A solitary town faces the setting sun.
It may happen that our plans go unused –
But don't say that you have few close friends.

1 See note to 2.23.1.

2 See note to 2.22.6.

3 Cold Food and the following Qingming festivals are tied to the solar calendar and occur in early April. Cooking fires were extinguished for Cold Food (hence the name).

4.8

送張舍人佐江州同薛據十韻

束帶趨承明，
守官惟謁者。
清晨聽銀虬，
薄暮辭金馬。
受辭未嘗易，
當御方知寡。
清範何風流，
高文有風雅。
忽佐江上州，
當自潯陽下。
逆旅到三湘，
長途應百舍。
香爐遠峰出，
石鏡澄湖瀉。
董奉杏成林，
陶潛菊盈把。
彭蠡常好之，
廬山我心也。
送君思遠道，
欲以數行灑。

4.8

Seeing off Secretarial Receptionist Zhang, who is going to Jiangzhou as an assistant to the prefect: matching Xue Ju, ten rhymes[1]

When they tied their sashes and hurried to Chengming Gate,[2]
There was only you, Receptionist, to watch over the officials.
In the clear dawn you heard the silver wyverne.[3]
At dusk, you took your leave at Gold Horse Gate.[4]
You received imperial commands, it was never easy;
You knew that your time for service there was limited.
How dashing was the pure model you provided!
And your lofty writings have the spirit of the *feng* and *ya*.[5]
Now you go off to be an assistant to a prefecture on the Jiang,
In the stretch below Xunyang.[6]
You'll travel until you arrive at the three Xiang;[7]
Your long road should require a hundred stays.
The distant peak of Incense Burner rises up;
The clear lake by Stone Mirror gushes forth.[8]
Dong Feng's apricot trees have become a forest;[9]
Tao Qian's chrysanthemums fill your hands.[10]
I have always been fond of Pengli Lake;
Mount Lu is what I'm thinking of.
I see you off as you brood on your long road ahead;
I want to relieve your worries with these few lines of verse.

---

1 South of the Jiang, further to the west of Wuhan.

2 Chengming was the name of a palace gate during the Wei dynasty where court audiences were held.

3 Clepsydras often had a mouth made of silver in the form of a dragon.

4 A palace gate from the Han era reserved for officials.

5 Two divisions of the *Shijing*.

6 A town in Jiangzhou.

7 The area around Lake Penghu, in the central Jiang valley. Zhang would pass through this area while heading east toward Jiangzhou.

8 Both scenic spots around Jiangzhou. Incense Burner is one of the peaks of Mount Lu 廬山.

9 See note to 1.5.12.

10 The recluse and poet Tao Qian was particularly fond of chrysanthemums.

4.9

送韋大夫東京留守

人外遺世慮，
空端結遐心。
曾是巢許淺，
始知堯舜深。
蒼生詎有物，
黃屋如喬林。
上德撫神運，
沖和穆宸襟。
雲雷康屯難，
江海遂飛沉。
天工寄人英，
龍袞瞻君臨。
名器苟不假，
保釐固其任。
素質貫方領，
清景照華簪。
慷慨念王室，
從容獻官箴。
雲旗蔽三川，
畫角發龍唫。

4.9

Seeing off Grand Master Wei to his post as Regent in the eastern capital[1]

I abandoned worldly cares outside of society,
And vain speculations formed in my daydreaming mind.
But actually Chaofu and Xu You were shallow;[2]
I only now know the depths of a Yao or a Shun.
How can the common people have worries
When the carriage canopy of the ruler is like a sheltering tree?
His supreme virtue brings calm to unearthly destinies;
Modesty and mildness dignify his imperial breast.
When the clouds thundered, he calmed a gathering of troubles;
Flying and swimming creatures then were free amid the rivers and lakes.
The work of Heaven he entrusted to the finest of men;
In his dragon robes he tranquilly looked down from the ruler's perch.
If reputation and rank are not falsely granted,
He can make firm the responsibilities of protecting and governing.
With robes of white and a square collar,
A pure light shines from your splendid official hatpin.
Fervently you keep the royal house uppermost in your mind,
While you calmly present official remonstrances.
Now cloud-banners cover the Three Streams,
And painted horns utter their dragon cries.[3]

---

1 This was Wei Zhi, the recipient of 2.14. A regent managed the affairs of the secondary capital when the emperor was away.

2 Two mythical recluses in early antiquity.

3 A reference to imperial troops, which had recently retaken the Luoyang area from rebel forces.

晨揚天漢聲，
夕捲大河陰。
窮人業已寧，
逆虜遺之擒。
然後解金組，
拂衣東山岑。
給事黃門省，
秋光正沉沉。
壯心與身退，
老病隨年侵。
君子從相訪，
重玄其可尋。

4.10

資聖寺送甘二

浮生信如寄，
薄宦夫何有。
來往本無歸，
別離方此受。
柳色藹春餘，
槐陰清夏首。
不覺御溝上，
銜悲執杯酒。

At dawn they utter sounds that reach to Heaven's River;
At dusk they roll back the waters on the south bank of the great Yellow River.
Those in hardship have had their estates restored,
And the rebellious barbarians have been presented as prisoners.
Afterwards you will remove your armor
And dust off your robes, departing for the peak of East Mountain.[1]
I am a Supervising Secretary in the Chancellery,
Which is filled right now with autumn light.
Youthful heart and body have both withdrawn;
Old age and sickness progress with the years.
But if you, sir, come to visit me,
Perhaps we could seek the mystery of mysteries together.

4.10

Seeing off Gan Two at Zisheng Temple[2]

This floating life is truly like a sojourn;
What is it really to have a lowly office?
Coming and going, never a homecoming,
And now we are handed a separation.
The hue of willows is lush in the remains of spring;
Sophora shade is clear in the beginning of summer.
Unconsciously, by the bank of the imperial canal,
We hold our ale cups and harbor our sorrow.

---

1 See note to 2.23.1.

2 Located in the Chongren Ward of Chang'an.

4.11

留別山中溫古上人兄并示舍弟縉

解薜登天朝，
去師偶時哲。
豈惟山中人，
兼負松上月。
宿昔同遊止，
致身雲霞末。
開軒臨潁陽，
臥視飛鳥沒。
好依盤石飯，
屢對瀑泉歇。
理齊少狎隱，
道勝寧外物.
舍弟官崇高，
宗兄此削髮。
荊扉但灑掃，
乘閒當過拂。

4.11

On parting with my elder cousin His Eminence Wengu from the mountains; also shown to my younger brother Jin[1]

Shedding my recluse's weeds, ascending Heaven's court,
I am leaving you, Master, to meet with the wise men of the age.
How is this not only letting down the men of the mountains,
But also letting down the moonlight in the pines?
Formerly we roamed and relaxed together,
And we exerted our utmost at the edge of the sunset clouds.
Opening our casement, we would look down on Yingyang;[2]
Reclining, view the flying birds disappear.
We were fond of eating while propped on a flat rock,
Or often resting while facing the waterfalls.
With the same principles we soon grew familiar with reclusion;
When the Way triumphs, one prefers to live beyond material things.
My younger brother is serving in Chonggao;[3]
While you, cousin, had your head shaved here.
Just be sure to put your thorn-wood gate in order –
When I have some time off I'll come to visit.

1 Written when Wang Wei was ending a period of seclusion on Mount Song near Luoyang.
2 About 20 kilometers south-southeast of Luoyang.
3 The Han era name for Dengfeng 登風, southeast of Luoyang.

4.12

觀別者

青青楊柳陌，
陌上別離人。
愛子遊燕趙，
高堂有老親。
不行無可養，
行去百憂新。
切切委兄弟，
依依向四鄰。
都門帳飲畢，
從此謝賓親。
揮涙逐前侶，
含悽動征輪。
車徒望不見，
時時起行塵。
余亦辭家久，
看之涙滿巾。

4.12

Seeing people parting

How green the lanes through poplar and willow –
And on the lanes, people who are parting.
Beloved sons travel to Yan and Zhao
While there are aged parents in the high hall.
If the sons do not go, they will have no resources to care for them;
But once they leave, many new worries arise.
Earnestly the brothers are entrusted,
And vanish on the horizon in every direction.
After the farewell banquet at the capital gate ends,
From that moment they take leave of their guests and their kin.
Wiping away the tears, they chase after their former companions;
Filled with sadness, they start the wheels of their journey.
Those left behind can no longer make out the carriage escort,
Though from time to time dust is stirred by their going.
I too have been long parted from my home;
When I see them the tears fill my kerchief.

4.13

別弟縉後登青龍寺望藍田山

陌上新別離，
蒼茫四郊晦。
登高不見君，
故山復雲外。
遠樹蔽行人，
長天隱秋塞。
心悲宦游子，
何處飛征蓋。

4.14–4.15

盧象: 別弟妹二首

1.

兩妹日成長，
雙鬟將及人。

1 These two poems as well as 4.24 are also attributed to Lu Xiang 盧象 in a number of significant collections, including the *Quan Tang shi* and the *Tang shi ji shi*. The long occasional title given to the poems in the Lu Xiang corpus ("On the Fifteenth of the Eighth Month I stopped in the country. I held a banquet to celebrate our family moving to a new estate. Before long I returned to Wenshang.

4.13

After parting with my younger brother Jin, I climb up to Blue Dragon Temple and gaze out at the hills of Lantian

On the lane after newly parting with you:
Evening gloom everywhere in the vast fields.
I climb high but I cannot see you;
Home mountains are beyond the clouds.
Distant trees shade the traveler,
The long sky conceals the autumn frontier.
My heart grieves for one wandering on official business.
Whither flies his traveling carriage?

4.14–4.15

Lu Xiang: Parting from my younger siblings[1]

1.

My two little sisters grow bigger every day;
Their paired hair buns show they're almost grown up.

My young siblings especially lamented this parting and I composed these three poems" 八月十五日象自江東止田園移莊慶會未幾歸汶上小弟幼妹尤嗟其別兼賦是詩三首), combined with suggestions that the speaker is living at places unassociated with Wang Wei in our current biographical data, tend to gravitate against Wang's authorship. Zhao Diancheng also doubted Wang's authorship in spite of including them in the collection.

已能持寶瑟，
4 自解掩羅巾。
念昔別時小，
未知疎與親。
今來始離恨，
8 拭淚方慇懃。

2.

小弟更孩幼，
歸來不相識。
同居雖漸慣，
4 見人猶未覓。
宛作越人語，
殊甘水鄉食。
別此最為難，
8 淚盡有餘憶。

4.16

別綦毋潛

端笏明光宮，
歷稔朝雲陛。
詔看延閣書，

They can already hold a zithern properly
And untie and wrap their gauze scarves for themselves.
I remember they were young when I parted with them last,
When I didn't feel particularly close to them.
Now for the first time I feel regret at parting,
And I earnestly wipe away tears.

2.

My little brother was even younger;
When I came home I didn't recognize him.
Though we gradually got used to living together
He is still too shy to seek me out.
He has acquired a slight Yue accent,
And he is especially fond of food from Jiangsu.
Parting from him is most difficult of all;
When my weeping ends, I still continue to think of him.

4.16

Parting with Qiwu Qian

Holding your office tally respectfully at Mingguang Palace,[1]
For a succession of years you have attended court on the cloud stairs.
You were commanded to examine books in the Yan'ge;[2]

1 West of Weiyang Palace in Han times.
2 Yan'ge – Han era imperial library. Qian had been Editor in the Palace Library.

高議平津邸。
適意輕微祿，
虛心削繁禮。
盛得江左風，
彌工建安體。
高張多絕弦，
截河有清濟。
嚴冬爽群木，
伊洛方清泚。
渭水冰下流，
潼關雪中啟。
荷蓧幾時還，
塵纓待君洗。

1 The Han minister Gongsun Hong 公孫弘 was enfeoffed as the Marquis of Pingjin. He built a lodge at his mansion where he invited talented scholars to help him make policy.

2 I.e., he could write in the rugged, plain style characteristic of early third-century poets, as well as the more rhetorically elaborate style of the Southern Dynasties.

3 The Ji River shared its banks with the Yellow River for some distance before flowing on in a separate channel – but it supposedly maintained its clear waters even while sharing space with the muddy Yellow.

There were lofty debates at the Pingjin Mansion.[1]
You were pleased to scorn your trivial salary;
With humble mind you dispensed with excessive formalities.
Already possessing in full the southern manner,
You were also skilled in the Jian'an style.[2]
High and piercing notes often come from the most excellent strings;
You were the clear Ji cutting itself off from the Yellow River.[3]
The harsh winter has deadened all the trees,
The Yi and Luo waters are now clear and fresh.
Ice is flowing down the Wei River current;
And snow opens up on the Tong Pass.[4]
When will you return with your weed basket?[5]
Dirty hatstrings are waiting for you to wash them.[6]

---

4 These four lines describe Qian's travels from Luoyang to the west in late winter.

5 *Analects* 18.7 tells of the disciple Zilu 子路 encountering an old hermit carrying a basket for weeds. The man treated Zilu to a rustic dinner and had him stay overnight. Wang is asking when his friend will return to the hermit life.

6 The minister of the state of Chu, Qu Yuan (third century BCE) was upset that the king would not listen to his advice. He wandered a riverbank until he met a fisherman, and he complained to him about his lack of political success. The fisherman replied by singing a song: "When the waters of the Canglang are clear, I wash my hatstrings in them; when the waters are muddy, I wash my feet." Wang is telling Qiwu Qian that he can serve in office at a more propitious time, or alternately he can cleanse himself in reclusion.

4.17

新晴野望

新晴原野曠，
極目無氛垢。
郭門臨渡頭，
4 村樹連溪口。
白水明田外，
碧峰出山後。
農月無閒人，
8 傾家事南畝。

4.18–4.21

晦日游大理韋卿城南別業四首（四聲依次用各六韻）

1.

與世澹無事，
自然江海人。
側聞塵外游，
4 解驂軛朱輪。

4.17

Gazing out on the fields after the weather clears

After the weather clears, the level fields are vast
With no smoke or dirt as far as the eye can see.
The outer city gate overlooks the ford,
4 And the village trees stretch to the mouth of the stream.
White waters brighten beyond the fields
And jade peaks rise behind the hills.
In these farming months no one is idle –
8 Each family is busy on the southern acres.

4.18–4.21

On the last day of the first month, traveling to the estate south of the city owned by Wei, Chief Minister of the Court of Judicial Review: four poems (Following set tonal categories, each with six rhymes)

1.

You are tranquil and have no affairs with the world,
And so have naturally become a man of the rivers and lakes.
When you heard that someone was visiting your home beyond the dust,
4 You unharnessed your team, chocked your vermillion carriage wheels.[1]

1 I.e., Wei decided to stay at home in order to entertain his guests.

極野照暄景，
上天垂春雲。
張組竟北阜，
汎舟過東鄰。
故鄉信高會，
牢醴及家臣。
幸同擊壤樂，
心荷堯為君。

2.

郊居杜陵下，
永日同攜手。
人里藹川陽，
平原見峰首。
園廬鳴春鳩，
林薄媚新柳。
上卿始登席，
故老前為壽。
臨當遊南陂，
約略執盃酒。
歸與絀微官，
惆悵心自咎。

In the remotest country there shines warm sunlight;
In the highest sky the spring clouds hang down.
You have spread banquet tents all over the north hill,
Let boats drift by to the neighbors to the east.
Truly an impressive assembly in your home village!
The viands and fine ale are even served to family servants.
We are lucky to share the joy of peg-throw;[1]
Our hearts receive Yao as our ruler.

2.

You live in the suburbs, below Duling;
We hold hands together throughout the long day.
Villages thick with trees on the north bank of the stream;
Above the level plain we see the top of the peak.
The spring doves cry over the garden stove;
The fresh willows are charming amid the forest brush.
The Senior Minister has just ascended to his mat,
Making his first toasts to venerable old men.
As we are about to stroll to the southern lake,
I am dilatory in my drinking.
Let me go home and give up this trivial office!
Despairing, I rebuke myself in my heart.

1 An ancient game from the time of sage ruler Yao 堯 in which players attempt to hit pieces of wood from a distance with other pieces of wood. It is recorded that old men with nothing to do would play this game and sing a song about their contentment.

3.

冬中餘雪在，
墟上春流駛。
風日暢懷抱，
山川多秀氣。
雕胡先晨炊，
庖膾亦後至。
高情浪海嶽，
浮生寄天地。
君子外簪纓，
埃塵良不啻。
所樂衡門中，
陶然忘其貴。

4.

高館臨澄陂，
曠望蕩心目。
澹蕩動雲天，
玲瓏映墟曲。
鵲巢結空林，
雉雊響幽谷。
應接無閒暇，
徘徊以躑躅。

3.

In the middle of winter some snow remains;
In the hamlet the spring current hurries on.
The scenery expands, makes our feelings euphoric;
Many delicately lovely scenes amid the hills and streams.
Wild rice is steamed before dawn,
And fine meat dishes are also brought in later.
Your lofty sentiments drift carefree to the lakes and peaks;
Our floating life is lodged between heaven and earth.
A true gentleman considers hatpin and hatstrings of office inessential,
Truly no different than dust and dirt.
What we delight in, within the rustic gate,
Is to forget all status in our delight.

4.

Your lofty lodge overlooks the clear pond;
Gazing out on the vastness unsettles heart and eye.
The water trembles, shaking the cloudy sky;
Its sparkling is set off against the village.
Magpies build their nests in the empty wood;
Pheasants' cries echo in the remote valleys.
I have not the leisure to take all this in;
I hesitate and cannot go on.

紆組上春隄，
側弁倚喬木。
弦望忽已晦，
後期洲應綠。

4.22

冬日游覽

步出城東門，
試騁千里目。
青山橫蒼林，
赤日團平陸。
渭北走邯鄲，
關東出函谷。
秦地萬方會，
來朝九州牧。
雞鳴咸陽中，
冠蓋相追逐。
丞相過列侯，
羣公餞光祿。
相如方老病，
獨歸茂陵宿。

With office seal-cords we climb the spring embankment;
With our caps askew we lean on the lofty trees.
From full moon to crescent it has passed to month's end;
12 And when we meet once again, the islets should be green.

4.22

Sightseeing on a Winter Day

As I walk out of the city's east gate,
I let my vision travel for a thousand li.
Green hills are traversed by the gray woods;
4 A red sun sinks round on the level plain.
North of the Wei my vision rushes off to Handan,
And to the east of the pass, coming out of Hangu.
People from a myriad places assemble in Qin country;
8 Governors from every province are coming to court.
Roosters crow in Xianyang,
Caps and carriages follow one after another.
Chief ministers call upon the noblemen,
12 Lords banquet with the Chief Minister of Imperial Entertainments.
Sima Xiangru, now old and sick,
Returns alone to spend the night at Maoling.[1]

1 The Han poet Sima Xiangru fell ill towards the end of his life and retired from office. He then lived near Maoling, near the tomb of Emperor Wu.

4.23

自大散以往深林密竹磴道盤曲四五十里至黃牛嶺見黃花川

危徑幾萬轉，
數里將三休。
回環見徒侶，
隱映隔林丘。
颯颯松上雨，
潺潺石中流。
靜言深溪裏，
長嘯高山頭。
望見南山陽，
白日靄悠悠。
青皋麗已淨，
綠樹鬱如浮。
曾是厭蒙密，
曠然消人憂。

4.23

Going on from Dasan Pass, there are deep forests and dense bamboo.
The Stone Path twists about for forty or fifty li until it arrives
at Brown Ox Ridge, where you can see Yellow Flower Stream.[1]

The steep path twists several myriad times;
You have to rest every several li.
Moving back and forth, I see other travelers
Now hidden, now visible through the forested hills.
The rain soughs among the pine trees;
The stream babbles over the stones.
We chat quietly in the deep ravine,
Then give prolonged whistles atop the high mountains.
I gaze far off to the south slope of Zhongnan Mountain;
The white sun is dim and lost in mist.
The verdant riverbank is lovely and pure;
The green trees are so dense they seem to float.
I have grown tired of the closed-in vegetation;
This vast space dissipates my worries.

---

1 Dasan Pass was located in the southwest corner of Qizhou 岐州, south of the Wei River and west of the capital of Chang'an.

4.24

盧象: 休假還舊業便使

謝病始告歸，
依依入桑梓。
家人皆佇立，
相候柴門裏。
時輩皆長年，
成人舊童子。
上堂嘉慶畢，
顧與姻親齒。
論舊忽餘悲，
目存且相喜。
田園轉蕪沒，
但有寒泉水。
衰柳日蕭條，
秋光清邑里。
入門乍如客，
休騎非便止。
中飯顧王程，
離憂從此始。

4.24

Lu Xiang: On my time off I return to my old estate before going on my official mission[1]

Pleading illness I finally announce my return home;
With a sense of longing I enter our mulberries and catalpas.
Family members all are standing there,
Waiting for me within the scrap-wood gate.
Those in my generation are now full in years,
While former children are now adults.
After I ascend the hall and celebrate with my parents,
I turn back and take my place with marriage kin.
We discuss old matters – suddenly lingering sorrow comes;
But we are happy that there are those who are still with us.
Our fields and gardens have gradually turned to weeds;
There is only the water from the chill stream.
Withered willows grow bleaker every day;
The autumn sunlight shines clear on the village.
My visit home is brief, as though I were just a visitor;
I cannot halt my mount at my own convenience.
In the midst of my meals I must heed my official mission;
Sorrow of parting begins from now on.

1 Probably by Lu Xiang, not by Wang Wei. See note to 4.14–15.

4.25

早入滎陽界

汎舟入滎澤，
茲邑乃雄藩。
河曲閭閻隘，
川中烟火繁。
因人見風俗，
入境聞方言。
秋野田疇盛，
朝光市井喧。
漁商波上客，
雞犬岸旁村。
前路白雲外，
孤帆安可論。

4.26

宿鄭州

朝與周人辭，
暮投鄭人宿。
他鄉絕儔侶，

4.25

Entering the Yingyang region early in the morning[1]

My drifting boat enters Ying marsh;
This town is a strategic strongpoint.
At the river's bend the village lanes are narrow,
And smoky fires are rife along the watercourse.
I observe local customs through the people;
Entering the region I hear local dialect.
The farmland is rich in this autumn country;
The towns are noisy in the light of dawn.
Fishermen and peddlers among the river's travelers;
Chickens and dogs in the village by the banks.
The road before me goes beyond the clouds;
In my solitary boat how can I tell how I feel?

4.26

Spending the night at Zhengzhou[2]

At dawn I parted with the people of Zhou;[3]
By dusk pass the night with the people of Zheng.
In another land, cut off from companions;

1 4.25 and 4.26 were all written during Wang Wei's journey to his appointment to Jizhou in Shandong, 721. Yingyang was located in Zhengzhou, a district not too far east of Luoyang.

2 See note to 4.25.

3 I.e., the eastern capital of Luoyang.

4 孤客親僮僕。
宛洛望不見，
秋霖晦平陸。
田父草際歸，
8 村童雨中牧。
主人東皋上，
時稼遶茅屋。
蟲思機杼鳴，
12 雀喧禾黍熟。
明當渡京水，
昨晚猶金谷。
此去欲何言，
16 窮邊徇微祿。

4.27

渡河到清河作

汎舟大河裏，
積水窮天涯。
天波忽開拆，
4 郡邑千萬家。
行復見城市，

---

1 The Jing flows between Yingyang and Zhengzhou town northwards and then empties into the Yellow River.

A lone traveler, associating with serving boys.
I gaze back toward Wan and Luo but cannot see them;
An autumn downpour darkens the level plain.
Old farmers return from the grassy verge;
Village lads tend cattle in the rain.
The owners go up in their eastern fields,
The seasonal crop growing round their thatched houses.
The crickets grieve while loom and shuttle clack;
Sparrows clamor while the millet ripens.
At dawn I should ford the Jing River,[1]
Though yesterday eve I was still at Gold Valley.[2]
What can I say about this departure?
At a remote borderland, seeking to earn a trivial salary.

4.27

Composed while crossing the Yellow River and Arriving at Qinghe[3]

A boat floating on the vast Yellow River;
A mass of waters reaching to the edge of the sky.
Sky and waves suddenly split open –
A commandery town with a myriad homes.
As we move on I can see the town markets,

2 As in the opening couplet, Wang Wei describes the distance he has put between himself and Luoyang. Gold Valley was the name of the famous estate near Luoyang owned by the wealthy fourth-century nobleman Shi Chong 石崇.

3 Written during his time in Jizhou, 721–726. Qinghe was located in Hebei, somewhat north of Jizhou (in the Tang district of Beizhou 貝州).

宛然有桑麻。
回瞻舊鄉國，
8 淼漫連雲霞。

4.28

苦熱

赤日滿天地，
火雲成山嶽。
草木盡焦卷，
4 川澤皆竭涸。
輕紈覺衣重，
密樹苦陰薄。
莞簟不可近，
8 絺綌再三濯。
思出宇宙外，
曠然在寥廓。
長風萬里來，
12 江海蕩煩濁。
却顧身為患，
始知心未覺。
忽入甘露門，
16 宛然清涼樂。

And distinctly make out mulberry and hemp.
I turn back to gaze at my old homeland;
The broad waters reach to the sunset clouds.

4.28

Suffering from the Heat

The red sun fills heaven and earth;
Clouds of fire form into mountains and peaks.
Grass and trees are all scorched, are curling up;
The rivers and marshes are dry and parched.
Even light silk clothes seem too heavy to wear,
And the densest of trees provide too thin a shade.
One can't stand to get close even to light *guan* mats;[1]
Hemp cloth has to be washed over and over.
I long to pass beyond the cosmos,
And reside in the emptiness of the infinite.
There a constant breeze comes from a myriad li away,
And the rivers and lakes wash away all impure vexations.
I contemplate that the body brings me trouble,
And I now understand that my mind is not yet awakened.
I would enter at once through the gate of sweet dew;[2]
That would seem like a pure and cool delight.

1 For *guan* mats, see note to 1.10.17.
2 Common metaphor for nirvana.

4.29

納涼

喬木萬餘株，
清流貫其中。
前臨大川口，
豁達來長風。
漣漪涵白沙，
素鮪如游空。
偃臥盤石上，
翻濤沃微躬。
漱流復濯足，
前對釣魚翁。
貪餌凡幾許，
徒思蓮葉東。

4.29

Enjoying the Cool Weather

Tall trees, over ten thousand trunks –
A cool stream threads through the middle.
I look over the mouth of the great river;
Where it's broad and open, a constant breeze comes.
Gentle ripples soak the white sand;
Pale sturgeon seem to swim in air.
I lie on my back on a broad rock,
While toppling billows wash my trivial frame.
I rinse my mouth in the current and wash my feet;
In front of me, an old man angling.
How many of them are greedy for the bait?
I idly think of them, to the east of the lotus leaves.

王右丞集卷之五 古詩

5.1–5.3

濟上四賢詠三首

1.

崔錄事

解印歸田里，
賢哉此丈夫。
少年曾任俠，
晚節更為儒。
遯世東山下，
因家滄海隅。
已聞能狎鳥，
余欲共乘桴。

2.

成文學

寶劍千金裝，
登君白玉堂。

---

1 Composed while the poet was stationed in Jizhou, 721–726. "Ji" here is the Ji River, which flows by the district seat and into the Yellow River.

2 See note to 2.23.1.

https://doi.org/10.1515/9781501516023-005

Juan 5: Old style poems

5.1–5.3

In praise of the four worthies of the Ji: three poems[1]

1.

Office Manager Cui

He untied his seal of office, returned to his village in the fields;
How worthy was this eminent man!
When still a youth he was a knight-errant;
And in his later years be became a scholar.
Withdrawing from the world at the foot of East Mountain;[2]
He then made his home at a corner of the blue lakes.
I have already heard that he can be intimate with the gulls;[3]
I would like to float off on a raft with him.[4]

2.

Instructor Cheng

Jeweled sword, clothing worth a thousand in gold,
He ascended his lord's white jade hall.

---

3 The *Liezi* tells of a boy who befriended the gulls, but when he tried to demonstrate this to his father, the gulls would have nothing to do with him.

4 *Analects* 5.7: The Master imagines putting out to sea on a raft if the Way does not prevail, accompanied by his disciple Zilu.

身為平原客，
家有邯鄲娼。
使氣公卿坐，
論心游俠場。
中年不得志，
謝病客游梁。

3.

鄭霍二山人

翩翩繁華子，
多出金張門。
幸有先人業，
早蒙明主恩。
童年且未學，
肉食騖華軒。
豈乏中林士，
無人獻至尊。
鄭公老泉石，
霍子安邱樊。
賣藥不二價，
著書盈萬言。

He was himself a retainer for the Lord of Pingyuan;[1]
At home he had dancers from Handan.
He could express his mettle seated with lords and ministers;
He talked freely in the arena of the knights-errant.
But at middle age he did not achieve his aims;
So he resigned, claiming ill health, and went traveling about Liang.[2]

3.

The Two Mountain Men Zheng and Huo

Elegant sons from flourishing houses –
Most of them coming from the Jins or the Zhangs.[3]
They have the good fortune to possess a patrimony,
And received early on the largess of enlightened rulers.
They did not study when they were children;
They dined on meat, let their splendid carriages dash.
There is no lack of gentlemen living in the woods,
But there is no one to present them to His Majesty.
Sir Zheng grows old amid the streams and rocks;
Master Huo is at peace on his farming plot.
They sell herbs, don't haggle over the price;[4]
They write books filled with a myriad words.

1 A prominent Warring States nobleman from the state of Zhao famous for patronizing worthy men.

2 Probably alluding to Prince Xiao 孝 of Liang during the Western Han, who patronized men of letters.

3 Referring to the prominent Western Han statesmen Zhang Anshi 張安世 and Jin Midi 金日磾.

4 Han Kang 韓康 was a recluse who sold medicine in the marketplace. When during a spat with a potential buyer she revealed that she knew who he was, he was so piqued that he withdrew permanently into reclusion.

息陰無惡木，
飲水必清源。
吾賤不及議，
斯人竟誰論。

5.4–5.9

偶然作六首

1.

楚國有狂夫，
茫然無心想。
散髮不冠帶，
行歌南陌上。
孔丘與之言，
仁義莫能奬。
未嘗肯問天，
何事須擊壤。
復笑採薇人，
胡為乃長往。

They refuse to rest on inferior trees;
They will only drink from the clearest fountains.
I am of low rank and cannot make my opinions known;
In the end, who will speak for them?

5.4–5.9

Written at random: six poems

1.

There is a madman in the land of Chu,[1]
Muddled, without a thought in his head.
Loosened hair, no cap or sash,
He wanders singing on the southern lanes.
Confucius spoke with him,
But he would not praise benevolence or righteousness.
Never once willing to ask the Heavens;[2]
He has no need to play at peg-throw.[3]
And he also laughs at the bracken-pickers –[4]
How can *they* count as hermits?

1 In *Analects* 18.5, Confucius meets a madman from Chu named Jieyu 接輿, who criticized his attitude toward office-holding in a veiled song.

2 The Warring States poet and statesman Qu Yuan composed "Questioning Heaven" after exiled from court, based on paintings on mythical subjects he saw on the walls of a shrine. Here it suggests someone discontented with fate.

3 See note to 4.18.11.

4 See note to 2.22.6.

2.

田舍有老翁，
垂白衡門裏。
有時農事閒，
斗酒呼鄰里。
喧聒茅簷下，
或坐或復起。
短褐不為薄，
園葵固足美。
動則長子孫，
不曾向城市。
五帝與三王，
古來稱君子。
干戈將揖讓，
畢竟何者是。
得意苟為樂，
野田安足鄙。
且當放懷去，
行行沒餘齒。

3.

日夕見太行，
沉吟未能去。

2.

There is an old man in a country home,
Within a rustic gate, with white hair.
Sometimes when he's not out farming,
He'll invite the neighbors with a gallon of ale.
Midst the racket under his thatched eaves,
He'll sit, and then he'll get up again.
He doesn't find his short homespun jacket too thin;
He finds the mallows in his garden a fine enough treat.
The only thing he does is raise his sons and grandsons;
He has never gone to city or market.
The five emperors and the three kings
Since ancient times have been deemed superior men.[1]
They engaged in war or they surrendered their thrones,
And in the end, which ones were right?
Satisfied, pleased in my small way –
These country fields are hardly worth scorning.
I will just give free vent to my feelings,
Go wandering about, spend my last years hidden away.

3.

At dusk I see the Taihang Mountains;
But I hesitate – I cannot leave yet.

1 Five emperors of distant antiquity (culminating with Yao and Shun); and the three founding kings of the Xia, Shang, and Zhou.

問君何以然，
世網嬰我故。
小妹日成長，
兄弟未有娶。
家貧祿既薄，
儲蓄非有素。
幾迴欲奮飛，
踟躕復相顧。
孫登長嘯臺，
松竹有遺處。
相去詎幾許，
故人在中路。
愛染日已薄，
禪寂日已固。
忽乎吾將行，
寧俟歲云暮。

4.

陶潛任天真，
其性頗耽酒。
自從棄官來，
家貧不能有。
九月九日時，

I ask you – why is it so?
The net of the world is wrapped around me.
My little sisters are still growing day by day;
My brothers have yet to marry.
Our family is poor and my salary scant;
And our savings are not what they once were.
Several times I've wished to fly away,
But I've hesitated and looked back at them.
Sun Deng's "Long Whistle Terrace"
Is still there amid the pines and bamboo.[1]
It is not very far away,
But my acquaintances all block the road.
Yet the taint of desires grows slighter each day,
And I am daily firmer in my meditative practice.
At once let me go now!
Why wait for my twilight years?

4.

Tao Qian dedicated himself to a natural forthrightness;
By nature he was quite fond of ale.
But after he abandoned his official post,
His family was poor and he could not have it.
Once, on the ninth day of the ninth month,

1 A Jin-era recluse, and a friend of Ruan Ji's 阮籍. Both were fond of the Daoist yogic practice of whistling.

菊花空滿手。
中心竊自思，
儻有人送否。
白衣攜壺觴，
果來遺老叟。
且喜得斟酌，
安問升與斗。
奮衣野田中，
今日嗟無負。
兀傲迷東西，
蓑笠不能守。
傾倒強行行，
酣歌歸五柳。
生事不曾問，
肯愧家中婦。

5.

趙女彈箜篌，
復能邯鄲舞。
夫婿輕薄兒，
鬬雞事齊主。
黃金買歌笑，
用錢不復數。

His hands held chrysanthemum blooms in vain.
In his heart he thought to himself
That perhaps someone would bring ale to him.
Then a servant in white came with jug and goblet in hand;
And, as expected, granted it to the old man.
Then for a time, delighted, he poured it out,
Not asking if it came in quarts or gallons.
Shaking out my sleeves in this country field,
Today I sigh, delighted that I haven't betrayed my kerchief.[1]
Haughtily I confuse east and west,
And am unable to keep my raingear on.
I fall over but then force myself to go on,
Drunkenly sing as I return to my five willows.[2]
Never inquiring about the affairs of the world,
Which admittedly shames my wife.

5.

The girl from Zhao is strumming her harp,
And she is able to perform Handan dances.
Her husband is a philanderer,
Serves the lord of Qi with his cockfights.
He spends yellow gold to buy singers' smiles,
Not noting how much money he spends.

1 Tao Qian Drinking Ale #20: "If I don't drink as I please, / I will wantonly betray the kerchief on my head." He used the kerchief to strain his ale.

2 See note to 2.24.10.

許史相經過，
8 高門盈四牡。
客舍有儒生，
昂藏出鄒魯。
讀書三十年，
12 腰下無尺組。
被服聖人教，
一生自窮苦。

6.

老來懶賦詩，
惟有老相隨。
宿世謬詞客，
4 前生應畫師。
不能捨餘習，
偶被世人知。
名字本習離，
8 此心還不知。

The Xu and Shi clans frequently visit,[1]
And his high gate is filled with four-stallion teams.
In their guest house there is a scholar,
A dignified man from Zou and Lu.[2]
He has been studying for thirteen years,
But there is no sash of office tied below his waist.
He has dressed himself in the Sage's teachings
And has suffered from poverty all his life.

6.[3]

As I grow old, I am too lazy to compose poems,
And old age is my only companion.
Wrong to think I was a writer in a past life;
In a previous existence I must have been a painter!
I cannot give up these old habits,
Though by chance my contemporaries know me for them.
My name and style contradict my habits –[4]
And I still do not understand my own mind.

1 Two powerful marriage clans during the reign of Emperor Xuan of the Han.

2 I.e., a Confucian.

3 This poem is also preserved in the *Tangchao minghua lu* 唐朝名畫錄, which states that he inscribed it on his painting of his Wangchuan estate. *Tangren wanshou jueju* 唐人萬首絕句 also has lines 3–6 as an independent poem under the title *Ti Wangchuan tu* ("Written on a painting of Wang Stream") 題輞川圖. If this transmission is accurate, then this poem does not belong to the other five (which were written relatively early in his career).

4 Wang Wei's name (*ming*) and style (*zi*) together made up the Chinese name for the bodhisattva Vimalakīrti. Wang Wei suggests that Vimalakīrti's actions seem out of place for a poet and painter.

5.10

西施詠

豔色天下重，
西施寧久微。
朝為越溪女，
暮作吳宮妃。
賤日豈殊眾，
貴來方悟稀。
邀人傅脂粉，
不自著羅衣。
君寵益驕態，
君憐無是非。
當時浣紗伴，
莫得同車歸。
持謝鄰家子，
效顰安可希。

5.10

On Xi Shi[1]

Sensual beauty is valued by the whole empire;
So how could Xi Shi remain obscure for long?
In the morning she was a washerwoman in Yue;
In the evening she was a palace consort in Wu.
When she was lowly she was the same as everyone else;
They only realized her rarity when she acquired status.
She could order others to apply grease and face powder;
She did not have to put on her gauze robes by herself.
Favored by her lord, she grew in arrogance,
And in his love for her he no longer distinguished right from wrong.
Of the companions from her silk-washing days
None got to go home in her carriage.
You can inform the neighbor girl –
What could you hope for by scowling?[2]

1 Xi Shi was the poor girl from the state of Yue who was trained by the king and then sent as a present to the king of Wu in the hopes that her bewitching beauty would undermine the king's commitment to governing his state.

2 *Zhuangzi*, chapter 14 states that Xi Shi looked particularly lovely when she scowled as a result of heartburn. An ugly woman, seeing this, thought that if she scowled as well it would make her beautiful.

5.11

李陵詠（時年十九）

漢家李將軍，
三代將門子。
結髮有奇策，
少年成壯士。
長驅塞上兒，
深入單于壘。
旌旗列相向，
簫鼓悲何已。
日暮沙漠陲，
戰聲烟塵裏。
將令驕虜滅，
豈獨名王侍。
既失大軍援，
遂嬰穹廬恥。
少小蒙漢恩，
何堪坐思此。
深衷欲有報，
投軀未能死。
引領望子卿，
非君誰相理。

5.11

On Li Ling (written at nineteen)[1]

General Li of the house of Han
Was the scion of three generations of generals.
When he had just tied up his hair, he had amazing plans;
He was a valiant man while still a youth.
Long he drove forth the frontier lads
Deep into the ramparts of the khan.
Ranks with their banners faced each other,
And shrill flutes and drums sounded without end.
By sunset at the edge of the desert
Sounds of battle arose from the smoke and dust.
He was going to exterminate the arrogant brutes,
Not simply force their "eminent prince" into service.
But after he lost the support of the greater army,
He encountered the shame of living in a yurt.
From the time he was young he had received Han's favor –
How could he bear it when this came to mind?
Deep in his heart he wished to repay them,
To sacrifice himself – but he could not die yet.
He craned his neck and gazed off toward Su Wu –
"To whom can I explain, if not to you?"[2]

1 Li Ling was a western Han general who was captured by the Xiongnu after a military defeat. He remained with them after his family was executed by Emperor Wu of the Han to punish him for his surrender.

2 Su Wu 蘇武 was a Han emissary who was captured by the Xiongnu. While in captivity he met Li Ling. There is a corpus of poems supposedly exchanged between the two of them.

5.12

燕子龕禪師詠

山中燕子龕，
路劇羊腸惡。
裂地競盤屈，
插天多峭崿。
瀑泉吼而噴，
怪石看欲落。
伯禹訪未知，
五丁愁不鑿。
上人無生緣，
生長居紫閣。
六時自搥磬，
一飲尚帶索。
種田燒白雲，
斫漆響丹壑。
行隨拾栗猿，
歸對巢松鶴。
時許山神請，
偶逢洞仙博。
救世多慈悲，
即心無行作。

5.12

On the Meditation Master of Swallow Stupa[1]

Swallow Stupa is in the hills:
The road is hard, as bad as twisting sheep guts.
Riven ground vies in bending and turning;
Many steep cliffs thrust into the sky.
The waterfalls roar and emit spray;
Weird-shaped rocks seem about to fall.
Lord Yu never knew this place in his investigations;[2]
The five strongmen grieve that they can't burrow through.[3]
Your eminence has the conditions for non-rebirth;
You grew to adulthood in Purple Pavilion.[4]
At all hours you beat the chime stones yourself;
You drink but once a day, with a cord for a belt.
You plant the fields, burning off the white clouds;[5]
You hack at the lacquer trees – the sound echoes through the cinnabar ravine.
When you walk, you follow gibbons gathering chestnuts;
When you return, you face the cranes roosting in pines.
Sometimes you assent to requests from the mountain spirits;[6]
By chance you find grotto Transcendents playing draughts.
You have much compassion for saving the age;
There is no conscious action or volition in your immediate mind.

---

1 From the text of the poem, the location of the temple was in the mountains on the road from Shu to the capital.

2 The sage king Yu 禹 toured the land to understand its topography when he was attempting to control flooding.

3 Five legendary men of Shu who could move mountains through sheer physical strength.

4 Purple Pavilion was the name of a peak on Zhongnan.

5 A poetic exaggeration of clearing fields by fire.

6 This alludes to story about a monk on Mt. Lu who was contacted by the god of the mountain in a dream when the latter wished to receive the Buddhist precepts.

周商倦積阻，
蜀物多淹泊。
巖腹乍旁穿，
澗脣時外拓。
橋因倒樹架，
柵值垂藤縛。
鳥道悉已平，
龍宮為之涸。
跳波誰揭厲，
絕壁免捫摸。
山木日陰陰，
結跏歸舊林。
一向石門裏，
任君春草深。

5.13

羽林騎閨人

秋月臨高城，
城中管絃思。
離人堂上愁，
稚子階前戲。
出門復映戶，

The merchants of Zhou grow tired of the frequent roadblocks,
So that the goods of Shu have often stayed there.
So they have suddenly cut through the cliff, halfway up,
And the edge of the ravine will be opened in time.
Bridges now hang on a scaffold of inverted trees;
Fences are tied with drooping vines.
The bird paths have all been leveled off,
And the dragon-palace pools have dried up because of it.
Who now must splash or wade through the leaping waves?
No longer need you feel your way up steep walls.
The mountain trees are shaded from the sun;
You return to old woods and sit there in lotus pose.
All along you stay within the stone gate,
Surrendering to the thick spring growth.

5.13

The wives of the palace guard cavalrymen

The autumn moon looks down on the high city walls;
Within the walls, there is brooding over pipes and strings.
They grieve in the hall for their men gone away,
While young children play on the front steps.
They leave the gate – moonlight still shines on the door;

望望青絲騎。
行人過欲盡，
狂夫終不至。
左右寂無言，
相看共垂泪。

5.14

冬夜書懷

冬宵寒且永，
夜漏宮中發。
草白靄繁霜，
木衰澄清月。
麗服映頹顏，
朱燈照華髮。
漢家方尚少，
顧影慚朝謁。

5.15

早朝

皎潔明星高，
蒼茫遠天曙。
槐霧鬱不開，

They gaze far, looking for horses with their green silk equipage.
Soon no more people will pass by,
But their wild husbands will never come.
All around is silent; no one speaks.
They look at each other and their tears fall down.

5.14

Writing what I feel on a winter night

The winter night is cold and prolonged;
The clepsydra emits its sound in the palace.
The grass is white – thickly covered in frost;
The trees have withered – they glow in the clear moonlight.
Lovely clothing sets off an aging face;
The vermilion lamp shines on white hair.
The house of Han just now respects the young;
I look back on my shadow, too ashamed to go to court.

5.15

Morning court audience

Gleaming white, the bright stars are high;
Silver-gray, the distant sky turns to dawn.
Fog in the sophoras is thick and will not disperse;

城鴉鳴稍去。
始聞高閣聲，
莫辨更衣處。
銀燭已成行，
金門儼騶馭。

5.16–5.17

寓言二首

1.

朱紱誰家子，
無乃金張孫。
驪駒從白馬，
出入銅龍門。
問爾何功德，
多承明主恩。
鬬雞平樂館，
射雉上林園。
曲陌車騎盛，
高堂珠翠繁。
奈何軒冕貴，
不與布衣言。

4 City-wall crows cry, then slowly depart.
Then one first hears sounds in the lofty chambers;
No one can yet make out the wardrobe office.[1]
Silver tapers already have formed ranks;
8 The coachmen are in strict array at Gold Horse Gate.[2]

5.16–5.17

Moral fables: two poems

1.

Who is the one with vermilion seal-ribbons?
It is a scion of the Jins and the Zhangs.[3]
He owns black colts followed by white horses;
4 He frequents Bronze Dragon Gate.[4]
I ask you – what merit has he earned,
That he has received so much of an enlightened lord's favor?
He holds cockfights at Pingle Lodge,
8 He shoots pheasants at Shanglin Garden.[5]
Carriages and horsemen throng the curving lanes;
Pearls and kingfisher feathers abound in the high halls.[6]
Why is it that a nobleman of high office
12 Will not allow a commoner to speak?

1 Where officials could change into court uniforms or rest.
2 See note to 4.8.4.
3 See note to 5.3.2.
4 A gate tower in Han era Chang'an Palace, ornamented with bronze dragons.
5 Shanglin was an imperial hunting park during the Western Han. Pingle Lodge was a site there where cockfights and dog races were held.
6 Metonymy for palace women.

2.

君家御溝上，
垂柳夾朱門。
列鼎會中貴，
鳴珂朝至尊。
生死在八議，
窮達由一言。
須識苦寒士，
莫矜狐白溫。

5.18

雜詩

朝因折楊柳，
相見洛城隅。
楚國無如妾，
秦家自有夫。
對人傳玉椀，
映竹解羅襦。
人見東方騎，
皆言夫婿殊。
持謝金吾子，
煩君提玉壺。

2.[1]

Your house is on the imperial canal;
Drooping willows line the vermilion gate.
Ranked tripods bring the noblemen together;
Ringing horse pendants go to His Majesty's court.
Matters of life and death lie with the Eight Assessors;[2]
Success and failure hang on a single word.
You must acknowledge the scholars suffering from the cold;
Do not boast of your warm fox furs.

5.18

(Poem without topic)[3]

In the morning they break off willow branches,
Seeing each other at one corner of Luoyang.
"No one in Chu is as beautiful as I,
And I have my own husband at my home in Qin."
He faces her, passes her a jade cup;
Hidden in bamboo he undoes her silk gauze jacket.
"When people see the riders from the east,
All of them say my husband is most exceptional.
I give you thanks, fine officer –
But I would trouble you to take your fine jug and leave."

1 Also attributed to Lu Xiang in some texts.

2 A Zhou institution of eight classes of high-ranking notables who ruled on judicial matters.

3 This poem participates in the Luofu 羅敷 trope derived from *yuefu*, in which a woman resists the attentions of a would-be seducer by boasting of her own husband.

5.19

獻始興公（時拜右拾遺）

寧棲野樹林，
寧飲澗水流。
不用食粱肉，
崎嶇見王侯。
鄙哉匹夫節，
布褐將白頭。
任智誠則短，
守仁固其優。
側聞大君子，
安問黨與讎。
所不賣公器，
動為蒼生謀。
賤子跪自陳，
可為帳下不。
感激有公議，
曲私非所求。

5.19

Presented to the Duke of Shixing[1] (written when serving as Reminder in the Secretariat)

I would prefer to roost in a wood in the wilds;
I would prefer to drink from the current of a stream.
What use is being served with fine viands
When you must restlessly attend on princes and lords?
How lowly is the virtue of the common man!
He grows gray-haired in his coarse homespun.
I am truly deficient in the aptitude for wisdom;
But keeping to my duties is truly my strongpoint.
I have incidentally heard that you, sir,
Never consider faction or enemy in choosing people.
You would never barter away the benefits of public office,
But you always make plans on behalf of the common people.
This lowly one kneels to you to explain himself:
Could I become part of your retinue?
I am highly motivated when it comes to public policy;
Bias or selfishness is not what I seek.

1 The prominent statesman Zhang Jiuling 張九齡 (678–740).

5.20

哭殷遙

人生能幾何，
畢竟歸無形。
念君等為死，
萬事傷人情。
慈母未及葬，
一女纔十齡。
泱漭寒郊外，
蕭條聞哭聲。
浮雲為蒼茫，
飛鳥不能鳴。
行人何寂寞，
白日自淒清。
憶昔君在時，
問我學無生。
勸君苦不早，
令君無所成。
故人各有贈，
又不及生平。
負爾非一途，
痛哭返柴荊。

5.20

Mourning Yin Yao

How long can a human life last?
In the end, we return to the formless.
When I think that you, like all others, have died,
A myriad affairs wound my feelings.
Your loving mother has not yet been buried;
You have a daughter, barely ten.
Beyond the chill town outskirts, broad and vast,
I hear the desolate sound of wailing.
Floating clouds form a boundless mass,
And flying birds cannot cry out.
How still and lonely are the travelers!
And the sunlight grows somber and cheerless.
I recall when you were alive:
You asked me about studying Non-rebirth.[1]
My exhortations – alas – were not early enough –
In the end, you accomplished nothing.
Old friends may each have their gifts
That are not given before they die.
I have failed you in more than one way;
Sobbing sorely, I return to my rustic hut.

1 That is, how to achieve nirvana and prevent future rebirths in the world of suffering.

5.21

歎白髮

我年一何長，
鬢髮日已白。
俯仰天地間，
能為幾時客。
悵惆故山雲，
徘徊空日夕。
何事與時人，
東城復南陌。

5.21

Sighing over white hair

How long will my years last?
The hair at my temples grows whiter each day.
Amidst the cycles of Heaven and Earth
For how long can we be sojourners?
Grieving over the clouds on my homeland hills,
I pace about, wasting the days and nights.
Why am I with these people of my time
Once more in the south streets of this eastern city?

王右丞集卷之六 古詩

6.1

夷門歌

七雄雄雌猶未分，
攻城殺將何紛紛。
秦兵益圍邯鄲急，
魏王不救平原君。
公子為嬴停駟馬，
執轡愈恭意逾下。
亥為屠肆鼓刀人，
嬴乃夷門抱關者。
非但慷慨獻奇謀，
意氣兼將身命酬。
向風刎頸送公子，
七十老翁何所求。

https://doi.org/10.1515/9781501516023-006

Juan 6: Old style poems

6.1

The Ballad of Yi Gate[1]

Who would dominate the seven powers was yet to be decided;[2]
Such a confusion of cities attacked and commanders killed!
The siege of Handan by the troops of Qin became more urgent,
But the King of Wei would not rescue the Lord of Pingyuan.
The prince had halted his carriage team for the sake of Ying,
Grasping the reins, more respectful, his thoughts more compliant.
Zhu Hai was a market butcher, a man who wielded a knife,
While Hou Ying merely guarded the bolt on Yi Gate.
Not only did Ying present a fine scheme in his heroic way;
He also desired to repay the prince with his own life.
He faced the wind, slit his own throat to bid the prince farewell;
"What more could an old seventy-year-old man seek?"

---

1 This ballad alludes throughout to the biography of the Prince of Wei from the *Shiji*, chapter 77. Important details are as follows: When Qin attacked the state of Zhao, the King of Wei refused to come to Zhao's assistance, in spite of pleas from the Zhao prince, the Lord of Pingyuan. The king's brother, the prince of Wei (also known as the Lord of Xinling) decided to go to Zhao's rescue instead. Among his retainers was the old gatekeeper of Yi Gate, Hou Ying, who concocted a plan to seize control of the Wei army and use it to drive out the Qin forces; part of the plan involved Hou Ying's friend, the butcher Zhu Hai, who was employed to assassinate the Wei commander (earlier, Hou Ying had deliberately made the prince accompany him on a visit to the butcher and to wait for him in his carriage until his visit had ended – this was to test his humility). Hou Ying told the prince that he could not accompany him on the mission to Zhao because he was too old; instead, he told the prince he would slit his own throat on the day the prince put his plan into action, to prove his loyalty to him.

2 Seven Powers: The seven principal states of Warring States China.

6.2

新秦郡松樹歌

青青山上松，
數里不見今更逢。
不見君，
心相憶。
此心向君君應識，
為君顏色高且閑，
亭亭迥出浮雲間。

6.3

青雀歌

青雀翅羽短，
未能遠食玉山禾。
猶勝黃雀爭上下，
唧唧空倉復若何。

6.2

Song: The Pine Tree in Xinqin Commandery[1]

Green, green, the pine on the mountain;
For several li I didn't see you, and now we meet again;
When I didn't see you,
I remembered you in my heart.
You ought to know the feeling my heart has toward you;
The expression I have for you – lofty and relaxed,
Rising loftily from far away, among the floating clouds.

6.3

Song: The Blue Sparrow

The blue sparrow's wings are short,
It can never eat the distant grain of Jade Mountain.[2]
Yet it still surpasses the brown sparrows as they bicker up and down;
Squawking in an empty granary with nothing else they can do.

1 Located in the far northeast corner of Shaanxi.
2 Jade Mountain: another name for the home of the Queen Mother of the West.

6.4

隴頭吟

長安少年游俠客，
夜上戍樓看太白。
隴頭明月迥臨關，
隴上行人夜吹笛。
關西老將不勝愁，
駐馬聽之雙淚流。
身經大小百餘戰，
麾下偏裨萬戶侯。
蘇武纔為典屬國，
節旄落盡海西頭。

6.5

老將行

少年十五二十時，
步行奪取胡馬騎。
射殺山中白額虎，
肯數鄴下黃鬚兒。

6.4

Song: Mount Long[1]

The young men of Chang'an, wandering knights-errant,
Climb the garrison watchtower at night to watch Taibo.[2]
Bright moon over Mount Long shines far down upon the pass;
Soldiers above Mount Long play the bamboo flute at night.
West of the pass, the old general is overcome with grief;
He halts his horse and listens to it – his tears flow down.
He has personally endured over a hundred battles;
All other officers under his command are now lords of a myriad households.
Su Wu remains a Supervisor of Dependent Countries;
The yak-tail hairs of his staff all fell out in the vast western desert.[3]

6.5

Ballad: The Old General

When a young man – just fifteen or twenty,
You went on foot to capture the Hun cavalry.
You shot and killed a white-browed tiger in the mountains;
Hardly willing to take second-place to the brown-whiskered lad of Ye.[4]

---

1 A mountain on the border of Shaanxi and Gansu.

2 The planet Venus.

3 When the Han envoy Su Wu refused to surrender to the Xiongnu, they exiled him to Lake Baikal to herd sheep. He used his imperial envoy staff as a shepherd's staff, never letting it leave his side. Eventually all the hairs on its ornamental yak tail fell out.

4 Nickname for Cao Cao's son Zhang 彰, famed for his military prowess and courage.

一身轉戰三千里，
一劍曾當百萬師。
漢兵奮迅如霹靂，
虜騎崩騰畏蒺藜。
衛青不敗由天幸，
李廣無功緣數奇。

自從棄置便衰朽，
世事蹉跎成白首。
昔時飛雀無全目，
今日垂楊生左肘。
路傍時賣故侯瓜，
門前學種先生柳。
蒼茫古木連窮巷，
寥落寒山對虛牖。
誓令疏勒出飛泉，
不似潁川空使酒。

1 A prominent military leader during the reign of Emperor Wu of the Han, famous for his victories against the Xiongnu.

2 Another general of Emperor Wu's. He was famous for never achieving advancement, in spite of his great courage and daring.

3 This alludes to the story of the mythical archer Yi 羿, who promised to shoot a sparrow in the left eye and felt humiliated when he hit the right one instead.

4 See note to 3.1.8.

All alone you went from battle to battle over three thousand li;
With one sword you faced an army of a million.
Your Han troops sped as swift as thunderbolts;
The barbarian cavalry scattered in terror, fearing the thorns of their weapons.
Wei Qing was never defeated, enjoying the favor of Heaven;[1]
But Li Guang earned no merit due to his strange fate.[2]

Since you were cast aside, you have grown decrepit;
Stumbling in the affairs of life, your hair has turned gray.
In the past, not a single sparrow was allowed to keep both eyes;[3]
Now a tumor grows from your left elbow.[4]
At times you sell melons at the roadside, like a former marquis;[5]
You imitate the master who planted willows before his gate.[6]
In boundless green the aged trees stretch to your remote lane;
Deserted and lonely, the cold hills face your open window.
You swore an oath at Kashgar and produced a flowing stream;[7]
You're not like the general of Yingchuan who uselessly gave himself up to drink.[8]

5 The Qin era Marquis of Dongling 東陵侯 was forced to sell melons to make a living after he lost his position.

6 See note to 2.24.10.

7 When the general Geng Gong 耿恭 was besieged by Xiongnu and his men were dying of thirst, he prayed for a well to produce water and it did so. The Xiongnu were convinced that Heaven was on his side and broke off the siege.

8 The Former Han general Guan Fu 灌夫 was infamous for losing his temper when drinking. He was later executed for offending the wrong court faction.

賀蘭山下陣如雲，
羽檄交馳日夕聞。
節使三河募年少，
詔書五道出將軍。
試拂鐵衣如雪色，
聊持寶劍動星文。
願得燕弓射大將，
恥令越甲鳴吾君。
莫嫌舊日雲中守，
猶堪一戰立功勳。

6.6

燕支行（時年二十一）

漢家天將才且雄，
來時謁帝明光宮。
萬乘親推雙闕下，
千官出餞五陵東。

1 Literally, a war summons with feather attached, indicating the necessity of quick response or action.

2 General term for the areas of Shanxi and Henan.

3 When Yue attacked Qi, the Qi minister Yongmen Zidi 雍門子狄 killed himself, claiming that the charioteer of the king had once killed himself because a noise made by the hubcap of the carriage disturbed his ruler, and now the Yue troops were disturbing the Qi ruler with their noise. The Yue forces were so impressed by this act of loyalty they broke off their invasion.

Now below Helan Mountain the battle arrays are massing like clouds;
The call to arms galloping back and forth can be heard day and night.[1]
Emissaries are drafting young men around the Three Rivers;[2]
24 Imperial orders summon generals through the Five Circuits.
You try brushing off your armor that gleams as white as snow;
You intend to take up your jeweled sword that glitters with its constellation pattern.
You wish to obtain a bow of Yan and shoot their great generals;
28 You are ashamed to let the Yue troops disturb our lord.[3]
Don't worry about the example of the governor of Yunzhong from olden days;[4]
You can still establish merit in a single battle!

6.6

Ballad: Yanzhi (Written at twenty-one)

The Heaven General of the Han house is talented and valiant;
He comes to pay court to the Emperor at Mingguang Palace.[5]
The emperor himself at the imperial watchtowers urges on his myriad carriages;
4 A thousand officials grant him a farewell banquet east of the Five Barrows.[6]

---

4 The governor of Yunzhong, Wei Shang 魏尚, was particularly effective in defending his district against Xiongnu attacks, but he was later demoted. When the unfairness of this treatment was brought to Emperor Wen's attention, he restored Wei to his office.

5 An imperial residence in Han times.

6 A suburb of the capital where the first five Han emperors were buried.

誓辭甲第金門裏，
身作長城玉塞中。
衛霍纔堪一騎將，
朝廷不數貳師功。

趙魏燕韓多勁卒，
關西俠少何咆勃。
報讎只是聞嘗膽，
飲酒不曾妨刮骨。
畫戟雕戈白日寒，
連旗大旆黃塵沒。
疊鼓遙翻瀚海波，
鳴笳亂動天山月。

麒麟錦帶佩吳鉤，
颯踏青驪躍紫騮。
拔劍已斷天驕臂，
歸鞍共飲月支頭。
漢兵大呼一當百，
虜騎相看哭且愁。
教戰雖令赴湯火，
終知上將先伐謀。

1 See note to 4.8.4. The Han general Huo Qubing 霍去病 refused such a mansion as long as the Xiongnu remained alive.

He swears he will refuse a mansion within Gold Horse Gate;[1]
He himself will become a long wall at the Jade Gate Pass.[2]
Wei's and Huo's talents were only worth a cavalry general's value;[3]
8 The court would not value the Ershi General's merit above yours.[4]

There are many tough troops in Zhao, Wei, Yan, and Han;
How the chivalrous young men from west of the pass rage!
Until they take revenge on their enemy they only taste gall;[5]
12 They won't prevent their bones from being scraped as they drink ale.[6]
Painted halberds and carved pikes are cold in the daylight;
Linked banners and the huge pennants sink in clouds of brown dust.
The sound of drums turns about far in the sand waves of the Gobi;
16 Sounding reeds wildly shake in the moonlight of Heaven Mountain.

Wu daggers hang from brocade sashes with unicorn patterns;
Exuberant black steeds leap with dappled roans.
They pull their swords – already cut off the arms of Heaven's Brats;[7]
20 With returning saddles they drink together from the skulls of Tokharians.[8]
With a great shout, one Han soldier can withstand a hundred.
The barbarian horsemen look at each other and sob in grief.
Though he goes through boiling water and fire when he leads in battle,
24 In the end he knows the best general works out battle plans beforehand.

---

2 A barrier established by Emperor Wu of the Han, located in Gansu northwest of Dunhuang. It is frequently mentioned in frontier poetry.

3 The Han generals Wei Qing 衛青 and Huo Qubing. The line is saying that their value was far below that of the "Heaven General."

4 The Han general Li Guangli 李廣利 besieged the city of Ershi in Ferghana in order to obtain some of their fine horses. He subsequently was granted the title of "Ershi General."

5 Said to be the actions of the Yue king Goujian 句踐 until he inflicted revenge on Wu.

6 The Shu general Guan Yu 關羽 was suffering from a wound inflicted by a poisoned arrow. The doctor was forced to scrape the bone of the infected arm to remove the poison. During the operation, Guan Yu chatted and laughed as he drank ale.

7 A boastful name the Xiongnu gave themselves.

8 A tribal people during the Han era dwelling in Gansu, Xinjiang, and Qinghai.

6.7

桃源行（時年十九）

漁舟逐水愛山春，
兩岸桃花夾去津。
坐看紅樹不知遠，
行盡青溪不見人。

山口潛行始隈隩，
山開曠望旋平陸。
遙看一處攢雲樹，
近入千家散花竹。
樵客初傳漢姓名，
居人未改秦衣服。

居人共住武陵源，
還從物外起田園。
月明松下房櫳靜，
日出雲中雞犬喧。

驚聞俗客爭來集，
競引還家問都邑。
平明閭巷掃花開，
薄暮漁樵乘水入。

6.7

Ballad: Peach Blossom Spring (Written at nineteen)[1]

In his fishing boat he followed the water; he loved spring in the hills.
On the two banks, peach blossoms flanked the departing stream.
He sat and watched the red trees, not noticing how far he went;
When he came to the end of the blue creek he saw no one.

Stealthily he entered the mountain mouth – at first it curved and turned;
Then it opened up, and suddenly he viewed a plain stretching away.
Far away he could see one place with a copse of misty trees;
When he approached, he entered a thousand houses with patches of flowering bamboo.
The woodsman was the first to have contact with these men with Han-era names;
The residents had still not changed their Qin-era clothing.

The residents lived together at this Wuling source,
Beyond the things of this world they established fields and gardens.
The moon shone bright under the pines; their windows were tranquil.
The sun emerged from behind the clouds; the clamor of chickens and dogs.

Startled to hear of this traveler from the common world, they gathered together;
They vied in leading them to their homes and asked about the capital.
At dawn in the village lanes, they swept the petals away;
At dusk, the fishermen and woodcutters rode the creek back home.

1 See note to 2.22a.4.

初因避地去人間，
及至成仙遂不還。
峽裏誰知有人事，
世中遙望空雲山。
不疑靈境難聞見，
塵心未盡思鄉縣。
出洞無論隔山水，
辭家終擬長游衍。
自謂經過舊不迷，
安知峰壑今來變。

當時只記入山深，
青溪幾度到雲林。
春來徧是桃花水，
不辨仙源何處尋。

6.8

洛陽女兒行（時年十八）

洛陽女兒對門居，
纔可顏容十五餘。
良人玉勒乘驄馬，
侍女金盤鱠鯉魚。

At first in order to avoid the troubles they had left the human realm;
When they turned into Transcendents they then did not return.
In this gorge who would know about affairs of men?
Gazing here from the human world you could only see cloudy hills.
He did not suspect that such a numinous realm was a rare discovery;
His dusty mind was not yet free of longing for his home.[1]
He emerged from the cave, paying no heed to the intervening hills and streams;
He bid his family farewell, intending in the end to travel long for his own pleasure.
He thought he wouldn't get lost if he followed his former path;
How could he know that peaks and valleys would now change?

The first time he had only noticed how deep he had entered the hills,
And how many turns the blue stream took into cloudy woods.
Now that spring had come, everywhere there were peach flower waters;
He could no longer distinguish where to find his Transcendents' stream.

6.8

Ballad: The Girl from Luoyang (Written at eighteen)

The girl from Luoyang lives behind the gates opposite;
Judging from her features she must be a bit over fifteen.
Her fine husband rides a piebald horse with jade bridle;
Her maidservants serve minced carp on golden plates.

1 That is, a mind still concerned with the common world. It may also signify samsara, the world of suffering in Buddhism.

畫閣朱樓盡相望，
紅桃綠柳垂簷向。
羅帷送上七香車，
寶扇迎歸九華帳。

狂夫富貴在青春，
意氣驕奢劇季倫。
自憐碧玉親教舞，
不惜珊瑚持與人。

春牕曙滅九微火，
九微片片飛花璅。
戲罷曾無理曲時，
妝成祇是薰香坐。

城中相識盡繁華，
日夜經過趙李家。
誰憐越女顏如玉，
貧賤江頭自浣紗。

Painted galleries and vermilion mansions rise up facing each other;
Red peach blossoms and green willows droop by the eaves.
From gauze drapes they see off her seven-fragranced carriage;
A jeweled fan greets her return by the nine-flowered bedcurtain.

Her wild husband, wealthy and noble in the verdant spring –
By temperament prouder in his luxuries than Shi Jilun.[1]
He cherishes his Biyu, personally teaches her dances;[2]
He does not begrudge the coral he gives to others.

By dawn in the spring window the Nine Subtleties lamp is put out;[3]
Fragments of wick from the Nine Subtleties fly out the decorated window.
When she is finished with play, she has no time to practice her songs;
With cosmetics done, she can only sit amid fragrant incense.

Those he knows in the city are all flourishing families;
Day and night he visits the houses of the Zhaos and Lis.[4]
Who pities the girl from Yue with features like jade,
Poor and humble, washing her own silk by the river?[5]

---

1 Jilun is the polite name of Shi Chong, a prominent fourth-century aristocrat famous for his great wealth and extravagant tastes. Most famously, when Wang Kai 王愷 tried to compete with him in ostentation by presenting him with a coral tree, Shi Chong promptly smashed it and then repaid the present by giving Wang six or seven more splendid corals.

2 The name of a prince's concubine who appears occasionally in *yuefu* ballads.

3 This lamp is mentioned in an early record of marvels as a lamp put on display by Emperor Wu of the Han when visited by the Daoist goddess the Queen Mother of the West.

4 Possibly a reference to Zhao Feiyan 趙飛燕 and Li Ping 李平, two female favorites of Emperor Cheng of the Han. Here it describes the actions of the girl's husband.

5 See note to 5.10. Here the poor Xi Shi is contrasted with the Luoyang girl and her wealth.

6.9

黃雀癡

黃雀癡，
黃雀癡。
謂言青鷇是我兒，
一一口銜食，
養得成毛衣。
到大啁啾解游颺，
各自東西南北飛。
薄暮空巢上，
羈雌獨自歸。
鳳凰九雛亦如此，
慎莫愁思憔悴損容輝。

6.10

榆林郡歌

山頭松柏林，
山下泉聲傷客心。
千里萬里春草色，
黃河東流流不息。
黃龍戍上游俠兒，
愁逢漢使不相識。

6.9

The Brown Sparrow is Foolish

The brown sparrow is foolish,
The brown sparrow if foolish.
It believes "These blue fledglings are my children,"
And feeds them by mouth, one by one,
Raising them until they grow their feathers.
When they can sing aloud and know how to flutter about,
Each flies off, east, west, north and south.
Then at twilight, to its empty nest
The single female returns alone.
Even the nine chicks of the phoenix are like this –
Be sure not to let sad worries turn your beauty to a haggard pallor!

6.10

Song: Yulin Commandery[1]

On the mountain, a forest of pine and cypress;
At the foot of the mountain, the sound of the stream breaks a traveler's heart.
A thousand li, ten thousand li, the color of spring grass;
The Yellow River flows east, flows and never stops.
At the garrison at Huanglong, a wandering knight-errant
Is sad to meet a Han emissary and not recognize him.[2]

1 A Tang district now located in Inner Mongolia.

2 Huanglong was in present-day Liaoning. In frontier poetry, place names are often evoked for their romance and not for their geographical accuracy.

6.11

問寇校書雙溪

君家少室西，
為復少室東。
別來幾日今春風，
新買雙溪定何似。
餘生欲寄白雲中。

6.12

寄崇梵僧

崇梵僧，
崇梵僧，
秋歸覆釜春不還。
落花啼鳥紛紛亂，
澗戶山窗寂寂閒。
峽裏誰知有人事，
郡中遙望空雲山。

6.11

A question for Editing Clerk Kou of Twin Streams

Is your home west of Little House,
Or is it east of Little House?[1]
Several days since we parted, now a spring breeze.
So how is the Twin Streams estate you just bought?
I'd like to entrust the remaining years of my life to white clouds.

6.12

Sent to a monk from the Chongfan Monastery[2]

Chongfan monk,
Chongfan monk,
In autumn he returns to Fufu Village, but he doesn't come back in the spring.
Falling flowers and chirping birds are scattering everywhere,
While ravine door and mountain window are lonely and quiet.
Who knows if there are people doing anything within that gorge?
From the commandery gazing afar: hills with empty clouds.

1 Little House and Big House are the two peaks of Mount Song. Twin Streams was probably located in the area.

2 Chongfan ("Honoring the Buddha") Monastery was located in Jizhou, where Wang Wei was serving from 721 to 726. Fufu Village was located nearby.

6.13

同崔傅答賢弟

洛陽才子姑蘇客，
桂苑殊非故鄉陌。
九江楓樹幾回青，
一片揚州五湖白。
揚州時有下江兵，
蘭陵鎮前吹笛聲。
夜火人歸富春郭，
秋風鶴唳石頭城。
周郎陸弟為儔侶，
對舞前溪歌白苧。
曲几書留小史家，
草堂棊賭山陰墅。
衣冠若話外臺臣，
先數夫君席上珍。
更聞臺閣求三語，
遙想風流第一人。

1 This seems to be written for Cui and his brother when they were both living in the Jiangsu region (Yangzhou, Suzhou, and the Five Lakes).

2 Gusu: another name for Suzhou. This poem alludes to many locations around the Suzhou area and the Jiang delta.

3 Probably a reference to the expedition of the Prince of Yong 永王. He occupied the Jiangsu region, ostensibly to put down part of the An Lushan rebellion. However, he soon declared himself emperor and launched his own revolt.

6.13

Matching Cui Fu: "Answering my younger brother"[1]

Talented men from Luoyang, sojourners in Gusu;[2]
These are not the lanes of your home, these cinnamon tree gardens.
Several times have the maple trees at Nine Rivers turned green;
The Five Lakes gleam white through the whole swathe of Yangzhou.
Yangzhou is now filled with troops that have come down the river;[3]
In front of Lanling headquarters there is the sound of bamboo flutes.
Night fires: people returning to the walls near Fuchun;[4]
Autumn wind: the cries of a crane at Shitou City.[5]
Young Zhou Yu has made his younger brother Lu Yun his companion:
Together they dance "Front Stream" and sing "White Ramie".
Calligraphy is left on a curving armrest in a family of petty clerks;
They play Go in a thatched hut on their estate north of the mountains.[6]
When officials speak of provincial administrators,
They count you sir, as a treasure above all others.
I hear that State Affairs is still seeking those who think precisely –[7]
So I thought of you far off – the most cultivated man.

---

4 Fuchun was a river islet in the Qiantang River associated with southern dynasties poetry (Xie Lingyun specifically). It is often mentioned as a place of scenic beauty by poets visiting the region.

5 After the rout at the battle of Fei River 淝水 (383), the fleeing forces of Fu Jian 苻堅 heard the cry of a crane, mistook it for the pursuing enemy, and panicked.

6 These four lines describe the brothers in southern dynasties terms, emphasizing their elegance and talent (and their indifference to the military unrest): Zhou Yu 周瑜 was the young and dashing general of Wu during the Three Kingdoms period; Lu Yun 陸雲 was the talented younger brother of the talented Lu Ji 陸機. "Front Stream" and "White Ramie" are both *yuefu* titles. Wang Xizhi 王羲之 (303–361), considered one of the founders of the calligraphic art, once left some of his exquisite calligraphy on the armrest of one of his family's retainers. The Jin prime minister Xie An nonchalantly played Go at his mountain estate outside the capital while waiting to hear the result of the battle of the Fei River.

7 Literally, "seeking three words." Wang Yan 王衍 admired Ruan Xiu 阮修 for the three-word answer he gave to the question "Is Confucianism and Daoism the same or different?" He got him a post, and the world knew Ruan as the "three-word clerk."

6.14

同比部楊員外十五夜游有懷靜者季

承明少休沐，
建禮省文書。
夜漏行人息，
歸鞍落日餘。
豈知三五夕，
萬戶千門闢。
夜出曙翻歸，
傾城滿南陌。
陌頭馳騁盡繁華，
王孫公子五侯家。
由來月明如白日，
共道春燈勝百花。
聊看侍中千寶騎，
強識小婦七香車。
香車寶馬共喧闐，
箇裏多情俠少年。
競向長楊柳市北，
肯過精舍竹林前。
獨有仙郎心寂寞，
却將宴坐為行樂。

6.14

Matching a poem by Director Yang of the Bureau of Review:
"Strolling on the night of the fifteenth and thinking of the recluse Ji"[1]

You have little time off at Chengming Gate;[2]
At Jianli Palace you examine documents.[3]
During the night watches, passers-by are few:
Your home-bound saddle in the lingering sunset.
Who would think, on this night of the fifteenth,
That a thousand gates of ten thousand homes would lie open?
Going out in the night, returning at dawn,
The entire city fills the south streets.
On the streets they hurry about – everywhere bustle and crowds;
Princes, young noblemen, the families of the five marquis.
The whole time, the moon is bright as day;
Everyone says that the spring lanterns surpass all the flowers.
For a while we see the palace attendants, horsemen with a thousand jewels;
We strain to recognize young wives in their seven-scented carriages.
Scented carriages, jeweled horses together raise a clamor;
In the midst, passionate and chivalrous young men.
They race to Tall Poplar Palace, north of Willow Market;
How could they be willing to visit the *vihāra* in front of the bamboo grove?[4]
The Director is alone there, his mind is empty and at peace;
Sitting in meditation is his form of entertainment.

---

1 The fifteenth of the first month, or the Lantern Festival.

2 See note to 4.8.1.

3 Jianli ("Establishment of Propriety") was a Han era palace; because the Secretariat was located within its grounds, Wang Wei uses it for the palace where the current Secretariat and other offices were located.

4 *Vihāra*: originally a refuge for ascetics in Indian religions; later became a poetic term for a monastery.

倘覓忘懷共往來，
幸霑同舍甘藜藿。

6.15

故人張諲工詩善易卜兼能丹青草隸頃以詩見贈聊獲酬之

不逐城東游俠兒，
隱囊紗帽坐彈碁。
蜀中夫子時開卦，
4 洛下書生解詠詩。
藥欄花徑衡門裏，
時復據梧聊隱几。
屏風誤點惑孫郎，
8 團扇草書輕內史。
故園高枕度三春，
永日垂帷絕四鄰。
自想蔡邕今已老，
12 更將書籍與何人。

If I seek to forget my passions and associate with you,
I will be fortunate enough to lodge with you and find pigweed and bean leaves sweet.[1]

6.15

My friend Zhang Yin is a talented poet; he is also good at casting hexagrams, at painting, and at the different styles of calligraphy. Recently I received a poem from him, and thus have a chance to reply to him.

You don't chase after the chivalrous lads east of the city;
With back-rest pillow and silk cap you sit playing Go.
The gentleman from Shu sometimes reads divinations;[2]
The scholar from the Luo knows how to chant poems.[3]
At fences of shrubs and flowered paths, under a rustic gate,
Sometimes propped on your zither, sometimes leaning on your armrest.
You drop ink on the screen in error and fool Master Sun;[4]
With your grass calligraphy on round fans you can scorn Wang Xizhi.
In your home garden, pillowed on high, you pass the spring season;
You let your curtains down through the long day, cut off from all your neighbors.
I imagine that you've now grown old, like Cai Yong;
Then to whom are you planning to give your library?[5]

1 Typical food for an ascetic hermit.
2 Yan Junping 嚴君平, recluse of Western Han, who made a living casting fortunes.
3 Alludes to the old "capital" style of chanting poetry popular with some of the aristocrats following the fall of the north during the Six Dynasties period.
4 Sun Quan 孫權 requested a painting of Cao Buxing 曹不興. When the latter spotted the silk with ink by accident and then decided to turn it into a drawing of a fly, Sun tried to swat the fly away.
5 Though much older with a well-established reputation, Cai Yong 蔡邕 enthusiastically patronized Wang Can 王粲 and declared that he would give his family's library to him.

6.16

答張五弟

終南有茅屋，
前對終南山。
終年無客常閉關，
4 終日無心長自閒。
不妨飲酒復垂釣，
君但能來相往還。

6.17

贈吳官

長安客舍熱如煮，
無箇茗糜難御暑。
空搖白團其諦苦，
4 欲向縹囊還歸旅。
江鄉鯖鮓不寄來，
秦人湯餠那堪許。
不如儂家任挑達，
8 草屩撈蝦富春渚。

6.16

Reply to younger brother Zhang Five

At Zhongnan there is a thatched hut,
Which faces Zhongnan mountain in front.
No visitors at the end of my days, I often shut my door;
All day with no preoccupations, I can stay relaxed.
Nothing keeps us from drinking ale and going fishing.
Visiting, then going home – is that all you can do?[1]

6.17

Presented to an official from Wu

The Chang'an guest-house is boiling hot
With no tea-infused congee to mitigate the heat.
In vain you wave your white fan – this is the Truth of Suffering;[2]
You wish to take your blue book bag and head back home.
The shipment of salted carp from your river home doesn't arrive;
How could you tolerate the noodle soup of these Qin people?
"I'd rather let myself wander free,
Go shrimping in straw sandals on a Fuchun River islet."[3]

1 Rather than staying here with me as a hermit permanently.
2 The first of Buddhism's Four Truths of the Noble Ones: all existence is suffering.
3 See note to 6.13.7.

6.18

雪中憶李揖

積雪滿阡陌，
故人不可期。
長安千門復萬戶，
何處蹀躞黃金羈。

6.19

送崔五太守

長安廄吏來到門，
朱文露網動行軒。
黃花縣西九折坂，
玉樹宮南五丈原。
褒斜谷中不容幰，
惟有白雲當露冕。
子午山裏杜鵑啼，
嘉陵水頭行客飯。
劍門忽斷蜀川開，
萬井雙流滿眼來。

6.18

In the snow, thinking of Li Yi

Drifts of snow fill up the lanes;
An old friend can't keep our meeting.
Among the thousand gates and myriad doors of Chang'an
Where paces your gold-bridled horse?

6.19

Seeing off Prefect Cui Five

The Chang'an stable manager has come to your gate;
The carriage goes forth with its vermilion patterns and its netted screen.
West of Huanghua County, at Nine Bends Slope,
South of Jade Tree Palace, on Wuzhang Plain.[1]
In Baoye Valley not a single carriage can pass through;
There are only white clouds confronting your ceremonial cap of honor.
In Ziling Mountain the cuckoo cries;
The traveler dines at the source of the Jialing River.
Where Sword Gate suddenly rises sheer, the way to Shuchuan is opened;[2]
Then the ten thousand homes at the paired currents come to fill the eyes.[3]

1 Throughout this poem Wang Wei uses elements of Shaanxi and Sichuan topography to describe (somewhat loosely) Cui's passage to Sichuan. Huanghua county – part of Fengzhou, in Shaanxi.

2 Shuchuan is another name for Yizhou 益州, now part of Sichuan.

3 The traveler arrives in Chengdu, where a section of the Jiang divides into two, passing north and south of the city.

霧中遠樹刀州出，
天際澄江巴字回。
使君年幾三十餘，
少年白皙專城居。
欲持畫省郎官筆，
迴與臨邛父老書。

6.20

送李睢陽

將置酒，
思悲翁。
使君去，
出城東。
麥漸漸，
雉子斑。
槐陰陰，
到潼關。
騎連連，
車遲遲，
心中悲。

1 Another name for Yizhou, based on a prophetic dream in which Jin era Wang Jun dreamed that three knives hung in his bedroom (3 *dao* characters = *zhou* character) and one was then "added" (*yi*). He was then made prefect of Yizhou.

Distant trees in the mist emerge in Daozhou,[1]
On the horizon, the clear river twists like the character "ba."[2]
An emissary over thirty years of age;
A young man of fair complexion who is master of the town.
You will grasp the writing brush used by the Secretaries in State Affairs
And turn it to write a letter for the old men of Linqiong.[3]

6.20

Seeing off Li of Suiyang[4]

About to serve the ale,
I think sadly of you, venerable sir.
You, an emissary, depart,
Leaving by the east side of the city.
Wheat is tall and flourishing,
The young pheasants are mottled.
Sophora trees are shady
As you arrive at Tong Pass.
Your mounted entourage dawdles,
And your carriage moves slowly,
And you are sad in your heart.

---

2 Where the Baishui Jiang flows into the Jialing Jiang it is said to look like the character *ba* 巴.

3 When Sima Xiangru was serving the government in Shu, he had suggested that negotiations be opened with non-Chinese tribes in the southwest, and the government was amenable. He later discovered the notables in Shu as well as court ministers were opposed to the idea. He felt he could not openly withdraw his suggestion, so he wrote a letter opposing the plan, using Shu elders as personae.

4 Li Huan 李峘, a descendant of the imperial family; see 3.16. He was sent out to his post because of opposition to Yang Guozhong. Suiyang is another name for Songzhou in modern Henan.

宋又遠，
周間之。
南淮夷，
東齊兒。
碎碎織練與素絲，
游人賈客信難持。
五穀前熟方可為，
下車閉閣君當思。
天子當殿儼衣裳，
太官尚食陳羽觴，
彤庭散綬垂鳴璫。
黃紙詔書出東廂，
輕紈疊綺爛生光。
宗室子弟君最賢，
分憂當為百辟先。
布衣一言相為死，
何況聖主恩如天。
鸞聲噦噦魯侯旂，
明年上計朝京師。
須憶今日斗酒別，
慎勿富貴忘我為。

Song too is far away;
The Zhou lands lie in between.
The tribals of the south Huai,
The lads of eastern Qi:
With their trifling woven silks and raw silk skeins,
Those traveling merchants are difficult to manage.
You can only take action after the five grains are harvested;
Think whether to be an activist or close your gate to plan.[1]
The Son of Heaven in his hall donned his formal apparel,
The provisioners and stewards arrayed the wing-patterned goblets,
Beribboned officials dispersed from the crimson court, their girdle chimes ringing.
Imperial decrees on yellow paper were sent from the eastern wing;
Light taffetas and lined brocades give off a glistening light.[2]
Of all the scions of the imperial house, you are the most worthy;
And you are first among the vassals in bearing the ruler's worries.
You would die honorably at a single word from a commoner;
How much more so for a sagely lord whose grace is that of Heaven's?
Your simurgh carriage bells ring out with the Lu ruler's standard;[3]
Next year you will present your plans and come to the capital again.[4]
Then you must remember today, when we part over our drinking;
Don't forget me from your position of wealth and status!

1 The first part of the poem projects the responsibilities Li will have after arriving at his post.
2 The second part describes the ceremonies for his departure from the capital.
3 *Shijing* 299 describes the arrival of the marquis of Lu in his carriage, ornamented with banners and bells.
4 I.e., run out your term and return from the provinces.

6.21

寒食城東即事

清溪一道穿桃李，
演漾綠蒲涵白芷。
谿上人家凡幾家，
落花半落東流水。
蹴踘屢過飛鳥上，
鞦韆競出垂楊裏。
少年分日作遨遊，
不用清明兼上巳。

6.22

不遇詠

北闕獻書寢不報，
南山種田時不登。
百人會中身不預，
五侯門前心不能。
身投河朔飲君酒，
家在茂陵平安否。

1 For Cold Food, see note on 4.7.7. The Purification Festival would normally fall sometime between late March and mid-April.

2 Football and swings were popular on both Cold Food and Qingming.

6.21

Things encountered on the Cold Food Festival east of the city[1]

The single course of the clear stream runs through the peach and plum;
Rivulets surge against the green sweet-flag and drench the angelica.
Along the stream some households, few in number,
Where half the fallen blossoms fall into the east-flowing water.
The kickballs have soared over flying birds several times;
The tree swings contend as they emerge from the drooping poplars.[2]
Youths go out to have fun on the spring equinox,
They need not wait for Qingming or the Purification Festival.[3]

6.22

On being unsuccessful

I presented proposals at the north palace gate tower, but never got an answer;
On Zhongnan Mountain I planted my fields, but they yielded no harvest.
To the assembly of a hundred I was not invited;[4]
My mind is unable to seek preferment at the gates of the Five Marquis.
So I took refuge north of the Yellow River and I drink your ale –
I wonder if my family at Maoling is well or not?[5]

3 The Purification Festival was held on the third day of the third month of the lunar calendar, and so would fall sometime between late March and mid-April.

4 From the *Shishuo xinyu*, chapter 22: Fu Tao 伏滔 boasted to his son that he was invited to a gathering of a hundred people at the palace, and that when he arrived, the emperor first demanded to know if he was there.

5 See note to 4.22.14.

且共登山復臨水，
莫問春風動楊柳。
今人作人多自私，
我心不說君應知。
濟人然後拂衣去，
肯作徒爾一男兒。

Together we climb the hill and look down upon the water;
8 No one asks if the spring breeze stirs the willow trees.
Most who act as humans these days are selfish;
You should know how unhappy I am in my heart.
If those who would help me should brush off their robes and leave,[1]
12 How can I play this useless role as a man?

1 To act dismissively (to wash their hands of).

王右丞集卷之七 近體詩

7.1

奉和聖製賜史供奉曲江宴應制

侍從有鄒枚，
瓊筵就水開。
言陪柏梁宴，
新下建章來。
對酒山河滿，
移舟草樹迴。
天文同麗日，
駐景惜行杯。

1 At this time Xuanzong granted the title "auxiliary" to members of the Hanlin 翰林 Academy, an institution meant for men skilled in the various arts. The Qujiang was a public park located in the southeast corner of Chang'an.

https://doi.org/10.1515/9781501516023-007

Juan 7: Recent style poems

7.1

At imperial command, respectfully harmonizing with the imperial composition: "Granting Auxiliary Shi a banquet at the Qujiang"[1]

Zou and Mei among his attendants,[2]
Garnet banquet mats unrolled by the waterside.
To accompany the banquet at Cypress Rafters,
They have just come down from Jianzhang Palace.[3]
As they face their wine, it is filled with hills and rivers;
As they move their boats, plants and trees turn about them.
The constellations and the lovely sun
Both halt time, for they love the passing of our drinking cups.

2 Zou Yang 鄒陽 and Mei Cheng 枚乘, two prominent poets of the Western Han dynasty who were patronized by the Princes of Wu and Liang in turn during the Western Han. Here it stands in for the literati invited to the banquet.

3 Cypress Rafter Terrace and Jianzhang Palace were both built by Emperor Wu of the Han. The former was often used to host banquets for literary men.

7.2

從岐王過楊氏別業應教

楊子談經所，
淮王載酒過。
興闌啼鳥換，
4 坐久落花多。
逕轉迴銀燭，
林開散玉珂。
嚴城時未啟，
8 前路擁笙歌。

7.3

從岐王夜讌衛家山池應教

座客香貂滿，
宮娃綺幔張。
澗花輕粉色，
4 山月少燈光。
積翠紗窗暗，
飛泉繡戶涼。
還將歌舞出，
8 歸路莫愁長。

7.2

Written at the prince's command: Accompanying the Prince of Qi on a visit to the country estate of the Yang clan

To the place where Master Yang discusses classics
The prince of Huainan comes visiting, bearing ale.[1]
By the time our enthusiasm is satisfied, the singing birds have changed;
As we sit there long, falling blossoms grow many.
The path swerves, makes our silver candles turn back;
The forest opens, dispersing our jade bridle pendants.
By curfew law the city gates have yet to open;
On the road in front our musicians and singers throng.

7.3

Written at the prince's command: Accompanying the Prince of Qi to a night banquet at the mountain pond of the Wei family

The seated guests are replete with scented marten tails;[2]
Patterned silk screens are spread before the palace ladies.
Ravine blossoms lighten their powder's color;
The mountain moon adds a little to the lantern light.
Mid the massed deep-green vegetation, the silk windowpanes darken;
By the flying stream the ornamented doors are cool.
Still they bring forth the singers and dancers;
Let no one grieve that the return road is long.

1 The Han poet and philosopher Yang Xiong 揚雄 is the stand-in for the Yang clan here (though his surname is written with a different character); the Han prince and patron the Prince of Huainan 淮南 is a stand-in for the Prince of Qi.

2 Marten tails were an insignia of high office.

7.4

和尹諫議史館山池

雲館接天居，
霓裳侍玉除。
春池百子外，
4 芳樹萬年餘。
洞有仙人籙，
山藏太史書。
君恩深漢帝，
8 且莫上空虛。

7.5

同崔員外秋宵寓直

建禮高秋夜，
承明候曉過。

1 Yin Yin 尹愔, the author of the original poem Wang is answering, was a noted Daoist adept and received his official position through Xuanzong's patronage of the faith. The Historiography Institute was located on the grounds of the Daming 大明 Palace in Chang'an – hence the reference to its connection with "Heaven's dwelling" in the first line. "Institute" is also the word translated in the first line as "lodge."

2 Rainbow skirts are said to be worn by Daoist immortals. Here this line describes Yin Yin attending upon the emperor.

3 The Hundred Sons Pond was a pond located within the imperial precincts during the reign of Emperor Wu of the Han.

7.4

Harmonizing with Yin, Grand Master of Remonstrance:
The mountain pool at the Historiography Institute[1]

This lodge in the clouds connects with Heaven's dwelling,
Rainbow skirts attend on the jade stairs.[2]
This spring pool far surpasses the "Hundred Sons,"[3]
Fragrant trees live more than ten thousand years.
The grotto holds an immortal's register;
The library stores the grand historian's book.[4]
Your lord's grace is deeper than a Han emperor's;
So please do not rise into the air![5]

7.5

Matching Supernumerary Cui: "Office duty on an autumn night"

A night in high autumn at Jianli Palace;
We wait for dawn at Chengming so we can leave.[6]

---

4 In the Daoist faith, the term "register" (*lu*) is applied to documents granted to adepts by their masters specifying their attendant deities and declaring them as initiates. Library (literally, "mountain"): refers here to the Western Han historian Sima Qian's 司馬遷 comment that he was storing a copy of his history "in a famous mountain," i.e., the imperial library.

5 Ge Hong tells of the Daoist adept Heshang Gong 河上公. He was visited by Emperor Wen of the Han, who sought from him an explanation of passages in the *Laozi*. When Emperor Wen criticized the adept for not treating him with respect, he rose into the air and told the emperor that since he belonged to neither earth nor heaven he could not be considered an imperial subject.

6 Jianli ("Establishment of Propriety") was a Han era palace; because the Secretariat was located within its grounds, Wang Wei uses it for the palace where the current Secretariat resides. For Chengming, see note to 4.8.1. Wang and Cui are waiting for the gate to open at dawn so that they can leave the palace grounds and enter back into the city.

九門寒漏徹，
萬井曙鐘多。
月迴藏珠斗，
雲消出絳河。
更慚衰朽質，
南陌共鳴珂。

7.6

奉和楊駙馬六郎秋夜即事

高樓月似霜，
秋夜鬱金堂。
對坐彈盧女，
同看舞鳳凰。
少兒多送酒，
小玉更焚香。
結束平陽騎，
明朝入建章。

1 Because the River of Stars (the Milky Way) seems to progress south from the pole star, and the south is associated with the color red, "Scarlet River" became an epithet for it.

Within the nine palace gates the cold water-clocks empty out;
4 In a myriad wards the dawn bells are many.
The moon is far off, the pearled dipper is concealed;
Clouds dissipate, exposing the Scarlet River.[1]
Even more ashamed of this body withering away,
8 I let bridle pendants ring with yours on southern avenues.

7.6

Respectfully harmonizing with Imperial Consort Yang Six's poem: "Things encountered on an autumn night"[2]

High in the building the moon is like frost;
An autumn night in a fragrant hall.
We sit facing Lady Lu as she strums;[3]
4 Together we watch the dancing phoenixes.
Shao'er often brings us ale,
Little Jade burns more incense.
They then attire Pingyang's escort,
8 For at dawn he enters Jianzhang Palace.

---

2 Throughout, this poem implicitly compares the subject Yang to the Han general Wei Qing. Wei was the illegitimate son of a concubine of the Marquis of Pingyang. One of his half-sisters, Wei Zifu 子夫, was in the service of the marquis' principal wife (the Princess of Pingyang) and later won the favor of Emperor Wu of the Han; this brought the Wei family to prominence. Wei Shao'er was another one of his sisters, and the mother of another prominent general, Huo Qubing. When Wei Qing grew up, he entered the Princess' service. Later, when Wei Zifu was promoted to the palace, Wei Qing served at the Jianzhang Palace.

3 See note to 2.2.4.

7.7

酬虞部蘇員外過藍田別業不見留之作

貧居依谷口，
喬木帶荒村。
石路枉迴駕，
山家誰候門。
漁舟膠凍浦，
獵犬繞寒原。
唯有白雲外，
疏鐘聞夜猿。

7.8

酬比部楊員外暮宿琴臺朝躋書閣率爾見贈之作

舊簡拂塵看，
鳴琴候月彈。
桃源迷漢姓，
松樹有秦官。

1 In Danfu Prefecture in Shandong. A disciple of Confucius, Mi Buqi 宓不齊, served as an official there. He was so virtuous that he remained in his hall playing the zither and yet the district was put in order. The site of his hall was a local destination for visitors, mentioned in other Tang poems. The bamboo slips in line one evidently refer to old books stored in a library on the site.

7.7

Reply To Vice Director Su of the Bureau of Forestry and Crafts: He visits my mountain estate at Lantian and leaves upon not meeting me

My poor dwelling leans on the mouth of the valley;
Lofty trees flank the rustic village.
The rock-strewn road turned back your carriage on its futile visit;
4 For who attended at the gate of my mountain home?
Now fishing boats are stuck to the frozen bank;
And hunting dogs encircle the cold plain.
There is only, beyond these white clouds,
8 The sparse sounds of bells mingled with the gibbons at night.

7.8

Reply to a Poem by Vice Director Yang of the Bureau of Review: “Spending the night at Zither Terrace and on the following morning climbing up to the library, I sent you a poem on the spur of the moment”[1]

You brushed dust off the old bamboo slips to look,
While a sounding zither awaited the moonlight to be played.
Your Peach Blossom Spring causes Han people to be lost;
4 Among your pine trees, some have served as Qin officials.[2]

---

2 For Peach Blossom Spring, see note to 2.22a.4. When the first Qin emperor visited Mount Tai, he encountered a storm on the way down and took shelter under a tree. He then granted the tree an honorary court position. Wang is here describing Yang’s idyllic residence near Zither Terrace, which is as remote as the Peach Blossom Spring and surrounded by venerable trees.

空谷歸人少，
青山背日寒。
羨君棲隱處，
遙望白雲端。

7.9

酬嚴少尹徐舍人見過不遇

公門暇日少，
窮巷故人稀。
偶值乘籃轝，
非關避白衣。
不知炊黍否，
誰解掃荊扉。
君但傾茶椀，
無妨騎馬歸。

1 Tao Qian was wary of befriending powerful people, and resisted the overtures of the prominent official and nobleman Wang Hong 王弘. Wang then had one of Tao's friends prepare a banquet for him. Wang showed up at the banquet later and Tao then treated him as a friend. At the time Tao was suffering from a sore foot and had to be brought to the banquet in a palanquin. After this meeting, Wang could be depended on to supply Tao with wine. On one occasion, on the Double Ninth, Tao was lacking in wine and was delighted when Wang sent him

Few people return to your empty valley;
Your green hills are chill with their back to the sun.
I envy you the place where you roost in reclusion,
And gaze afar to the edge of white clouds.

7.9

Reply to Vice-Governor Yan and Secretary Xu coming to visit me and not finding me at home

Few days of leisure at your office gates;
In remote lanes, old friends are scarce.
If you had happened to meet me riding in a sedan chair,
It was not because I'm avoiding a white-robed servant![1]
I don't know if anyone there cooked millet for you –
And who there would know to sweep my rustic hut in welcome?[2]
You barely had a bowl of tea to drink
Then decided you might as well ride home.

---

some. In one version of the story, the wine was delivered by a "white robed servant." In later literature, a "white robed servant" came to mean a wine deliveryman, especially one sent by an official. Here, Wang Wei jokingly denies that he was "not at home" because he was trying to avoid the powerful officeholders Yan and Xu.

2 I.e., Wang is so poor he doubts there was anyone to look after the guests when they arrived in his absence.

7.10

慕容承攜素饌見過

紗帽烏皮几，
閒居懶賦詩。
門看五柳識，
年算六身知。
靈壽君王賜，
雕胡弟子炊。
空勞酒食饌，
特底解人頤。

7.11

酬慕容十一

行行西陌返，
駐幰問車公。
挾轂雙官騎，
應門五尺僮。
老年如塞北，

---

1 See note to 2.24.10.

2 An allusion to a passage in the *Zuo zhuan*, in which an old man's age is calculated by taking the character *hai* 亥 apart, resulting in "two at the head and two sixes in the body." The result was a calculation of 26,600 days, or about seventy-three years. In other words, Wang is saying that he is quite old.

7.10

Murong Cheng visits me, bringing vegetarian food

Muslin cap of office, armrest upholstered in black lambskin:
I live in idleness, too lazy to compose poems.
You recognize me when you see the five willows by my gate;[1]
You calculate my age – you know the sixes of the body.[2]
My zelkova-wood staff – a gift of my ruler;
My disciples steam wild rice gruel for me.
Merely that you make the effort to bring me food and ale
Especially cheers me up.

7.11

Reply to Murong Eleven

Going on and on, returning from the western streets,
I halt my carriage and ask after Lord Ju.[3]
Our wheels aligned – you have a pair of official escorts;[4]
Standing guard at your gate – lads five feet tall.
In your old age, you head off north of the frontier;

3 Ju Yin 車胤 was a handsome and clever Eastern Jin aristocrat much prized at parties – leading to the saying of the time, "It's not fun if Lord Ju isn't here." Wang Wei is designating Murong.

4 Literally, "touching wheel-hubs," a poetic cliché for carriages crowded side by side on a narrow street. Here it describes Murong's and the poet's conversation occurring between their two carriages.

強起離牆東。
為報壺丘子，
來人道住蒙。

7.12

酬張少府

晚年唯好靜，
萬事不關心。
自顧無長策，
空知返舊林。
松風吹解帶，
山月照彈琴。
君問窮通理，
漁歌入浦深。

7.13

喜祖三至留宿

門前洛陽客，
下馬拂征衣。
不枉故人駕，
平生多掩扉。

Forced to rise and abandon your reclusion east of the wall.[1]
For my sake report to Master Huqiu:[2]
The one who seeks him says he'll live in Meng.[3]

7.12

Reply to Assistant Magistrate Zhang

Late in life I only like quiet;
Worldly affairs do not bother my mind.
I observe myself: no long-term plans –
Know there's nothing to do save return to home woods.
A pine breeze blows on my untied sash,
And a mountain moon shines on my zither as I strum.
You ask about the principle of failure or success;
The fisherman's song enters deep into the riverbank.[4]

7.13

Happy that Zu Three has come to spend the night

Before my gate, a guest from Luoyang
Dismounts and brushes off his traveling clothes.
An old friend's carriage does not come in vain,
Though in the course of my life I've often shut my door.

---

1 See note to 1.2.12.
2 Master Huqiu was supposedly the teacher of the Daoist sage Liezi.
3 Meng was the home of Zhuangzi.
4 See note to 4.16.16.

行人返深巷，
積雪帶餘暉。
早歲同袍者，
高車何處歸。

7.13a

祖詠：答王維留宿

四年不相見，
相見復何為。
握手言未畢，
却令傷別離。
升堂還駐馬，
酌醴便呼兒。
語默自相對，
安用傍人知。

7.14

酬賀四贈葛巾之作

野巾傳惠好，
茲貺重兼金。
嘉此幽棲物，
能齊隱吏心。

Strollers return to their secluded lanes,
And accumulated snow bears the lingering sunlight.
You're a bosom friend from our earliest years –
8 So where else could your lofty carriage find refuge?

7.13a

Zu Yong: Reply to Wang Wei inviting me to spend the night

For four years we haven't seen each other –
We see each other, and what do we do?
Clasping hands, before our words are done
4 It brings on the heartbreak of parting.
We go up into your hall, my horses are stalled;
You pour out sweet ale and call the serving lad.
We fall silent then, and face each other:
8 What use for others to know?

7.14

Reply to He Four for his gift of a hemp headcloth

The rustic headcloth conveys your kind intentions;
This gift is worth more than the finest gold.
Delighting in this thing of secluded refuge –
4 It can be fitting for a hermit mind still serving in office.

早朝方暫挂，
晚沐復來簪。
坐覺囂塵遠，
思君共入林。

7.15

寄荊州張丞相

所思竟何在，
悵望深荊門。
舉世無相識，
終身思舊恩。
方將與農圃，
藝植老邱園。
目盡南飛鳥，
何由寄一言。

7.16

輞川閒居贈裴秀才迪

寒山轉蒼翠，
秋水日潺湲。

At morning court I hang it up for a while;
After washing in the evening I can pin it back on.
Then at once I feel far away from the noise and dust,
And imagine going with you together into the woods.

7.15

Sent to Zhang of Jingzhou, the head of the Department of State Affairs[1]

Where finally is the one I long for?
Grieving, I gaze toward remote Jingmen.
There is no one who knows me in all the age;
To the end of my life, I think of your old favors.
Now you will work on your farming plot;
You'll till and plant your old hills and gardens.
At the edge of sight, birds flying south:
How can I send you a single word?

7.16

Living at ease at Wangchuan: sent to Flourishing Talent Pei Di

The chill hills turn increasingly gray-green;
The autumn waters surge more daily.

1 Written to console Zhang Jiuling after Li Linfu 李林甫 ousted him from government in 737 and sent him to a post in exile at Jingzhou (in the central Jiang valley).

倚杖柴門外，
臨風聽暮蟬。
渡頭餘落日，
墟里上孤烟。
復值接輿醉，
狂歌五柳前。

7.17

冬晚對雪憶胡居士家

寒更傳曉箭，
清鏡覽衰顏。
隔牖風驚竹，
開門雪滿山。
灑空深巷靜，
積素廣庭閑。
借問袁安舍，
翛然尚閉關。

I lean on a cane outside my scrap-wood gate,
Facing the wind, listening to cicadas at dusk.
At the ford some lingering sunlight;
In the village, solitary smoke rises.
Again I meet Jieyu drunk,[1]
Madly singing in front of Five Willows.[2]

7.17

Facing the snow on a winter evening and thinking of the house of Layman Hu

Chill watch-drums convey the dawn marker;[3]
In the clear mirror I observe my features in decline.
Beyond the window the breeze shakes the bamboo;
I open the gate – snow covers the hills.
Air sprinkled with flakes – the deep lanes are still;
Piled-up white – broad courtyards are calm.
I ask after the lodging of Yuan An;[4]
In his lofty spirit he still keeps his door shut.

1 See note to 5.4.1.
2 See note to 2.24.10.
3 Dawn marker: the arrow in the clepsydra that indicates the time now points at dawn.
4 Yuan An 袁安 was a virtuous man of the Eastern Han. He remained in his house with door closed in a snowstorm nearly frozen to death, for he thought if he left to beg for food he would interfere with others who were hungrier than he was. The poet is comparing Hu to Yuan.

7.18

山居秋暝

空山新雨後，
天氣晚來秋。
明月松間照，
清泉石上流。
竹喧歸浣女，
蓮動下漁舟。
隨意春芳歇，
王孫自可留。

7.19

歸嵩山作

清川帶長薄，
車馬去閒閒。
流水如有意，
暮禽相與還。
荒城臨古渡，
落日滿秋山。
迢遞嵩高下，
歸來且閉關。

7.18

Living in the mountains: autumn dusk

In empty mountains, after new rains,
The weather turns to autumn as evening comes.
A bright moon shines in the pine trees,
A clear stream flows over the stones.
Noise in bamboos: washerwomen return.
Lotuses move: fishing boats go downstream.
Following its nature, spring fragrance fades;
My Prince, you can linger here.[1]

7.19

Written while returning to Mount Song

The clear stream is banded by tall bushes;
Cart and horse depart leisurely.
Flowing water seems to have a mind;
And twilight birds go home together.
The abandoned walls look over an ancient ford;
The setting sun fills the autumn hills.
And far away, on the heights of Mount Song,
I have come home and have shut my door.

1 The last line adapts "Summoning the Recluse" (*Zhao yinshi* 招隱士) from the *Chu ci*: "Return, O Prince, / You cannot long stay in the hills." Here it is inviting the poem's recipient to stay in the hills as a recluse.

7.20

歸輞川作

谷口疏鐘動，
漁樵稍欲稀。
悠然遠山暮，
獨向白雲歸。
菱蔓弱難定，
楊花輕易飛。
東皋春草色，
惆悵掩柴扉。

7.21

韋給事山居

幽尋得此地，
詎有一人曾。
大壑隨階轉，
羣山入戶登。
庖廚出深竹，
印綬隔垂藤。
即事辭軒冕，
誰云病未能。

7.20

Written while returning to Wangchuan

At the valley mouth, scattered bells sound;
Fishermen and woodcutters gradually grow few.
In the stillness of dusk in the distant hills,
4 I face white clouds alone as I go home.
Caltrop stems are fragile and cannot settle;
Willow blossoms are light and easily float.
On the east riverbank, the color of spring grass;
8 And disconsolate I close my scrap-wood door.

7.21

The mountain dwelling of Supervising Secretary Wei[1]

Seeking the remote, you found this place;
How could there have been anyone here before?
The great ravine follows the turns of your stairs;
4 The assembled mountains enter your door as they rise.
A kitchen set out among deep bamboo,
Official seal and cap-strings of office cut off by the drooping vines.
Because of current matters you resigned high-ranking coach and coronet;
8 Who could criticize you and think you incapable?

1 See note to 2.11.

7.22

山居即事

寂寞掩柴扉，
蒼茫對落暉。
鶴巢松樹徧，
人訪蓽門稀。
嫩竹含新粉，
紅蓮落故衣。
渡頭燈火起，
處處採菱歸。

7.23

終南山

太乙近天都，
連山到海隅。
白雲迴望合，
青靄入看無。
分野中峰變，
陰晴眾壑殊。
欲投人處宿，
隔水問樵夫。

7.22

Living in the mountains: things encountered

In the lonely stillness I shut my scrap-wood door;
In the vast wilderness I face the setting light.
Cranes nest everywhere in the pine trees;
4 Few people visit my wicker gate.
Tender bamboo are filled with fresh powder;
Red lotuses shed their former garments.
At the ford the lantern flames rise;
8 And everywhere the caltrop-pickers go home.

7.23

Zhongnan Mountain

Taiyi nears the capital of Heaven,[1]
A stretch of mountains reaches to the edge of the sea.
White clouds come together when you turn to gaze at them;
4 Blue mists disappear when you enter them and look.
Delineating the land, the central peak marks the change;[2]
Shadow and light are different in the multitude of ravines.
If you want to put up with someone for the night,
8 Inquire of that woodcutter across the stream.

---

1 Taiyi (also written 太一) represents the source of all things in Daoist thought. It is also associated in astrological and geomantic terms with the emperor, the imperial capital, and with the pole star. Because of its important location south of Chang'an, Zhongnan Mountain is also referred to as Taiyi.

2 Delineating the land (*fen ye*) refers to mapping territorial sections against the constellations. This line is asserting that the central peak of Zhongnan marks the boundary between one such section and another.

7.24

輞川閒居

一從歸白社，
不復到青門。
時倚簷前樹，
遠看原上村。
青菰臨水映，
白鳥向山翻。
寂寞於陵子，
桔槔方灌園。

7.25

春園即事

宿雨乘輕屐，
春寒著弊袍。
開畦分白水，
間柳發紅桃。
草際成棋局，
林端舉桔槔。
還持鹿皮几，
日暮隱蓬蒿。

7.24

Living at ease at Wangchuan

Once I returned to White Shrine,[1]
I never came back to the Blue Gate of the capital.[2]
At times I lean on the tree before my eaves
And distantly look at the villages on the plain.
Black wild rice is reflected at the water's edge,
While white birds go flitting before the hills.
How lonely is Master Wuling,
Turning the well sweep so he can water the garden.[3]

7.25

Things encountered in my spring garden

After last night's rain I put on my light clogs;
The spring is chill, so I don my tattered robe.
I till my plot, drain off the white water,
While red peach blossoms open amid the willows.
I draw a Go board at the edge of the grass,
And raise the well sweep by the side of the wood.
Still grasping my deer-hide armrest,
At dusk I hide myself in a thicket of fleabane and artemisia.

---

1 A neighborhood near Luoyang, and home of the famous Jin era recluse Dong Jing 董京. Since then, the name has been associated with hermits.

2 See note to 3.9.10.

3 Chen Zhongzi 陳仲子, known also from his dwelling in reclusion as Master Wuling. Mencius criticized him as being too extreme in carrying his desire to be free of all ties to others (3B.10). When the ruler of Chu tried to employ him and sent a gift of gold, he and his wife fled and he became a hired gardener.

7.26

淇上即事田園

屏居淇水上，
東野曠無山。
日隱桑柘外，
河明閭井間。
牧童望村去，
獵犬隨人還。
靜者亦何事，
荊扉乘晝關。

7.27

與盧象集朱家

主人能愛客，
終日有逢迎。
貰得新豐酒，
復聞秦女箏。
柳條疏客舍，
槐葉下秋城。
語笑且為樂，
吾將達此生。

7.26

Things encountered among fields and gardens by the Qi River[1]

I live in seclusion by the bank of the Qi;
Eastern fields are broad; no hills in sight.
The sunlight is darkened beyond mulberry and cudrania;
The river is bright in the midst of the hamlets.
Herd-boys head off toward the village;
Hunting dogs follow their masters home.
Indeed, what business does a man of quiet have?
While it's still daytime I close my thorn-wood door.

7.27

With Lu Xiang, a gathering at the Zhu house

The host is able to treasure his guests;
At end of day there is someone to greet us.
He buys some Xinfeng ale on credit,[2]
And again we hear the Qin-girl's cither.[3]
Willow branches are sparse by the lodging for guests;
Sophora leaves fall by the autumnal city walls.
We chat and laugh, make merry for a time;
I am going to master this life.[4]

---

1 The Qi flows south into the He about 150 kilometers east of Luoyang. Some scholars speculate that Wang Wei lived in retirement here for a time following his time in Jizhou (721–726).

2 An esteemed ale produced by the Xinfeng region (northeast of Lintong in Shaanxi).

3 Cither (*zheng* 箏): this is a variant of the *se* native to the Qin region and often played by professional female entertainers.

4 "Mastering Life" is the name of the nineteenth chapter of the *Zhuangzi*.

7.28

過福禪師蘭若

巖壑轉微逕，
雲林隱法堂。
羽人飛奏樂，
4 天女跪焚香。
竹外峰偏曙，
藤陰水更涼。
欲知禪坐久，
8 行路長春芳。

7.29

黎拾遺昕裴秀才迪見過秋夜對雨之作

促織鳴已急，
輕衣行向重。
寒燈坐高館，
4 秋雨聞疏鐘。
白法調狂象，
玄言問老龍。

7.28

Visiting the *araṇya* of Meditation Master Fu[1]

Through crags and ravines there turns a faint path,
And cloudy trees that conceal a Dharma hall.
Feathered beings fly by, playing music;
Apsaras kneel, burning incense.[2]
Beyond the bamboo, daybreak on one side of the peak;
In the wisteria shade the water is even more cool.
If you want to know if he's been long sitting in meditation:
The fragrant spring plants have grown tall by the roadside.

7.29

Reminder Li Xin and Flourishing Talent Pei Di visited me on an autumn night; we watched the rain

Cricket cries have turned urgent;
Light robes will soon be changed for heavy ones.
In chill lamplight we sit in the high lodge;
In autumn rain we hear sparse sounds of bells.
Pure Dharma controls mad elephants;
With arcane words we question Old Dragon.[3]

1 *Araṇya*: another term for a Buddhist monastery or temple.

2 Apsaras are female spirits in Indian and Buddhist lore. Here Wang juxtaposes them with Daoist Transcendents ("feathered beings").

3 "Mad elephant" is a Buddhist cliché for the uncontrolled passions. "Arcane words" is the term applied to much of the metaphysical speculation in which intellectuals engaged during the third and fourth centuries. Old Dragon (full name: Old Dragon Lucky, Lao Long Ji 老龍吉) is a Daoist sage mentioned in chapter 22 of the *Zhuangzi*. He died before he could convey his wisdom to his students.

何人顧蓬徑，
8 空愧求羊蹤。

7.30

晚春嚴少尹與諸公見過

松菊荒三逕，
圖書共五車。
烹葵邀上客，
4 看竹到貧家。
鵲乳先春草，
鶯啼過落花。
自憐黃髮暮，
8 一倍惜年華。

1 Jiang Xu 蔣詡 resigned his office during Wang Mang's usurpation and lived as a recluse in Duling, where he allowed the three paths to his house to become overgrown. Only two local friends, Yang Zhong 仰仲 and Qiu Zhong 求仲, were willing to venture to see him. here Wang Wei says he is unworthy of the effort Li Xin and Pei Di have made to visit him.

Who is it who asks after me on this overgrown path?
I'm only ashamed of the tracks of Qiu and Yang.[1]

7.30

In late spring Vice Governor Yan and several gentlemen come to visit me

Pines and chrysanthemums cover the three overgrown paths,[2]
Though I have here five cartloads of books.[3]
I boil mallows and invite fine guests,
Who have come to my poor home to view the bamboo.[4]
Magpies nurse hatchlings before the spring grass;
Orioles cry past the fallen blossoms.
I pity myself in my old gray-haired twilight;
Even more so because I cherish the spring season.

---

2 See note to 7.29.8.

3 See note to 2.24.1.

4 Once Wang Huizhi 王徽之 (a connoisseur of bamboo) went to an estate where the bamboo was reputed to be excellent. He arrived without an invitation. The owner attempted to act as host, but Wang simply ignored him.

7.31

過感化寺曇興上人山院

暮持筇竹杖，
相待虎溪頭。
催客聞山響，
歸房逐水流。
野花叢發好，
谷鳥一聲幽。
夜坐空林寂，
松風直似秋。

7.31a

裴迪：游感化寺曇興上人山院

不遠灞陵邊，
安居向十年。
入門穿竹徑，
留客聽山泉。
鳥囀深林裏，
心閑落照前。
浮名竟何益，
從此願棲禪。

7.31

Visiting the mountain cloister of His Reverence Tanxing at Ganhua Monastery[1]

At dusk, with a bamboo cane in hand,
He waits for me at Tiger Stream.[2]
He urges his guest to hear the mountain echoes;
We return to his house, pursuing the water flow.
Mountain flowers bloom, lovely in their clusters;
A valley bird issues one mysterious call.
At night I sit; the empty woods are still;
A breeze in the pines blows as constant as autumn.

7.31a

Pei Di: Traveling to the mountain cloister of His Reverence Tanxing at Ganhua Monastery

Not far from the side of Ba tomb mound
He has lived in peace for ten years.
Entering the gate, we penetrate to a bamboo path;
He detains his guests and has them listen to the mountain stream.
Birds warble in the deep woods;
The mind is idle before the setting sun.
Of what benefit is ephemeral fame?
From now on I wish to nest here and meditate.

---

1 Possibly an error for Huagan 化感 Monastery, located in Lantian.

2 The prominent fifth-century monk Huiyuan 慧遠 when he lived at Donglin Monastery on Mount Lu had a Tiger Stream nearby. Whenever he accompanied a departing visitor past it, they would hear a tiger roaring, warning Huiyuan not to leave the mountain.

7.32

夏日過青龍寺謁操禪師

龍鍾一老翁，
徐步謁禪宮。
欲問義心義，
遙知空病空。
山河天眼裏，
世界法身中。
莫怪銷炎熱，
能生大地風。

7.32a

裴迪：夏日過青龍寺謁操禪師

安禪一室內，
左右竹亭幽。
有法知不染，
無言誰敢酬。
鳥飛爭向夕，
蟬噪已先秋。
煩暑自茲退，
清涼何所求。

7.32

Visiting Blue Dragon Monastery on a summer day and paying a call on Meditation Master Cao[1]

Decrepit, a single old man
With slow steps comes to visit this hall of meditation.
I wish to inquire about the principle of the mind caught in principles,
And gain far-ranging understanding of the emptiness of empty illness.[2]
Hills and rivers lay within the divine eye;
Our world system exists within the dharmakāya.[3]
Do not find it strange that the blazing heat melts away –
For here can be born a breeze for all the earth.

7.32a

Pei Di: Visiting Blue Dragon Monastery on a summer day and paying a call on Meditation Master Cao

In calm meditation within a single room,
Where all around bamboo pavilions are secluded.
Possessing the Dharma, my knowledge is unsullied;
Without words – who would dare to reply?
Birds fly, hurrying towards evening;
Cicadas sound, already foretelling autumn.
Sultry heat here withdraws;
Where else could I look for such cool clarity?

---

1 Blue Dragon Monastery was located in the Xinchang ward of Chang'an.

2 A general comment on *śunyatā* and more specifically the central situation of the *Vimalakīrti Sutra*, in which the bodhisattva Vimalkīrti feigns illness as a skillful means to lecture on Emptiness and No-duality.

3 One of the Three Bodies of the Buddha in Mahayana doctrine: the cosmic Buddha, which incorporates all real existence.

7.33

鄭果州相過

麗日照殘春，
初晴草木新。
牀前磨鏡客，
4 林裏灌園人。
五馬驚窮巷，
雙童逐老身。
中廚辦麤飯，
8 當恕阮家貧。

7.34

過香積寺

不知香積寺，
數里入雲峰。
古木無人逕，
4 深山何處鐘。

7.33

Zheng of Guozhou visits[1]

The lovely sun shines in the waning spring;
When it first clears, the plants and trees are renewed.
Before the couch, the mirror-polishing wayfarer;[2]
4 In the forest, the garden-watering man.[3]
Your five-horse team startles my remote lane;
My pair of servant boys chase after my aged self.
My kitchen prepares coarse fare for you,
8 But you should tolerate the poverty of Ruan's house.[4]

7.34

Visiting the Temple of Incense Amassed

Not knowing of the Temple of Incense Amassed,
I went several miles into cloudy peaks.
Old trees – paths empty of people.
4 Deep mountains – somewhere the sound of a bell.

1 In eastern Sichuan, about 140 kilometers north of the Jiang.

2 The Daoist transcendent Master Bearing-Pan would visit the markets of Wu with a pan that could be used to polish mirrors. He would employ a form of magic when polishing that would diagnose illnesses. He thus obtained a reputation as a great healer.

3 See note to 7.24.8.

4 This alludes to the "poor" side of the Ruan family under the Wei dynasty: Ruan Ji and Ruan Xian 咸 (who saw their poverty as a mark of virtue), as opposed to the wealthy branch.

泉聲咽危石，
日色冷青松。
薄暮空潭曲，
安禪制毒龍。

7.35

過崔駙馬山池

畫樓吹笛妓，
金椀酒家胡。
錦石稱貞女，
青松學大夫。
脫貂貰桂醑，
射雁與山廚。
聞道高陽會，
愚公谷正愚。

The sound of the stream chokes on sharp rocks,
And the color of sunlight chills in green pines.
At dusk, by the curve of an empty pool,
Peaceful meditation will control poison dragons.

7.35

Visiting the mountain pool of Imperial Consort Cui

In a painted mansion, entertainers playing bamboo flutes;
Golden vessels from the wine-shop maid.
A decorated stone named after the Chaste Girl;[1]
Green pines imitating the Court Gentleman Tree.[2]
He doffs his marten cap and pawns it for osmanthus flower brew;
He shoots geese and delivers them to his mountain kitchen.
I've heard of the parties at Gaoyang Pool;[3]
And the master of Foolish Valley is truly foolish.[4]

---

1 An ornamental stone in the consort's garden resembles the "Chaste Girl" rock on a mountain near a gorge of the Kuang River in Guangdong.

2 See note to 7.8.4.

3 Shan Jian 山簡 was a Jin era general particularly fond of drinking. While stationed in Jingzhou, he used to frequent and drink at a garden pool called the Gaoyang Pond. Here Wang Wei is comparing parties at the Consort's pond to Wang Jian's drinking bouts.

4 The Valley of Master Foolish. Located in Shandong, originally named for an anecdote connected to a local farmer; by Wang Wei's time it was a designation for a hermit's surroundings (for more details see note to 9.15–9.17). Here Wang Wei ironically suggests that the consort is in fact not a fool but a wise hermit.

7.36

送李判官赴東江

聞道皇華使，
方隨皁蓋臣。
封章通左語，
冠冕化文身。
樹色分揚子，
潮聲滿富春。
遙知辨璧吏，
恩到泣珠人。

1 In the southern part of modern Guandong province.
2 “Brilliant flowered” is a poetic locution for a messenger, drawn from *Shijing* 163.
3 In the Han, middle-ranking officials were granted the right to ride in carriages with black canopies. Gradually this became associated specifically with high-ranking officials serving in the provinces. Li is going off to serve his superior in Dongjiang.

7.36

Seeing off Administrative Assistant Li on his way to the Dongjiang[1]

I've heard that the "brilliant flowered" emissary[2]
Is just now following the minister in his black carriage canopy.[3]
Sealed dispatches will communicate the petitions of barbarians;
In cap of office you will morally transform the tattooed ones.
The hue of the trees reveals the Yangzi ford;
The roar of the tide fills Fuchun.[4]
I know that far away, this officer who can perceive a jade disk[5]
Will extend his grace to the pearl-weeping mermen.[6]

---

4 Yangzi: at one time, a ford on the lower Jiang; also a county in the Tang. Fuchun: see note to 6.13.7.

5 Zhu Hui 朱暉 of the Eastern Han assisted his superior Wang Cang 王蒼 in recovering a jade disk that had been appropriated by a secretary of the Chamberlain of Revenues. Zhu Hui was able to distinguish the disk from a distance as it was being held by the secretary.

6 A Chinese myth describes a race of ocean-dwelling creatures in the southern seas who weep pearls.

王右丞集卷之八 近體詩

8.1

送封太守

忽解羊頭削，
聊馳熊軾轓。
揚舲發夏口，
按節向吳門。
帆映丹陽郭，
楓攢赤岸村。
百城多候吏，
露冕一何尊。

https://doi.org/10.1515/9781501516023-008

Juan 8: Recent style poems

8.1

Seeing off Governor Feng

At once you untie your sheep-head dagger,[1]
And will hasten your carriage with its bear-shaped crossbar.[2]
Your barque will spread its sails and set forth from Xiakou,
Then you will halt your whip at Wumen.
Your sails will stand out against the city walls of Danyang,
And maple trees will cluster at the Redbank villages.[3]
So many clerks are waiting for you in your hundred towns;[4]
And how honored will you be as you display your ceremonial cap![5]

1 "Sheep head": describes a triangular-shaped blade. This suggests that Feng is leaving a military office to take up the civil office of governor.

2 In Han times, the carriages of nobility were ornamented with a crossbar in the shape of a crouching bear. Consequently, in medieval writing "bear-shaped crossbar" became a metonymic expression for a regional governor.

3 Xiakou: At Wuchang, in the central Yangtze valley. Wumen: Another name for Suzhou. Danyang and Redbank are both located along the lower Jiang valley. Wang Wei is describing Feng's journey to his post in these couplets, both by water and by land.

4 See note to 4.3.8.

5 Emperor Ming of the Han was so impressed by the good administration of Guo He 郭賀, he rewarded him with a ceremonial robe and ornamental cap and commanded that he wear it in public so that the common people could see this recognition of his virtue.

8.2

送嚴秀才還蜀

寧親為令子，
似舅即賢甥。
別路經花縣，
還鄉入錦城。
山臨青塞斷，
江向白雲平。
獻賦何時至，
明君憶長卿。

8.3

送張判官赴河西

單車會出塞，
報國敢邀勳。
見逐張征虜，
今思霍冠軍。

---

1 A reference to He Wuji 何無忌, who joined Liu Yu's 劉裕 revolt against Huan Xuan 桓玄 at the end of the Eastern Jin dynasty. Huan Xuan remarked that He was a formidable foe because he was just like his uncle Liu Laozhi 牢之.

2 A poetic reference to Heyang County in Henan. Pan Yue once served as magistrate there and planted a large number of peach and plum trees, so that the county earned this nickname.

8.2

Seeing off Flourishing Talent Yan on his return to Shu

Soothing one's parents is the mark of a fine son;
Just like your uncle, a worthy nephew.[1]
The road you take in parting will pass through Flower County;[2]
In returning home you'll enter Brocade City.[3]
Hills break off at the edge of the green pass;
The river is level as it stretches to white clouds.
When will the rhapsody you submitted to the court arrive?
Then an enlightened lord will think of Changqing.[4]

8.3

Seeing off Administrative Assistant Zhang on his way to Hexi[5]

Your single carriage will surely head out the pass;
You'll repay the country – not daring to focus on your own achievements.
Presently you'll follow after Zhang Attack-the-Caitiffs;
Now you're thinking about Huo the army leader.[6]

---

3 Abbreviation for Brocade Official City (just south of Chengdu), so called because the official in charge of overseeing the brocade industry had his headquarters there.

4 See note to 2.24.4.

5 The headquarters of the military commissioner, located in Liangzhou (Gansu). Qizhou was southeast of Chang'an, in southern Shaanxi.

6 Zhang Fei 張飛 of Shu received the title of "attacking the catiffs general." The Han general Huo Qubing was enfeoffed as the "army leading marquis."

沙平連白雪，
蓬卷入黃雲。
慷慨倚長劍，
8 高歌一送君。

8.4

送岐州源長史歸（源與余同在崔常侍幕中時常侍已沒）

握手一相送，
心悲安可論。
秋風正蕭索，
4 客散孟嘗門。
故驛通槐里，
長亭下槿原。
征西舊旌節，
8 從此向河源。

The sand is level, it stretches to the white snow;
The tumbleweed pulls up its roots and enters the brown clouds.
Full of valor, you lean on your long sword,
8 While a lofty song sees you off.

8.4

Seeing off Administrator Yuan of Qizhou on his way home (Yuan and I both served in the retinue of Attendant-in-Ordinary Cui; at this time, the Attendant had already passed away)[1]

We clasp hands, as we see each other off;
Our hearts grieve, but how can we discuss it?
The autumn wind just now blows desolate;
4 And guests scatter at the gate of the Lord of Mengchang.[2]
The old post station connects with Sophora Village;
The guest house sits below Althea Plain County.[3]
The old pennants and insignia of the western campaigns
8 From now on will head toward the source of the Yellow River.[4]

1 Cui Xiyi was Wang Wei's superior in the frontier district of Hexi from 737 until Cui's untimely death the following year.

2 A nobleman from the state of Qi during the Warring States era famous for patronizing talented men and taking in retainers. This refers to the departure of Cui Xiyi's staff after his death.

3 Locations through which Yuan will pass on his way home from Hexi.

4 This perhaps suggests that after Cui Xiyi's death the region will become unstable and break out in warfare.

8.5

送張道士歸山

先生何處去，
王屋訪毛君。
別婦留丹訣，
驅雞入白雲。
人間若剩住，
天上復離群。
當作遼城鶴，
仙歌使爾聞。

8.6

同崔興宗送衡岳瑗公南歸

言從石菌閣，
新下穆陵關。
獨向池陽去，
白雲留故山。

---

1 King's House Mountain: in Shanxi, near Yangcheng 陽城. The Eastern Han Daoist Mao Bodao 毛伯道 cultivated the Way there and achieved immortality.
2 The Daoist Xu Mai 許邁 after his parents died abandoned his wife and went off traveling among famous mountains; it was believed that he later attained immortality.
3 See note to 1.5.9.

8.5

Seeing off Daoist Master Zhang on his return to the hills

Master, to where are you departing?
You'll visit Lord Mao on King's House Mountain.[1]
You'll bid your wife farewell, keep the cinnabar secret,[2]
Driving your chickens before you, you'll enter white clouds.[3]
How can you live long in the human realm?
In heaven you'll part once more from the crowd.
You will become a heron at Liao city;[4]
You will get to hear the Transcendent's song.

8.6

Matching Cui Xingzong: "Seeing off Master Yuan of Heng Marchmount on his return south"[5]

From Stone Mushroom Lodge,
You recently descended on Muling Pass.[6]
Alone you left for Chiyang,[7]
Leaving white clouds behind on your former mountain.

---

4 The Transcendent Dingling Wei 丁令威 was from Liaodong in northeastern China. He transformed into a crane and flew to the city walls of his hometown, where he sang a song about becoming immortal and urging others to follow his path.

5 For the preface to this poem, see 19.9 below. The Heng was the southern of the five marchmounts, located in Hengzhou on the Xiang River (modern Hunan).

6 Stone Mushroom Lodge: one of the peaks of Mount Heng. Yuan would have to pass through Muling Pass in Hubei on the way to the capital.

7 A Han era name for a district in the capital region (Jingyang).

綻衣秋日裏，
洗鉢古松間。
一施傳心法，
惟將戒定還。

8.6a

崔興宗：同王右丞送瑗公南歸

行苦神亦秀，
泠然溪上松。
銅瓶與竹杖，
來自祝融峰。
常願入靈嶽，
藏經訪遺踪。
南歸見長老，
且為說心胸。

You patch your robe in the autumn sunlight,
Wash your begging bowl under ancient pines.
Now that you've disseminated the Dharma of mind-transmission,
Nothing to do but return home with your precepts and meditation.

8.6a

Cui Xingzong: Matching Assistant Director of the Right Wang:
"Seeing off Master Yuan on his return south"

In the pain of travel your spirit also prospers,
Clear and cool, like a pine by a stream.
With your copper washing vase and bamboo staff
You come from Zhurong Peak.[1]
I've always hoped to go to the sacred marchmounts,
Store my classics away and go visiting historical sites.
When you return South and see the elder monks there
Tell them for me what my heart desires.

1 One of Heng's peaks.

8.7

送錢少府還藍田

草色日向好，
桃源人去稀。
手持平子賦，
4 目送老萊衣。
每候山櫻發，
時同海燕歸。
今年寒食酒，
8 應得返柴扉。

8.8

錢起: 晚歸藍田酬王維給事贈別

卑棲却得性，
每與白雲歸。

1 See note to 2.22a.4.

2 Pingzi was the polite name for the Eastern Han poet Zhang Heng 張衡. When he became frustrated in office, he composed a "Rhapsody for Returning to the Fields."

8.7

Seeing off District Defender Qian on his return to Lantian

The hues of the grass are finer daily;
And few people depart from my Peach Blossom Spring.[1]
With Pingzi's rhapsody held in my hand,[2]
My eyes bid farewell to Laolai dressed in his motley.[3]
You always wait for the mountain cherries to bloom,
At times returning with the sea swallows.
This year when the Cold Food ale is ready[4]
You should be able to return to your scrap-wood door.

8.8

Qian Qi: Returning to Lantian in the evening: replying to a poem Supervising Secretary Wang Wei presented to me on parting[5]

I find my nature, even though I live lowly;
I always go home with the white clouds.

3 When an old man of seventy, Master Laolai dressed in motley clothing and pretended to be a small child in order to comfort his still living parents. He was considered one of the paragons of filial piety. This line suggests that Qian is returning to Lantian to look after his parents.

4 See note to 4.7.7.

5 The Zhao Diancheng edition mistakenly attributes this poem to Wang Wei and places it here. This is Qian Qi's response to 8.7.

徇祿仍懷橘，
看山免採薇。
暮禽先去馬，
新月待開扉。
霄漢時回首，
知音青瑣闈。

8.9

送邱為往唐州

宛洛有風塵，
君行多苦辛。
四愁連漢水，
百口寄隨人。
槐色陰清晝，
楊花惹暮春。
朝端肯相送，
天子繡衣臣。

1 When Lu Ji 陸績 visited Yuan Shu 袁術 at the age of six in the company of his father, he took three oranges away with him hidden in the folds of his gown. He was discovered and he confessed he was taking them home for his mother. Here it refers to Qian Qi's desire to be filial.

In search of salary, I still harbored oranges;[1]
4 I viewed the hills, avoided picking bracken.[2]
Evening birds fly before my departing horse,
The new moon waits for me to open the door.
Sometimes I turn my head towards the Starry River,
8 Toward my intimate friend within the blue chain-patterned gates.[3]

8.9

Seeing Qiu Wei off to Tangzhou[4]

There is windblown dust over Wan and Luo;
There will be much hardship for you on your way.
Your "Four Griefs" will stretch to Han waters;[5]
4 Your hundred mouths entrusted to people in Sui.[6]
Sophora tree hues shade the clear daytime;
Willow catkins tug at you in the late spring.
The highest in court are willing to see you off:
8 One of the emperor's ministers in his embroidered robe.

---

2 See note to 2.22.6. Qian is suggesting he was willing to serve, though wished to live as a recluse.

3 Qian Qi is gazing toward the capital and thinking of Wang Wei in his palace post. "Starry River" here is a poetic substitution for the palace. Palace gates and doors were painted with a chain-link pattern.

4 About 270 kilometers south of Luoyang.

5 "Four Griefs" is a cycle of poems attributed to the Han poet Zhang Heng when he was depressed over his lack of success. Wang is suggesting that Qiu Wei will compose his own "Four Griefs" in his new surroundings.

6 "Hundred mouths" is idiomatic for all the people of an extended household. Qiu has entrusted them to connections in Suizhou in Hubei (about 150 kilometers north-northeast of Wuhan).

8.10

送元中丞轉運江淮

薄稅歸天府，
輕徭賴使臣。
歡沾賜帛老，
恩及卷綃人。
去問珠官俗，
來經石劫春。
東南御亭上，
莫使有風塵。

8.11

送崔九興宗游蜀

送君從此去，
轉覺故人稀。
徒御猶回首，
田園方掩扉。

1 Tax collection on transported goods was one of the tasks of the Transport Commissioner, as well as drafting labor.
2 Literally, "soak," "permeate." Government policy sometimes granted gifts of silk to the aged.
3 Said to be one of the customs of mermen. Compare 7.36.8 and note.

8.10

Seeing off Yuan, Vice Censor-in-Chief and Transport Commissioner, to the Jiang and Huai

Scant taxes are given back to the imperial storehouses;
The emissary takes responsibility for light corvée duties.[1]
Your delight will come to the elders presented with silk;[2]
Your benevolence will reach to the men rolling bolts of raw gauze.[3]
You will go off to ask about the customs of Pearl Office County;[4]
And will come back again during the spring of the anemone.[5]
To the southeast, above Yuting Station,
Don't let there be wind or dust.[6]

8.11

Seeing off Cui Nine Xingzong on his travels to Shu

I see you off – from now you depart;
I feel more and more that my friends grow few.
You drive on alone, yet still turn your head;
In fields and gardens I am shutting my door.

---

4 A prefecture in Guangxi (also known as Hepu) famous for its pearls. Wang is likely exaggerating the distance Yuan is going for poetic purposes (Pearl Office County was nowhere near the Jiang and Huai region).

5 It was believed that anemones (which were mistaken for flowers) "blossomed" in the spring (actually, feelers were mistaken for blossoms).

6 There were likely rebellions in the area at the time. These lines allude to a poem by the southern dynasties poet Yu Jianwu 庾肩吾: "At Yuting I turn back to gaze / wind and dust, a thousand li of gloom."

出門當旅食，
中路授寒衣。
江漢風流地，
游人何歲歸。

8.12

送崔興宗

已恨親皆遠，
誰憐友復稀。
君王未西顧，
游宦盡東歸。
塞迥山河淨，
天長雲樹微。
方向菊花節，
相待洛陽扉。

Once you leave your gates, you'll be eating at inns;
You'll be sent winter clothes while still on the road.
The Jiang and Han valleys are scenic lands;
What year will the traveler return?

8.12

Seeing off Cui Xingzong

I already resent that all my kin are far away;
So who pities me that my friends are few as well?
The emperor has yet to turn back west to Chang'an,
And traveling officials are all heading east to him.[1]
The frontier is far, the hills and rivers pure;
The sky is long, cloudy trees faint.
Just in the festival of chrysanthemums,[2]
Wait for me at the door of your Luoyang house.

1 This poem was written when Xuanzong was residing at the subsidiary capital of Luoyang, while Wang Wei was in Chang'an (probably around 734).

2 The festival of the Double Ninth (ninth day of the ninth month).

8.13

送平淡然判官

不識陽關路，
新從定遠侯。
黃雲斷春色，
畫角起邊愁。
瀚海經年到，
交河出塞流。
須令外國使，
知飲月支頭。

8.14

送孫秀才

帝城風日好，
況復建平家。
玉枕雙文簟，
金盤五色瓜。
山中沽魯酒，
松下飯胡麻。
莫厭田家苦，
歸期遠復賒。

8.13

Seeing off Administrative Assistant Ping Danran

You don't recognize the road to Yang Pass,
Since you're just now following the Marquis of Pacifying the Remote.[1]
Brown clouds cut off the spring colors;
4 A painted horn gives rise to frontier grief.
It will take you a year to reach the Gobi;
The Yarkhoto River comes flowing from out of the frontier.
You must command the emissaries to foreign lands:
8 "Learn to drink from a Tokharian skull."[2]

8.14

Seeing off Flourishing Talent Sun

Scenery is fine in the imperial city,
Even more so at Jianping's house.[3]
Jade pillows, paired-pattern bamboo mats,
4 Gold plates with rainbow melons.
In the hills they only sell weak Lu wine,
And eat sesame under the pines.
But don't despise the hardship of your home in the country;
8 My own time to return is distant and far away.[4]

---

1 The Yang Pass was in Gansu and led to points west. "Pacifying the Remote" was a title granted to the Eastern Han general Ban Chao 班超.

2 See note to 6.6.20.

3 Song (southern dynasties) Prince of Jianping (either Liu Hong 劉宏 or Liu Jingsu 劉景素), both patrons of scholars.

4 That is, Sun may regret that he must abandon the luxuries of city life by returning to his rural homestead, but at least he *can* go home, unlike the poet.

8.15

送劉司直赴安西

絕域陽關道，
胡沙與塞塵。
三春時有雁，
萬里少行人。
苜蓿隨天馬，
蒲桃逐漢臣。
當令外國懼，
不敢覓和親。

8.16

送趙都督赴代州得青字

天官動將星，
漢地柳條青。
萬里鳴刁斗，
三軍出井陘。

1 Headquarters of the Anxi military governor, in Xinjiang.

2 See note to 8.13.2.

3 This is flattering Liu, suggesting that he might accomplish the same sort of thing the Han emissary Zhang Qian 張騫 and the Han General Li Guangli managed – to compel Ferghana to send tribute horses (see 6.6.8 and note), and to bring alfalfa and grapes for cultivation in China.

8.15

Seeing off Rectifier Liu on his way to Anxi[1]

In a remote realm, the road to Yang Pass:[2]
Western sands and frontier dust.
Geese are seen throughout the spring,
But few travelers for ten thousand li.
Alfalfa came with the fine Ferghana horses;
And grapes followed after the Han minister.[3]
Just make those foreigners fear us,
So they dare not seek a marriage alliance![4]

8.16

Seeing off Commander-in-Chief Zhao on his way to Daizhou;
I received the rhyme "qing" [green][5]

In the constellation of officials the Commander Star trembles;[6]
While down in Han lands the willow branches are green.
Over ten thousand li they sound their cookpot-clappers;[7]
The three armies have set out from Well Gorge.[8]

4 During the Han, the northern Xiongnu tribes were dealt with either through marriage alliances with the Chinese imperial house or through attempts at military conquest.

5 Daizhou: in northern Shanxi, about 150 kilometers north of Taiyuan.

6 An astrological omen of war.

7 Used to announce the night watches in military camps.

8 A frontier pass in Hebei.

忘身辭鳳闕，
報國取龍庭。
豈學書生輩，
窗間老一經。

8.17

送方城韋明府

遙思葭菼際，
寥落楚人行。
高鳥長淮水，
平蕪故郢城。
使車聽雉乳，
縣鼓應雞鳴。
若見州從事，
無嫌手板迎。

1 Dragon Court (Longting) was a ritual center for the Xiongnu.

2 Fangcheng: county in Tangzhou prefecture; see note to 8.9. This was the heart of the old state of Chu.

3 Ying was the capital of the state of Chu.

4 Two allusions of good magistracy. Yuan An (Eastern Han) wondered why Lu Gong's district of Zhongmou 中牟 was spared a plague of insects and sent an emissary there to find out. The emissary was struck by the fact that a child would not take a pheasant because it was looking after her chicks. Yuan assumed that

With no regard for himself he departs Phoenix Gate-tower;
To repay his country he'll capture Dragon Court.[1]
How could he imitate those bookish scholars,
Who grow old by the window with a single classic text?

8.17

Seeing off Magistrate Wei of Fangcheng[2]

I think of you far away, at the edge of reeds and rushes,
Where Chu travelers are few and far between.
High-flying birds above the long Huai waters;
A plain of scrub covers the old Ying City.[3]
The emissary hears the pheasant nurturing its chicks,
The district drums respond to the rooster's cry.[4]
If you meet the staff of the Prefect,
Don't demur to greet them with tally in hand.[5]

---

this air of benevolence came from Lu, and that it prevented the insect plague from arriving. Deng You 鄧攸 (Jin dynasty) was such a good magistrate, the local people tried to prevent him from leaving. When they tried to block his boat, he was forced to stay until he could sneak out at night. This inspired a song: "Bang, they beat the fifth-watch drum, / When roosters cry at the brink of dawn. We pulled at Master Deng but couldn't keep him, / We push out Magistrate Xie but he won't leave."

5 The official tally was proof of office. The new magistrate would be expected to meet with the staff of his superior, the Prefect.

8.18

送李員外賢郎

少年何處去，
負米上銅梁。
借問阿戎父，
4 知為童子郎。
魚箋請詩賦，
橦布作衣裳。
薏苡扶衰病，
8 歸來幸可將。

8.19

送梓州李使君

萬壑樹參天，
千山響杜鵑。
山中一半雨，
4 樹杪百重泉。

8.18

Seeing off the worthy son of Vice Director Li

Where are you off to, young man?
To carry rice up Mount Copper-bridge.[1]
I inquired about you, Rong, from your father;
And learned that you are a Gentleman Youth.[2]
They'll request poems and rhapsodies on fish-scale patterned paper,
And they'll make your robes from the cotton-tree.[3]
The tear-grass herb helps those who are old and ill;
When you come back, please bring some with you!

8.19

Seeing off Prefect Li of Zizhou[4]

In a myriad ravines the trees are level with the sky;
A thousand hills echo with the cuckoo.
In these hills, after even a partial rain,
Hundred layers of streams come down from branch-tips.

1 Mount Copper-bridge is in Shu in Hezhou, evidently the home district of the young man. Confucius' disciple Zilu once claimed to have carried rice over a hundred *li* to his parents.

2 Ruan Ji was a contemporary of Wang Hun's 王渾, but felt much more at home with Hun's son Wang Rong 戎. Gentleman Youth (*tongzi lang*) was a title granted to youths in the Han-Wei period who showed a knowledge of the Confucian tradition.

3 Both famous products of Shu.

4 In Sichuan, about 100 kilometers northeast of Chengdu.

漢女輸橦布，
巴人訟芋田。
文翁翻教授，
不敢倚先賢。

8.20

送張五諲歸宣城

五湖千萬里，
況復五湖西。
漁浦南陵郭，
人家春穀溪。
欲歸江淼淼，
未到草萋萋。
憶想蘭陵鎮，
可宜猿更啼。

1 Wen Weng was a Han-era magistrate in Shu who worked hard to improve living conditions and to change the local (non-standard, "barbarian") customs. The poet is suggesting that in spite of the oddness of local habits (cotton, taro fields), a talented and activist magistrate will be able to guide his people to a more enlightened way of life. Some interpret the last line as meaning, "Don't you dare imitate (unlike Wen Weng) those early worthies who pursued non-action as the best way to govern."

The women of Han will pay with cotton cloth;
The people of Ba will litigate over taro fields.
In spite of all, Wen Weng bestowed his instructions;
8 Do you not dare to rely on this former worthy?[1]

8.20

Seeing off Zhang Yin Five on his return to Xuancheng[2]

A million li of the Five Lakes,
And furthermore to the west of the Five Lakes.[3]
A fishing bank outside the city walls of Nanling,
4 Houses of people on Chungu stream.
As you're about to return, the Jiang is spreading its flood;
Before you arrive, the grass will be lush and thick.
I imagine you at Lanling Stronghold;
8 Is it right for the gibbons to continue their cries?[4]

2 See note to 3.19. This poem describes in detail Zhang's journey from the capital: South to the Han River, then southwards to the Jiang, and then to Nanling in Xuanzhou.

3 Five Lakes: Probably Taihu and adjoining lakes. Xuanzhou is about 70 km southwest of Taihu.

4 I.e., should the gibbons be crying and making you homesick?

8.21

送友人南歸

萬里春應盡，
三江雁亦稀。
連天漢水廣，
孤客郢城歸。
鄖國稻苗秀，
楚人菰米肥。
懸知倚門望，
遙識老萊衣。

8.22

送賀遂員外外甥

南國有歸舟，
荊門泝上流。
蒼茫葭菼外，
雲水與昭邱。
檣帶城烏去，
江連暮雨愁。

8.21

Seeing off a Friend on his return south

After a myriad li the spring should end,
With geese fewer by the Three Jiang.[1]
Stretching to the sky, the Han waters are broad;
A lone traveler returns to Ying city.
Rice sprouts ripen in the state of Yun;[2]
Wild rice fattens among the people of Chu.
I imagine your parents leaning on the gate and gazing,[3]
Recognizing Laolai's motley from afar.[4]

8.22

Seeing off Vice-Director He Sui's nephew

There is a returning boat in the southern lands;
At Jingmen it advances upstream.[5]
The green is vast beyond reeds and rushes,
Where cloud-hid waters join with Zhao Hill.[6]
The mast departs, carrying city crows;
The Jiang is bleak as it joins with the evening rain.

---

1 Possibly Baling (near Dongting Lake), where the Jiang, Fengjiang, and Xiangjiang meet.
2 A small Spring and Autumn era state destroyed by Chu. Located near the modern city of Wuhan.
3 From a *Zhanguo ce* anecdote, leaning on a gate refers to parents anxiously awaiting the return of their child.
4 See note to 8.7.4.
5 In the central Jiang valley.
6 Zhao Hill is the tomb mound of King Zhao of Chu.

猿聲不可聽，
莫待楚山秋。

8.23

送楊長史赴果州

褒斜不容幰，
之子去何之。
鳥道一千里，
猿啼十二時。
官橋祭酒客，
山木女郎祠。
別後同明月，
君應聽子規。

8.24

送邢桂州

鐃吹喧京口，
風波下洞庭。

It is best not to hear the cries of the gibbons,
So do not wait for autumn in the Chu hills.

8.23

Seeing Off Administrator Yang on His Way to Guozhou[1]

Baoye Valley is too narrow for your carriage;[2]
You're leaving, but where are you going?
Only a path for birds for a thousand li;
Gibbons cry all hours of the day.
A traveler sacrificing to the road god on the public bridge;
The temple to the Maiden in a mountain wood.[3]
After we part, we share the same bright moon;
You should listen to the cries of the cuckoo.[4]

8.24

Seeing off Xing of Guizhou[5]

Handbells and flutes resound in Jingkou;[6]
Windblown waves descend from Dongting.

---

1 See note to 7.33.
2 Near Baocheng in Liangzhou, southwest of the capital (on the way to Shu).
3 The Maiden was worshipped near Baocheng (possibly associated with Daoist sects in Shu).
4 Whose cries supposedly sounded like the phrase, "Best to go home!"
5 In Guangxi.
6 Not too far from Yangzhou.

赭圻將赤岸，
4 擊汰復揚舲。
日落江湖白，
潮來天地青。
明珠歸合浦，
8 應逐使臣星。

8.25

送宇文三赴河西充行軍司馬

橫吹雜繁笳，
邊風捲塞沙。
還聞田司馬，
4 更逐李輕車。
蒲類成秦地，
莎車屬漢家。
當令犬戎國，
8 朝聘學昆邪。

Russet Boundary, and then Redbank;[1]
Striking the waves, your barque will spread its sails.
At sunset, rivers and lakes turn pale;
The tide comes in, Heaven and Earth darken.
Bright pearls will return to Hepu;[2]
And you should follow the emissary stars.[3]

8.25

Seeing off Yuwen Three to Hexi to take the post of adjutant[4]

Bamboo flutes combine with a profusion of barbarian reeds;
The border wind curls up the frontier sand.
I hear yet that Adjutant Tian
Will go off to follow Light Carriage Li.[5]
Pulei has now become Qin territory,
And Shaju subject to the house of Han.[6]
Force the countries of the Dog Rong
To pay us court in imitation of the Hunye![7]

1 Both locations on the lower Jiang.
2 See note to 8.10.5. Xing will ensure the pearl trade in the region.
3 An astrologer recognized two emissaries sent to him from the court because he saw two stars enter the astrological counterpart of his district.
4 See note to 8.3.
5 Two figures from Han military history. Light Carriage Li was the nickname of Li Cai 李蔡.
6 Both Han era nomad kingdoms, in places now located in eastern Xinjiang.
7 The Hunye were a tribe of Xiongnu (modern Gansu) that surrendered to the Han after its ruler was threatened by the Shanyu.

8.26

送孫二

郊外誰相送，
夫君道術親。
書生鄒魯客，
才子洛陽人。
祖席依寒草，
行車起暮塵。
山川何寂寞，
長望淚霑巾。

8.27

送崔三往密州覲省

南陌去悠悠，
東郊不少留。
同懷扇枕戀，
獨解倚門愁。

8.26

Seeing off Sun Two

Beyond the outskirts, who will see you off?
You, a gentleman familiar with the Daoist arts,
A scholar, a sojourner of Zou and Lu,[1]
A talent, a man of Luoyang.
The parting banquet mat spread over cold grasses,
The moving carriage stirs up the twilight dust.
How lonely and quiet the mountains and streams!
I gaze afar and the tears soak my kerchief.

8.27

Seeing off Cui Three on his way to Mizhou to see his parents[2]

On southern lanes you depart, moving on and on;
We can't detain you for a moment in the eastern suburbs.
With you I hold dear a fan-and-pillow affection;[3]
But you alone are able to relieve the grief of those who lean on
the gate.[4]

1 Pre-imperial states associated with Confucian scholarship.
2 Mizhou: located on the southern coast of Shandong.
3 An outstanding act of filial piety: fanning the parents at their pillow and couch during the summer.
4 See note to 8.21.7.

路遶天山雪，
家臨海樹秋。
魯連功未報，
且莫蹈滄洲。

8.28

送邱為落第歸江東

憐君不得意，
況復柳條春。
為客黃金盡，
還家白髮新。
五湖三畝宅，
萬里一歸人。
知禰不能薦，
羞為獻納臣。

1 On the northwest frontier. This poem was probably composed when Wang Wei was serving in the northwest with Cui Xiyi.

2 Lu Zhonglian 魯仲連 was a famous orator of the Warring States period. He became a recluse (poetic, "tread on blue islet") rather than accept a fiefdom that would cause him to be subordinate to others.

3 The Jiang delta region.

Your road circles the snow on Heaven Mountain;[1]
At home will meet autumn with its seaside trees.
Lu Zhonglian has yet to be rewarded for his achievements;
But for the time being, do not tread on some blue islet![2]

8.28

Seeing off Qiu Wei upon his failing the examinations and returning to Jiangdong[3]

I feel for you, that you have been disappointed;
The more so in this season of willow branches.[4]
As a stranger here, you've spent all your gold;[5]
You return home, with hair just turned white.
To the Five Lakes, to your three-*mou* homestead,
You return, one man traveling ten thousand li.
I know that you're a Mi Heng, but could not recommend you;
I am ashamed that I'm a censorate official.[6]

---

4 Willow branches were presented to people departing, as a poetic wish that they might be detained ("willow" and "detain" are pronounced the same).

5 This echoes a phrase in *Zhanguo ce* about Su Qin's 蘇秦 attempt to attract the attention of the King of Qin with numerous letters, all of which were ignored. Soon he had spent all of his money in his efforts to be heard.

6 The third-century scholar Mi Heng 禰衡 was a young genius but also possessed of an unyielding personality. The older scholar Kong Rong 孔融 wrote a famous letter recommending him to Cao Cao when he was still a teenager. Wang is apologizing for not using his own position to further his friend's career.

8.29

漢江臨汎

楚塞三湘接，
荊門九派通。
江流天地外，
山色有無中。
郡邑浮前浦，
波瀾動遠空。
襄陽好風日，
留醉與山翁。

8.30

登辨覺寺

竹徑從初地，
蓮峰出化城。
窗中三楚盡，
林上九江平。
輭草承趺坐，
長松響梵聲。
空居法雲外，
觀世得無生。

8.29

Drifting on the Han River

Chu borderlands – the Three Xiang Rivers meet;
Jingmen – the nine tributaries join.
The river flows beyond Heaven and Earth;
The mountain's color between being and nothingness.
The district boroughs float on the farther bank;
The river waves shake the distant sky.
Wonderful is Xiangyang's scenery –
I'll stay and get drunk with an old mountain man.

8.30

Climbing to the Monastery of Discerning Enlightenment[1]

The bamboo path links with the first stage of the bodhisattva's course;
A city of illusion rises from Lotus Peak.[2]
From the window, the three lands of Chu stretch to their end;
Above the forest, the Nine Rivers level off.
Soft grasses accept seated meditators;
Tall pines echo with the sound of sutra chants.
I dwell in emptiness beyond the cloud of the Dharma,
Observe the world, obtain Non-rebirth.

---

1 The landscape described here suggests that the temple is located at Mount Lu in the central Yangtze valley.

2 City of illusion: in a parable from the *Lotus Sutra*, a guide conjures an imaginary city to bring comfort to some weary travelers; it serves as a metaphor for skillful means. Mount Lu had a Lotus Peak, though Wang Wei is also suggesting a place fit for preaching sutras as well. In general, the monastery becomes a place of wisdom and skillful means for the traveler set on becoming a bodhisattva.

8.31

涼州郊外游望

野老才三戶，
邊村少四鄰。
婆娑依里社，
簫鼓賽田神。
灑酒澆芻狗，
焚香拜木人。
女巫紛屢舞，
羅襪自生塵。

8.32

觀獵

風勁角弓鳴，
將軍獵渭城。
草枯鷹眼疾，
雪盡馬蹄輕。
忽過新豐市，
還歸細柳營。
回看射鵰處，
千里暮雲平。

8.31

Gazing afar on the outskirts of Liangzhou[1]

Rustic old men, barely three households:
A border village with few neighbors.
Whirling, they head toward the village shrine;
4 With pipes and drums they sacrifice to the field god.
Sprinkling ale, they give libations to straw dogs;
Burn incense, bow before wooden effigies.
The shamanka dances a profusion of steps:
8 Dust rises from her silken stockings.

8.32

Observing the hunt

The wind is sharp; the horn-tipped bows ring out:
The general is hunting at Weicheng.
The grass is dry: the hawk's eye keen;
4 Snow has melted: the horses pace lightly.
Suddenly they pass Xinfeng Market,[2]
Then return to Slender Willow Camp.[3]
Turn back and look to where the hawk was shot:
8 For a thousand li, the evening clouds are level.

1 Composed 737–738 while in service with Cui Xiyi.
2 A town near the capital, famous for its ale.
3 A training camp near the capital during the Han dynasty, erected by the general Zhou Yafu 周亞夫.

王右丞集卷之九 近體詩

9.1

春日上方即事

好讀高僧傳，
時看辟穀方。
鳩形將刻杖，
龜殼用支牀。
柳色春山映，
梨花夕鳥藏。
北窗桃李下，
閑坐但焚香。

9.2

汎前陂

秋空自明迥，
況復遠人間。
暢以沙際鶴，
兼之雲外山。
澄波澹將夕，
清月皓方閒。
此夜任孤棹，
夷猶殊未還。

https://doi.org/10.1515/9781501516023-009

Juan 9: Recent style poems

9.1

Things encountered on a spring day at a mountain monastery

They're fond of reading "The Lives of Eminent Monks";
Often they observe the methods for avoiding grains.[1]
Figures of doves carved on their staffs,
They prop their couches with tortoise shells.[2]
Willow hues set against the spring hills;
Pear blossoms hide the evening birds.
By the north window, under peach and plum,
I sit idly, just burning incense.

9.2

Drifting on the front lake

The autumn sky is bright and high;
The more so with people far away.
I delight in the cranes at the edge of the sand
And the hills that rise beyond the clouds.
The limpid wavelets turn tranquil with the dusk;
Clear moonlight gleams in the peaceful calm.
Tonight I resign myself to a single oar;
Drifting and not returning yet.

---

1 Removing grains from one's diet is a necessary step in becoming a Daoist Transcendent.

2 Both images refer to ancient Han customs appropriate for the very aged.

9.3

游李山人所居因題屋壁

世上皆如夢，
狂來或自歌。
問年松樹老，
有地竹林多。
藥倩韓康賣，
門容向子過。
翻嫌枕席上，
無那白雲何。

9.4

登河北城樓作

井邑傅巖上，
客亭雲霧間。
高城眺落日，
極浦映蒼山。
岸火孤舟宿，
漁家夕鳥還。
寂寥天地暮，
心與廣川閒。

9.3

Traveling to Mountain Recluse Li's residence; I then wrote this on the wall of the house

The world of men is all like a dream;
When madness comes, sometimes I sing to myself.
I ask the age of the old man under the pines;
He has some land, with many bamboo groves.
For medicine he asks Han Kang to sell to him;[1]
His gate will admit Master Xiang when he visits.[2]
Though I do dislike it, I can't prevent
The white snow from falling on pillow and mat.

9.4

Written when climbing the gate tower at Hebei[3]

The town stands above Fu cliff;[4]
The guesthouse rests among clouds and mist.
From the high city wall, I gaze out on the setting sun,
And the farther bank, distinct against the gray-green hills.
Fire on the riverside – a lone boat passes the night;
Fishermen's houses – evening birds return.
Lonely and desolate, twilight on heaven and earth;
My mind is as calm as the broad current.

---

1 See note to 5.3.11.

2 Xiang 向 (or Shang 尚) Ziping 子平 was a Han era man who went off traveling to the five mountains after his family was grown and married.

3 In the Tang district of Shanzhou 陝州 in southwestern Shanxi.

4 Fu Cliff was said to be the home of the Shang era recluse Fu Shuo 傅說.

9.5

登裴迪秀才小臺作

端居不出戶，
滿目望雲山。
落日鳥邊下，
秋原人外閒。
遙知遠林際，
不見此簷間。
好客多乘月，
應門莫上關。

9.6

被出濟州

微官易得罪，
謫去濟川陰。
執政方持法，
明君無此心。
閭閻河潤上，
井邑海雲深。
縱有歸來日，
多愁年鬢侵。

9.5

Written when climbing the small terrace of Flourishing Talent
Pei Di

You don't leave the door of your settled dwelling;
Cloudy hills are everywhere you gaze.
The setting sun descends beside the birds;
The autumn plain is calm beyond human presence.
Afar, I know that from my distant forest edge
I cannot see the eaves of your house.
You're fond of many guests who come to enjoy the moon –
So your porter never locks the gate.

9.6

I am sent to Jizhou[1]

Easy for a minor official to offend;
Now I am exiled to the south bank of the Ji River.
Those in power have applied the law;
An enlightened ruler had no such intentions.[2]
Village lanes rise above riparian ground;
Towns are hidden deep in sea clouds.
Even if there is a day for my return,
I grieve much at the gray invading my temples.

---

1 Composed in 721, when first learning of his appointment to distant Jizhou in Shandong.

2 I.e., officials in power are responsible for the poet's exile, not the emperor.

9.7

千塔主人

逆旅逢佳節，
征帆未可前。
窗臨汴河水，
門渡楚人船。
雞犬散墟落，
桑榆蔭遠田。
所居人不見，
枕席生雲烟。

9.8

使至塞上

單車欲問邊，
屬國過居延。
征蓬出漢塞，
歸雁入胡天。
大漠孤烟直，
長河落日圓。
蕭關逢候騎，
都護在燕然。

---

1 Not identified; probably the name of a temple.

9.7

My host at Thousand Pagodas[1]

I encounter a fine season at the hostel;
But my journeying sails can't proceed yet.
The windows overlook the waters of the Bian;
Boats from Chu cross over by the gates.[2]
Chickens and dogs are scattered through the village;
Mulberry and elm shade the distant fields.
I see no one who is living here;
From pillow and mat clouds and mist arise.

9.8

Sent to the frontier on a mission

A single carriage is investigating the borders,
Where the tribute states stretch beyond Juyan.[3]
Traveling tumbleweeds emerge from the Han frontier;
Returning geese enter northern barbarian skies.
From the great desert a lone line of smoke rises straight;
By the long river the setting sun is round.
At Xiao Pass he meets an army scout:[4]
"The Protector-General is at Yanran Mountain."[5]

---

2 This likely takes place near a northern section of the Grand Canal (sometimes given the name of the Bian River, whose course it followed), hence the boats from Chu.

3 Or "[the carriage] passes the tribute state of Juyan," or "the supervisor of tribute states passes Juyan." Now in Inner Mongolia.

4 In Ningxia, Yuanzhou prefecture.

5 Now in Inner Mongolia. After a victory against the leader of the Xiongnu, the Eastern Han general Dou Xian 竇憲 proceeded deep into foreign territory and erected a stele commemorating his victory on this mountain (with an inscription by the famous historian Ban Gu 班固).

9.9

晚春閨思

新妝可憐色，
落日卷羅帷。
鑪氣清珍簟，
牆陰上玉墀。
春蟲飛網戶，
暮雀隱花枝。
向晚多愁思，
閒窗桃李時。

9.10

戲題示蕭氏外甥

憐爾解臨池，
渠爺未學詩。
老夫何足似，
弊宅倘因之。
蘆筍穿荷葉，
菱花罥雁兒。

9.9

Boudoir thoughts in late spring

Recent make-up, and adorable hue;
She rolls up the gauze drapes in the setting sun.
Incense from the burner purifies the precious mat;
The shadow of the wall ascends the jade stairs.
Spring insects fly through the lattice doors,
Sparrows at dusk are shaded by the flowering branches.
Toward evening she has many melancholy thoughts –
By the idle window in the season of peach and plum.

9.10

Composed as a joke and shown to my maternal nephew of the Xiao clan

I love that you overlook the pool;[1]
Your old man never took up verse.
I, an old geezer, am hardly good enough to resemble you,[2]
Though perhaps I can leave you my battered old house.[3]
Reed shoots poke through the lotus leaves;
Caltrop flowers snag on goslings.

---

1 An allusion to the Eastern Han scholar Zhang Zhi 張芝, who studied by a pool and turned the water black with his ink. Wang Wei is saying that the nephew is an avid scholar.

2 See note to 8.2.2.

3 Wei Shu 魏舒 (Jin era) was adopted by the Ning 甯 family, who was told by a geomancer that their house would produce an outstanding nephew.

郗公不易勝，
莫著外家欺。

9.11

秋夜獨坐

獨坐悲雙鬢，
空堂欲二更。
雨中山果落，
燈下草蟲鳴。
白髮終難變，
黃金不可成。
欲知除老病，
惟有學無生。

9.12

待儲光羲不至

重門朝已啟，
起坐聽車聲。
要欲聞清佩，
方將出戶迎。

It wasn't easy for Master Chi to prevail;
8 So don't end up bullying your maternal relations![1]

9.11

Autumn night, sitting alone

Alone I sit, grieving over my graying temples.
Empty hall, nearing the second watch.
In the rain the mountain fruit fall;
4 Under the lamp, weed crickets cry.
White hair, impossible to change in the end,
Just as gold cannot be created.[2]
If you wish to know how to rid yourself of old age and illness:
8 There is only the study of Non-rebirth.

9.12

Waiting for Chu Guangxi, who never came

The double gates have been open since dawn;
I rise, sit down again when I hear the sound of a carriage.
It seems like I hear the clear sound of your pendants,
4 Then I go out to welcome you at the door.

---

1 When Wang Xianzhi 王獻之 and his brother Huizhi 徽之 visited their uncle Chi Yin 郗愔, they always acted with great politeness. After Chi Yin's son Chao 超 died, they started treating Yin with rudeness. Yin remarked that they wouldn't dare treat him like that if his son were still alive.

2 A reference to the two main goals of Daoist alchemists: elixirs for immortality, and the secret for turning base metals into gold.

晚鐘鳴上苑，
疏雨過春城。
了自不相顧，
臨堂空復情。

9.13

聽宮鶯

春樹遶宮牆，
宮鶯囀曙光。
欲驚啼暫斷，
移處弄還長。
隱葉棲承露，
排花出未央。
游人未應返，
為此思故鄉。

9.14

早朝

柳暗百花明，
春深五鳳城。

1 Bronze pillars erected by Emperor Wu of the Han for the collection of condensed dew (the dew was used for the decoction of immortality elixirs).

Evening bells ring in the upper garden;
Sparse rain passes over the city walls in spring.
I understand now that we won't see each other –
8 I stand in the reception hall – again, my feelings all in vain.

9.13

Listening to orioles in the palace

Spring trees surround the palace walls,
And palace orioles warble in the morning light.
Just startled, their cry is halted for a moment;
4 They move, their prolonged chirping resumes.
Hidden in leaves, they nest on the dew-collecting pillar;[1]
Pushing aside flowers, they emerge from Weiyang Palace.[2]
A traveler who has yet to return,
8 Because of this, longs for home.

9.14

Early dawn

Willows are dark, all the various flowers bright;
Spring is deep in Five Phoenix City.[3]

2 An imperial palace of the Han era.

3 During the reign of the mythical Shao Hao 少昊, five phoenixes appeared, each of different colors, to dance on the capital city walls. This is a poetic locution for the capital.

城烏睥睨曉，
4 宮井轆轤聲。
方朔金門侍，
班姬玉輦迎。
仍聞遣方士，
8 東海訪蓬瀛。

9.15–9.17

愚公谷三首（青龍寺與黎昕戲題）

1.

愚谷與誰去，
唯將黎子同。
非須一處住，
4 不那兩心空。
寧問春將夏，

1 The famous scholar and jester of Emperor Wu's during the Han. For Gold Horse Gate, see note to 4.8.4.

2 A court lady during the reign of Emperor Cheng of the Western Han renowned for her virtue. She is most famous for supposedly composing the poem "Song of Resentment"怨歌行 lamenting her loss of the ruler's favor.

3 Reference to Emperor Wu's desire to find the secret of immortality – here, by employing magicians ("masters of methods") to find the islands of the Transcendents. This poem may be a satire on Xuanzong's similar Daoist interests.

4 Name for a residence of a recluse. The *Shuo yuan* has original story: "Duke Huan 桓 of Qi went out hunting, and entered a valley in pursuit of a deer. He saw an old man and asked him, 'What valley is this?' He replied, 'It's the Valley of Master Foolish.' 'Why?' 'It's named after me.' 'You don't look so foolish, as far as I can

City crows – dawn on the parapets;
4 Palace well – sound of the sweep.
Dongfang Shuo attends at Gold Horse Gate,[1]
Ban Jieyu greets his carriage of jade.[2]
I hear that he still is sending masters of methods
8 To the eastern sea to find the isles of Peng and Ying.[3]

9.15–9.17

The Valley of Master Foolish: three poems[4] (written in jest with Li Xin at Qinglong Monastery)

1.

Who will go to Foolish Valley with me?
I can only go with Master Li.
Not because we must live in the same place –
4 Rather, we have no choice, because both our minds are empty.
Then why ask if it's spring or summer,

---

see. How is that naming it after you?' 'Let me explain. I once possessed a cow. It gave birth to a heifer, and when it grew up I sold it and bought a colt. A young man said, "A cow can't give birth to a horse." And he took the colt away from me. A neighbor heard of this and thought I was foolish, and so he named this valley the Valley of Master Foolish.' Duke Huan replied, 'You really were stupid! Why did you give him the colt?' He then went home. The following morning he told this to Guan Zhong 管仲. Guan Zhong straightened the folds in his robe and bowed twice. 'I am the foolish one. If a Yao had been on the throne and a Jiu Yao was acting as minister of justice, would there be anyone stealing colts? Then if an old man encountered aggression such as this, he would not have given up his colt. He gave it up because he knew that the system was unfair. Allow me to withdraw and rectify things.'"

誰論西復東。
不知吾與子，
若箇是愚公。

2.

吾家愚谷裏，
此谷本來平。
雖則行無跡，
還能響應聲。
不隨雲色暗，
只待日光明。
緣底名愚谷，
都由愚所成。

3.

借問愚公谷，
與君聊一尋。
不尋翻到谷，
此谷不離心。
行處曾無險，
看時豈有深。
寄言塵世客，
何處欲歸臨。

And who debates about going west or east?
But I don't know whether it's you or I
Who can be Master Foolish there.

2.

My house is in Foolish Valley –
But this valley has always been flat.
And even though my actions leave no traces,
I can still respond to others like an echo to a sound.
This place doesn't need the clouds to darken;
And it just waits for the sun to brighten up.
Why is it called Foolish Valley?
It's becomes that way if you act foolish.

3.

Inquiring after the Valley of Master Foolish,
For a time I go seeking with you.
But don't seek it and you'll get there anyway –
Because this valley isn't separate from the mind.
Never a path there that's treacherous;
There are no depths when you look.
I send word to those in the dusty world –
Where is it you're planning on going?

9.18

雜詩

雙燕初命子，
五桃新作花。
王昌是東舍，
宋玉次西家。
小小能織綺，
時時出浣紗。
親勞使君問，
南陌駐香車。

9.19

過秦皇墓 （時年十五）

古墓成蒼嶺，
幽宮象紫臺。
星辰七曜隔，
河漢九泉開。
有海人寧渡，
無春雁不迴。

1 Conventional handsome man in many Tang poems.
2 A Warring States poet from Chu famous for his physical beauty.
3 A trope taken from *yuefu* poems describing a lovely girl named Mochou 莫愁.

9.18

(Poem without topic)

A pair of swallows first call for their chicks;
The five peach trees have just bloomed.
Wang Chang is her neighbor to the east;[1]
Song Yu occupies the western house.[2]
When very little she could already weave patterned silks;[3]
From time to time she goes out to wash gauze.
She personally compels the emissary to inquire,
As he halts his fragrant carriage in the southern lane.[4]

9.19

Visiting the tomb mound of the First Emperor (composed at fifteen)

The old tomb mound turned to a green ridge;
This underworld palace mimics the Violet Terrace.[5]
Stars and planets – these seven luminaries are in their places;
The river of stars spread out over the Nine Streams.[6]
There is a sea, but what man would cross it?[7]
No spring here – geese will not return.

---

4 See note to 5.18.

5 Violet Terrace: both the name of an imperial palace and a term for Daoist palaces in Heaven, so this may be mocking the Qin emperor's desire for eternal life.

6 Descriptions of the tomb note that stars and planets were painted on the roof (the Seven Luminaries are the sun, moon, and five known planets). Nine Streams is a term for the underworld.

7 The tomb was said to contain a lake of mercury. This may also refer to the emperor's futile attempts to discover the islands of the immortals in the eastern sea.

更聞松韻切，
疑是大夫哀。

9.20–9.23

故太子太師徐公挽歌四首

1.

功德冠群英，
彌綸有大名。
軒皇用風后，
傅說是星精。
就第優遺老，
來朝詔不名。
留侯常辟穀，
何苦不長生。

2.

謀猷為相國，
翊贊奉乘輿。

---

1 See note to 7.8.4.

2 This was Xiao Song 蕭嵩, appointed to this position in 736. He died in 749. "Coffin Pulling Song" is a form of conventional dirge.

3 The Yellow Emperor discovered his minister Feng Hou after a prophetic dream revealed the man's name to him. When Fu Shuo, a minister of the Shang emperor Wuding died, he became a star in the "tail" constellation.

And I also hear the sharp harmony of the pine trees,
That seems like a lament from some minister of state.[1]

9.20–9.23

Four coffin-pulling songs for the Grand Preceptor of
the Heir Apparent, the Duke of Xu[2]

1.

His achievement and conduct surpassed all worthy men;
Embracing all things, he had great renown.
The Yellow Emperor made use of Feng Hou,
And Fu Shuo became the spirit of a star.[3]
He retired to his estate, an old statesman honored;
When he came to court, an edict allowed him to omit his name.[4]
The Marquis of Liu always avoided grains;
So how could it be that he was not long-lived?[5]

2.

Devising plans, he served the state as minister;
He assisted the ruler, attending upon his carriage.

4 Officials were required to give their name and position on any documents they submitted at court; this was waived in the case of particularly honored or high-ranking ones.

5 The Han minister Zhang Liang 張良 practiced many proto-Daoist habits for the sake of his health, including avoiding eating grains. Xiao Song was also a devout Daoist.

劍履升前殿，
貂蟬託後車。
齊侯疏土宇，
漢室賴圖書。
僻處留田宅，
仍纔十頃餘。

3.

舊里趨庭日，
新年置酒辰。
聞詩鸞渚客，
獻賦鳳樓人。
北首辭明主，
東堂哭大臣。
猶思御朱輅，
不惜汙車茵。

---

1 This line is probably meant to state simply that the emperor enfeoffed Xiao Song in a manner similar to the ancient Zhou rulers.

2 When the Qin was overthrown and Liu Bang 劉邦 (the future emperor Gaozu) and his allies entered the capital, Liu Bang's minister Xiao He 蕭何 was careful to obtain and then hide away Qin's official documents – which later proved of great use when Liu founded the Han.

3 Simurgh Islet: poetic designation of the Chancellery.

Allowed to keep sword and shoes when ascending the throne hall,
In marten and cicada pin he was entrusted to the entourage.
Made Marquis of Qi, the emperor allotted him land;[1]
The House of Han relied on the documents he procured.[2]
He only kept a farm for himself in a remote region,
Barely ten or so hectares in size.

3.

In his old village, he was tutored by his father;
And when each New Year came, it was a time for holding banquets.
Hearing poems, he was a sojourner on the Simurgh Islet;[3]
Presenting rhapsodies, a man in the Phoenix Mansions.[4]
With head buried toward the north, he bids leave of his enlightened lord;[5]
In the eastern hall they mourn the great minister.[6]
I still remember him driving his vermilion carriage,
Not caring if his cushions were soiled.[7]

---

4 Phoenix Mansions: a designation of residence of imperial princesses. This may be a reference to Xiao Heng 衡, Xiao Song's son, who married a Tang princess.

5 Standard burial procedure, according to the *Liji*.

6 Ritual specified that rulers should mourn those who have died in the eastern hall of the palace.

7 Alluding to the Western Han official Bing Ji 丙吉. His carriage driver once got drunk and threw up in Bing's carriage. Bing refused to dismiss him, saying that putting up with some soiled cushions was better than destroying the man's livelihood.

4.

久踐中台座，
終登上將壇。
誰言斷車騎，
空憶盛衣冠。
風日咸陽慘，
笳簫渭水寒。
無人當便闕，
應罷太師官。

9.24–9.26

故西河郡杜太守輓歌三首

1.

天上去西征，
雲中護北平。
生擒白馬將，
連破黑雕城。

1 The middle of the three asterisms referred to as the Three Eminences; they correspond to the high government positions known as the Three Dukes (the middle one being the Director of Works, later associated with Councilor-in-Chief).

2 Alludes to Xiao's time as Military Commissioner of Hexi.

3 The scenery surrounding the funeral procession.

4.

Long he trod the Central Eminence asterism,[1]
In the end he ascended to the altar of commander-in-chief.[2]
Who would think he would sever himself from war carriages and cavalry;
4 And we remember in vain this illustrious official.
The scenery in Xianyang is dreary;
Reeds and flutes are cold along the Wei waters.[3]
No one is appropriate to fill his position;
8 Best to leave vacant the post of Grand Preceptor.

9.24–9.26

Three coffin-pulling songs for the Late Prefect Du of Xihe Commandery[4]

1.

He departed on a western campaign, riding off into the distant sky;
The Yunzhong prefect guarded Beiping.[5]
He captured the White Horse general alive;[6]
4 In succession destroyed the cities of the men with scarred foreheads.[7]

4 The subject is Du Xiwang 杜希望, the father of the historian Du You 佑. He was active as a military official on the frontier. There are also four coffin-pulling songs for him by Cen Shen. He died ca. 746.

5 Reference to two Han military officials whose competence kept the Xiongnu from attacking their prefectures: Li Guang 李廣 at Beiping, and Wei Shang 魏尚 at Yunzhong.

6 A Xiongnu leader killed by Li Guang.

7 In pre-imperial times, men of Wu were said to blacken their teeth and scarify their foreheads. Here, general term for barbarians.

忽見芻靈苦，
徒聞竹使榮。
空留左氏傳，
誰繼卜商名。

2.

返葬金符守，
同歸石窌妻。
卷衣悲畫翟，
持翣待鳴雞。
容衛都人慘，
山川駟馬嘶。
猶聞隴上客，
相對哭征西。

3.

塗芻去國門，
祕器出東園。
太守留金印，
夫人罷錦軒。

---

1 Term for Du; allusion to the tally system of issuing military orders common in early China.

2 Alluding to Du Yu 杜預, who composed his commentary on the *Zuo zhuan* only after an outstanding military career.

3 Confucius's disciple Bu Shang later taught in Fenzhou, located at Xihe.

Suddenly we suffer from seeing the straw funeral effigies,
In vain we hear now of the glory of the emissary with bamboo tallies.[1]
Only his commentary on Master Zuo has been left to us;[2]
Who now will continue the fame of Bu Shang?[3]

2.

The prefect of the metal tally comes back to be buried,
Returning together with Shiliu's wife.[4]
Rolling up her robes, we lament her pheasant feather ornaments;[5]
Holding our funeral fans, we await cockcrow.
By the ceremonial guard the capital citizens are anguished;
By hills and streams the teams of horses whinny.
Still I hear that the men of Longshang
Face one another and sob for the West-Pacifying General.[6]

3.

The clay funeral carriage and its straw effigies leave the capital gate;
His coffin emerges from the palace's East Garden.
The prefect leaves behind his metal seal of office;
His lady has given up her carriage with brocade curtains.

---

4 *Zuo zhuan*, Duke Cheng 2 tells of a woman fleeing an enemy army who first inquired whether the marquis and the army commander (her father) had successfully escaped capture; only after learning they were safe did she seek to escape herself. The marquis honored her sense of propriety and rewarded her husband with the city of Shiliu. This suggests that Du was brought home to be buried with his wife.

5 This refers to the earlier mourning for Du's wife.

6 Comparing Du to Latter Han general Geng Bing 耿秉, who served at Liangzhou and was popular with the local Xiongnu, who bitterly mourned his death.

旌旐轉衰木，
簫鼓上寒原。
墳樹應西靡，
長思魏闕恩。

9.27–9.28

故南陽夫人樊氏輓歌二首

1.

錦衣餘翟茀，
繡轂罷魚軒。
淑女詩長在，
夫人法尚存。
凝笳隨曉旆，
行哭向秋原。
歸去將何見，
誰能返戟門。

2.

石窌恩榮重，
金吾車騎盛。

1 A Han prince died out in his fief, still hoping that he could return to the capital. After he died, all of the trees on his grave fell to the west in the direction of the capital.

Banners turn toward the withered trees;
Flutes and drums rise from the cold moor.
The trees on his mound ought to fall to the west,
8 For he always thought of the grace granted from the palace
watchtowers.[1]

9.27–9.28

Two coffin-pulling songs for the late Madam Fan, Duchess of Nanyang

1.

Left behind – her carriage in brocade with pheasant feather screens;
Left too her carriage with carved wheel hubs and fish-scale patterns.
The poem about the virtuous woman will exist forever;[2]
4 And the lady's model behavior is still preserved.
The slow and murmuring pipes follow the dawn pennants,
We walk sobbing toward the autumn moors.
When we return again, what will we see?
8 Who could go back to her home's halberd gate?[3]

2.

The honor bestowed on Shiliu was substantial;[4]
Carriages and riders from the Imperial Insignia Guards are plentiful.[5]

---

2 Reference to the epithalamium of *Shijing* 1.

3 Officials and noblemen of a certain rank were allowed to erect a gate made of halberds to display their status.

4 See note on 9.25.2.

5 Madam Fan's husband was a commander of the right Imperial Insignia guard.

將朝每贈言，
入室還相敬。
疊鼓秋城動，
懸旌寒日映。
不言長不歸，
環珮猶將聽。

9.29–9.30

吏部達奚侍郎夫人寇氏輓二首

1.

束帶將朝日，
鳴環映牖辰。
能令諫明主，
相勸識賢人。
遺挂空留壁，
迴文日覆塵。
金蠶將畫柳，
何處更知春。

1 Her husband was Daxi Xun 達奚珣, who was later executed for surrendering to An Lushan. Written ca. 743–745.

2 This image is drawn from one of Pan Yue's poems mourning the death of his wife.

Every time he went to court, she would give him advice;
When he came home again, they would treat each other with respect.
Beating drums – the city walls in autumn shake;
The cold sun shines on the hanging funeral banners.
Silent, we do not return for a long time;
We still listen for the sound of her jade waist pendants.

9.29–9.30

Two coffin-pulling songs for Madam Kou, the wife of Vice Minister Daxi of the Ministry of Personnel[1]

1.

She tied his sash on days when he went to court,
And his waist pendants would shine in the dawn light through the window.
She could make him remonstrate with an enlightened lord,
And persuade him to recognize worthy men.
Hangings she left behind vainly remain on the walls;[2]
Her palindrome poem daily gathers dust.[3]
Gold silkworms and painted willow –[4]
When will she ever know the spring season again?

---

3 Alludes to a famous example of female authorship: The fourth-century woman Su Hui 蘇蕙 composed a palindrome of 841 characters into a brocade and sent it to her unfaithful husband Dou Tao 竇滔.

4 Gold ornaments in the shape of silkworms were often buried with the dead in early times, and later became a stand-in for burial objects in general. A "painted willow" was a form of funeral carriage.

2.

女史悲彤管，
夫人罷錦軒。
卜塋占二室，
行哭度千門。
秋日光能澹，
寒川波自翻。
一朝成萬古，
松柏暗平原。

9.31–9.35

恭懿太子輓挽歌五首

1.

何悟藏環早，
纔知拜璧年。
翀天王子去，

1 In Zhou times, there were female scribes appointed to record the actions of the queen. Later on, this became a general term for female scribes. They characteristically employed a crimson-colored writing brush, which later became a general symbol for female authorship.

2 The two peaks of Mount Song.

3 The twelfth son of Suzong, Zhao 佋, who died in 760 at the age of eight. He was posthumously granted the title of Grand Prince and the name Gongyi.

4 When Yang Hu 羊祜 was a child, he requested that his nurse give him a gold ring that he claimed to own. When the nurse replied that he had no such ring, he went to a neighbor's house and found a buried ring that was the possession

2.

The female scribes lament with their crimson brushes;[1]
The lady has surrendered her brocade carriage.
They divined a grave plot located at the Two Houses;[2]
We walk sobbing past a thousand gates.
The light is so pale from the autumn sun;
The waves of the cold stream topple down.
One morning turns into an eternity;
Pine and cypress are dark on the level plain.

9.31–9.35

Five coffin-pulling songs for Crown Prince Gongyi[3]

1.

How early he became aware of buried rings![4]
He barely knew the year for worshipping the jade disk.[5]
Soaring into the sky, Wangzi Qiao has departed;[6]

---

of a son who had died there earlier. People speculated that he was the reincarnation of the boy. Here it seems to be a general comment on the late prince's cleverness.

5 *Zuo zhuan* Duke Zhao 13: King Gong 共 could not decide which of his five sons should be appointed heir apparent. He secretly buried a jade disk at a shrine and prayed that the spirits would make the appropriate son worship at the place where it was buried. Only the youngest child, the future King Ping 平, worshipped at that very spot.

6 The Transcendent Wangzi Qiao 王子喬 was originally the crown prince Jin 晉 of King Ling 靈 of Zhou. He was fond of playing the reed organ. Later he disappeared, riding a white crane.

對日聖君憐。
樹轉宮猶出，
笳悲馬不前。
雖蒙絕馳道，
京兆別開阡。

2.

蘭殿新恩切，
椒宮夕臨幽。
白雲隨鳳管，
明月在龍樓。
人向青山哭，
天臨渭水愁。
雞鳴常問膳，
今恨玉京留。

1 After the Jin court fled the north in the early fourth century, the Emperor Ming 明 when still a child was asked whether the sun or the lost capital of Chang'an was closer. First he replied, "Chang'an, because I have never heard of anyone coming from the sun." Then he changed his answer and said, "The sun, because I can see it, but I can't see Chang'an."

2 When the Han emperor Cheng 成 was a boy, he was summoned by his father Emperor Yuan 元. He was late in attending on his father because he refused to take a shortcut that would make him cross a road reserved for the emperor's

When his son faced the sun, the sagely lord treasured him.[1]
Winding through the trees, he has already left the palace;
The nomad fifes grieve – the horses refuse to go on.
Though he was permitted to cross the imperial way,
The capital must now open a separate funeral lane for him.[2]

2.

In thoroughwort halls the recent favor is earnest;
In pepper palace, evening mourning is profound.[3]
The white clouds follow his phoenix pipes,[4]
The bright moonlight remains at Dragon Gate tower.[5]
People sob, facing the green hills;
The sky grieves, looking down on the Wei waters.
At cock-cry, he would always ask about his parents' meals;[6]
Now we mourn that the Jade Capital has detained him.[7]

---

carriage. His father, impressed, issued an edict granting him special permission to do so.

3 Both terms for the women's residence in the palace. "Recent favor" refers to the posthumous granting of crown prince status.

4 See note to 9.31.3.

5 Dragon Gate tower: Where the prince had lived in the palace.

6 Alludes to a description of King Wen in the *Liji* that shows him inquiring after his father's health at earliest dawn and making sure that his meals pleased him.

7 See note to 1.3.6.

3.

騎吹凌霜發，
旌旗夾路陳。
禮容金節護，
冊命玉符新。
傅母悲香褓，
君家擁畫輪。
射熊今夢帝，
秤象問何人。

4.

蒼舒留帝寵，
子晉有仙才。
五歲過人智，
三天使鶴催。
心悲陽祿館，
目斷望思臺。
若道長安近，
何為更不來。

1 Gold-tallied one – refers to a high ranking official. Here, probably refers to the Metropolitan Governor, who was ordered by the emperor to oversee the prince's funeral.

2 A reference to posthumous honors.

3 Zhao Jianzi 趙簡子 (Spring and Autumn era) during an illness had a visionary dream in which he went to the palace of God on High (*di*) and shot two bears.

4 Cao Chong 曹沖, a son of Cao Cao's, was known to be particularly clever, though he died only at the age of twelve. When Cao Cao was given an elephant and was

3.

Cavalry music comes forth, braving the frost;
Pennants are displayed, lining the road.
The gold-tallied one guards the standards of ritual;[1]
The emperor has newly made him crown prince with a jade tally.[2]
His godfather and his nurse grieve over his scented swaddling,
The lord's household throngs around the painted carriage wheels.
Now he shoots a bear as he dreams of God on High;[3]
Whom now can we ask about weighing an elephant?[4]

4.

Cangshu kept the emperor's affection after his death;[5]
The son Jin had the talent of a Transcendent.[6]
At four years old, he surpassed others in wisdom;
The Three Heavens have sent a crane to hurry him away.[7]
His mother's heart grieves over Yanglu lodge;[8]
His father strains to make out the Longing Terrace.[9]
If he said that Chang'an is nearby,
Why is it that he comes no more?[10]

---

wondering how it could be weighed, Chong suggested putting it in a boat, marking how far down the boat sank, then filling the boat with weighable things until it reached the same level.

5 Cao Chong (see 9.33.8). His polite name was Cangshu.

6 See note to 9.31.3.

7 In one Daoist cosmological model, the Heavens are divided into "Three Clarities": Jade Clarity, Highest Clarity, and Great Clarity.

8 In the Han, the Yanglu Lodge was where palace ladies gave birth.

9 Liu Ju 劉據, the crown prince of Emperor Wu of the Han, was unjustly accused of witchcraft and eventually hanged himself. The emperor, when he discovered his son's innocence, built "Longing for My Son Terrace" (*si zi tai*) on the location of his death.

10 See note to 9.31.4.

5.

西望昆池闊，
東瞻下杜平。
山朝豫章館，
4 樹轉鳳凰城。
五校連旗色，
千門疊鼓聲。
金環如有驗，
8 還向畫堂生。

5.

To the west we gaze toward the breadth of Kunming Lake;
To the east, look toward the plain below Duling.
The hills face the Yuzhang Lodge;
4 The trees turn about Phoenix city.[1]
The sight of the linked banners of the Five Colonels,[2]
The sound of drums beating at a thousand gates:
If the story of the gold ring holds true,
8 He will be born once more in painted halls.[3]

1 These are all poetic Han-era names for places around the capital.
2 Five Colonels were five army officers prominent in the Han army. Here, indicates the participation of the military at the funeral.
3 See note to 9.31.1.

王右丞集卷之十 近體詩

10.1

奉和聖製從蓬萊向興慶閣道中留春雨中春望之作應制

渭水自縈秦塞曲，
黃山舊繞漢宮斜。
鑾輿迴出仙門柳，
閣道迴看上苑花。
雲裏帝城雙鳳闕，
雨中春樹萬人家。
為乘陽氣行時令，
不是宸游重物華。

https://doi.org/10.1515/9781501516023-010

Juan 10: Recent style poems

10.1

Respectfully harmonizing with the imperial composition
"On the covered walkway from Penglai Palace to Xingqing Palace,
detaining spring: gazing out on the rain": to imperial command

The Wei waters bend as they turn about the Qin frontiers;
Yellow Mountain as of old inclines and coils around the Han Palace.[1]
His simurgh carriage emerges afar from the willows at
  the Transcendent's gate;
4 From the covered walkway he turns and sees the imperial garden
  flowers.
Amid the clouds in the emperor's city – paired phoenix gate-towers;
In the rain, spring trees – ten thousand people's homes.
Taking advantage of the spring air, he has issued a timely command –
8 It is not an imperial excursion just because he values the scenery!

1 Site of a palace in Han times.

10.2

大同殿生玉芝龍池上有慶雲百官共睹聖恩便賜宴樂敢書即事

欲笑周文歌宴鎬，
遙輕漢武樂橫汾。
豈如玉殿生三秀，
詎有銅池出五雲。
陌上堯樽傾北斗，
樓前舜樂動南薰。
共歡天意同人意，
萬歲千秋奉聖君。

10.3

敕賜百官櫻桃（時為文部郎中）

芙蓉闕下會千官，
紫禁朱櫻出上蘭。
纔是寢園春薦後，
非關御苑鳥銜殘。

1 A song attributed to Shun: “The warmth of the south wind / can relieve my people’s anger.”

10.2

Angelica appeared growing at the Datong Hall, and auspicious clouds were seen over the Dragon Pool. This was seen by all the court officials. The sagely ruler then graciously granted a banquet and music. I dared write describing what I saw there.

One will smile at King Wen of the Zhou, singing and banqueting at Hao,
Scorn that long ago Emperor Wu of the Han played music in crossing the Fen.
How could these compare with a thrice-flowering herb arising from the jade halls?
How could they have had brass rain-basins giving rise to five-colored clouds?
In the lanes the northern dipper is tipped into Yao's goblets;
Before the hall, Shun's music performs "southern warmth."[1]
Together we delight that heaven's and men's intentions are the same;
For ten thousand years, a thousand autumns, we attend on our sagely lord.

10.3

Cherries granted to the court officials by the emperor
(at the time serving as a director in the Ministry of Personnel)

Below the hibiscus gate-towers the thousand officials gather;
A vermillion cherry tree of the Purple Tenuity has emerged from Shanglan Belvedere garden.[2]
It is just after the presentation of spring fruit at the imperial mausolea –
It has nothing to do with feeding leftovers to the imperial garden birds.

2 Purple Tenuity: constellation linked with the imperial palace, so substitute for the palace itself. The Shanglan Belvedere was a Han-era palace structure with attached gardens.

歸鞍競帶青絲籠，
中使頻傾赤玉盤。
飽食不須愁內熱，
大官還有蔗漿寒。

10.3a

崔興宗： 和王維敕賜百官櫻桃

未央朝謁正逶迤，
天上櫻桃錫此時。
朱實初傳九華殿，
繁花舊雜萬年枝。
全勝晏子江南橘，
莫比潘家大谷梨。
聞到令人好顏色，
神農本草自應知。

Returning saddles compete in carrying blue-thread-handled baskets;
Court eunuchs repeatedly pour them out from red jade plates.
Eating our fill, no need to worry that we'll contract a fever;[1]
8 The Court Provisioners still have chilled cane sugar juice for us.

10.3a

Cui Xingzong: Harmonizing with Wang Wei: "Cherries granted to the court officials by the emperor"

The court audience at Weiyang palace windingly advances;
This is when Heaven above bestows us with a cherry tree.
Its vermilion fruit just now are brought from Jiuhua Hall;
4 Its profuse blossoms were mixing in with the branches of the holly trees.
They surpass by far Master Yan's oranges south of the Jiang;
Don't bother to compare them with the Pan estate Great Valley pears.[2]
I've heard it said that the fruit can put one in a good mood;
8 It should be known about in Shennong's Materia Medica.[3]

1 Eating too many cherries was said to generate excessive warm *qi* in the body.
2 In his "Living in Idleness" rhapsody, Pan Yue mentions the pears of "Sir Zhang's Great Valley," reputed to be particularly sweet.
3 Han dynasty pharmacological work.

10.4

敕借岐王九成宮避暑應教

帝子遠辭丹鳳闕，
天書遙借翠微宮。
隔窗雲霧生衣上，
卷幔山泉入鏡中。
林下水聲喧語笑，
巖間樹色隱房櫳。
仙家未必能勝此，
何事吹笙向碧空。

10.5

和賈舍人早朝大明宮之作

絳幘雞人送曉籌，
尚衣方進翠雲裘。
九天閶闔開宮殿，
萬國衣冠拜冕旒。
日色纔臨仙掌動，
香煙欲傍袞龍浮。

10.4

The emperor has loaned the Prince of Qi the Jiucheng Palace
for avoiding the heat: at princely command

The imperial prince has distantly retreated from the cinnabar phoenix watchtowers;
An imperial order lends him afar this palace in azure mists.
Beyond the windows, the clouds and mist seem to rise from our clothes;
As we roll up the curtains, the mountain stream enters into the mirrors.
Below the wood, the sound of water drowns out speech and laughter;
Before the cliffs, the color of the trees conceals the window lattices.
The homes of Transcendents would not necessarily be able to surpass this;
So why should Wangzi Qiao play his reed organ and ascend into the jade-green sky?[1]

10.5

Harmonizing with Secretariat Drafter Jia: "Morning audience at
the Daming Palace"

The scarlet-turbaned rooster-man transmits the dawn tally;[2]
The Wardrobe Steward has just presented the robes with their kingfisher-feather clouds.
The Grand Gate to the Nine Heavens has just opened the palace halls;
Officials from the myriad lands bow before His coronet tassels.
Sunlight just now moves over the Immortal's palms;[3]
Incense smoke is floating beside the imperial dragon robes.

---

1 See note to 9.31.3.

2 A guard given the task of announcing the coming of dawn. The tally here is one of the arrows used to mark time in the palace clepsydras.

3 Dew-collecting statues; see note to 9.13.5.

朝罷須裁五色詔，
珮聲歸向鳳池頭。

10.5a

賈至：早朝大明宮呈兩省僚友

銀燭朝天紫陌長，
禁城春色曉蒼蒼。
千條弱柳垂青瑣，
百囀流鶯遶建章。
劍佩聲隨玉墀步，
衣冠身惹御爐香。
共沐恩波鳳池裏，
朝朝染翰侍君王。

10.5b

杜甫：奉和賈至舍人早朝大明宮

五夜漏聲催曉箭，
九重春色醉仙桃。
旌旗日暖龍蛇動，
宮殿風微燕雀高。

1 Both Wang Wei and Jia Zhi had official duties drafting government documents. Phoenix Pool was a poetic cognomen for the Secretariat.

When the audience is over, we must trim our five-colored fiats;
8 The sound of our pendants returns to the Phoenix Pool.[1]

10.5a

Jia Zhi: Morning audience at the Daming Palace: shown to my two colleagues at the office

Silver tapers face the sky; the capital lanes are long.
In the forbidden city spring colors are gray in the dawn.
A thousand branches of fragile willows hang down over the blue chain-patterned gates;[2]
4 With a hundred trills the sweet-throated orioles surround the Jianzhang palace.[3]
Tinkle of sword-pendants follow the tread on jade stairs;
Robed and capped forms brush up against the imperial burner incense.
Together we bathe in the waves of His grace in Phoenix Pool;
8 Morning after morning we stain our brushes in the service of our lord.

10.5b

Du Fu: Respectfully harmonizing with Drafter Jia Zhi:
"Morning audience at the Daming Palace"

At the fifth watch, the clepsydra's sound hastens the dawn arrow;
Autumn colors in the nine-layer palace makes drunk the Transcendents' peaches.
The sun warms the pennants as their snakes and dragons tremble;
4 The wind is gentle in palace halls as swallows and sparrows fly high.

2 See note to 8.8.8.
3 See note to 7.1.4.

朝罷香煙攜滿袖，
詩成珠玉在揮毫。
欲知世掌絲綸美，
池上于今有鳳毛。

10.5c

岑參： 奉和中書舍人賈至早朝大明宮

雞鳴紫陌曙光寒，
鶯囀皇州春色闌。
金闕曉鐘開萬戶，
玉階仙仗擁千官。
花迎劍珮星初落，
柳拂旌旗露未乾。
獨有鳳皇池上客，
陽春一曲和皆難。

Audience ended – incense smoke fills our sleeves;
Verses finished – pearls and jades come from flourished writing brushes.
If you want to know generations in charge of the beauty of silken threads:
Until now there has been phoenix down on the pool.[1]

10.5c

Cen Shen: Respectfully harmonizing with Secretariat Drafter
Jia Zhi: "Morning audience at the Daming Palace"

The cock crows over the capital lanes; the daybreak light is chill.
Orioles trill in the imperial precincts; spring hues are waning.
By gold watchtowers the dawn bells open ten thousand doors;
On the jade stairs, Transcendents' standards cause to throng a thousand officials.
Blossoms greet sword-pendants as the stars begin to set;
Willows brush the pennants – the dew has yet to dry.
Alone there is a man from Phoenix Pool –
His single song of "Rising Spring" is a challenge to match![2]

1 "Silken threads" – the elegant writing on government edicts. Du Fu is complimenting Jia and his father, who also served as a Secretary.

2 "Rising Spring" was said to be a song so elegant it could only be matched by a dozen or so people. This is complimenting Jia Zhi.

10.6

和太常韋主簿五郎溫湯寓目

漢主離宮接露臺，
秦川一半夕陽開。
青山盡是朱旗繞，
4 碧澗翻從玉殿來。
新豐樹裏行人度，
小苑城邊獵騎迴。
聞道甘泉能獻賦，
8 懸知獨有子雲才。

10.7

苑舍人能書梵字兼達梵音皆曲盡其妙戲為之贈

名儒待詔滿公車，
才子為郎典石渠。
蓮花法藏心懸悟，
4 貝葉經文手自書。

1 The springs at Mount Li were close to a site where Emperor Wen of the Han had erected an "open terrace" for observing astronomical phenomena.
2 Reference to a rhapsody composed by the Han poet and philosopher celebrating a detached imperial palace.

10.6

Harmonizing with Recorder Wei Wulang of the Court of Imperial Sacrifices: "Things seen at the warm springs"

The Han ruler's detached palace connects with an open terrace;[1]
Half of the Qin rivers are revealed in the evening light.
The green hills are all surrounded by vermilion pennants;
4 The jade-green streams on the contrary turn through the jade halls.
Travelers cross amid the Xinfeng trees;
Mounted hunters return beside the small garden town.
I've heard it said that Yang Xiong was able to present a rhapsody on Sweet Springs,
8 And I suppose that only you are possessed of his talent.[2]

10.7

Secretariat Drafter Yuan can write Sanskrit and understands its sounds. I playfully wrote this to fathom fully the marvelousness of this and presented it to him.

Esteemed scholars awaiting their summons fill the Gate Traffic Control Office;[3]
You, a talented man, serve as a Director, and preside over the Stone Channel chamber.[4]
Your mind alone has awakened to the Lotus Flower tripitaka;
4 Your own hand can copy the writings of sutras on pattra palm leaves.

3 Originally a Han institution; it was in charge of accepting memorials, tribute articles, and vehicles used to fetch those summoned to court.

4 I.e., the imperial library.

楚辭共許勝揚馬，
梵字何人辨魯魚。
故舊相望在三事，
8 願君莫厭承明廬。

10.7a

苑咸: 酬王維（並序）

王員外兄以予嘗學天竺書。有戲題見贈。然王兄當代詩匠。又精禪理。枉採知音。形於雅作。輒走筆以酬焉。且久未遷。因而嘲及。

蓮花梵字本從天，
華省仙郎早悟禪。
三點成伊猶有想，
4 一觀如幻自忘筌。
為文已變當時體，
入用還推間氣賢。

1 Literally, “Lu and fish” – proverbial for two characters that get miswritten for each other and thus are used as examples of misreading in general.

2 Chengming Stove – in Han times, an area outside of the library where low-ranking palace attendants would pass the night.

All endorse your Chu-style compositions as superior to Yang Xiong and Sima Xiangru;
And in Sanskrit writing, who else could make difficult distinctions?[1]
Your old associates have hope that you will attain position as one of the three dukes;
8 But I hope you won't grow tired of the Chengming stove![2]

10.7a

Yuan Xian: Answering Wang Wei (with preface)

Brother Wang the Vice Director sent me a teasing poem once because I had studied the writing of India. Brother Wang is a poetic craftsman of our age and is also conversant with the principles of meditation – and yet he has stooped to choose me as a friend and formed his thoughts into an elegant composition for me. I immediately hurried my brush to answer him – and also because he has not been promoted for some time in office, I took the opportunity to tease him as well.

The lotus-flower Sanskrit letters came originally from Heaven;
And you, a Director in State Affairs, awakened to meditation early on.
When three dots form the letter "i," then there are things to ponder;[3]
4 With one glance, all becomes illusion – one forgets the fish-trap.[4]
In writing prose, you have already altered the style of the time;
Employed in office, you still recommend extraordinary worthies.[5]

---

3 In the *Nirvana Sutra* (chapter 3), the Buddha uses the three dots that come together to form the Sanskrit "i" as a metaphor for how Dharma, the Buddha, and Wisdom must come together to have meaning. Each dot by itself is meaningless.

4 A proverb from the *Zhuangzi*: Just as one may abandon the fish-trap once the fish are caught, so one may abandon words once they successfully convey meaning.

5 Literally, men with *qi* that fills up the space between Heaven and Earth.

應同羅漢無名欲，
故作馮唐老歲年。

10.8

重酬苑郎中并序時為庫部員外

頃輒奉贈。忽枉見酬。敘末云。且久不遷。因而嘲及。詩落句云。應同羅漢無名欲。故作馮唐老歲年。亦解嘲之類也。

何幸含香奉至尊，
多慚未報主人恩。
草木豈能酬雨露，
榮枯安敢問乾坤。
仙郎有意憐同舍，
丞相無私斷掃門。
揚子解嘲徒自遣，
馮唐已老復何論。

1 Feng Tang served under Emperor Wen of the Han; he was offered a position under Emperor Jing but turned it down. He was again offered a post under Emperor Wu, but by this time he was in his nineties, and so his son was offered the post instead.

As with arhats, you should have no desire for fame;
8 That's why you are like Feng Tang in the years of his old age.[1]

10.8

A reply in turn to Secretariat Drafter Yuan (with preface; at the time I was Director of the Bureau of Provisions)

Not long ago I offered a poem to Drafter Yuan, and he suddenly deigned to grant me a reply. At the end of his note he says, "also because he has not been promoted for some time in office, I took the opportunity to tease him as well." The end of the poem reads: "As with arhats, you should have no desire for fame; / That's why you are like Feng Tang in the years of his old age." That is also a way of "disarming ridicule."[2]

How fortunate that I can attend on His Majesty with fragrance in my mouth;[3]
I am often ashamed that I have yet to repay my lord's grace.
Plants and trees can fully requite the dew and the rain;
4 And how can they inquire of Heaven whether they will flourish or wither?
You deliberately took pity on one of your colleagues;
But the Chief Minister is impartial; he rejects special pleading.[4]
Master Yang wrote "Disarming Ridicule" only to relieve himself;
8 But Feng Tang is already old, so what more is there to say?

---

2 "Disarming Ridicule" is a rhapsody composed by Yang Xiong in which he defends his low position and failure to advance his career.

3 Staff of the Department of State Affairs were expected to put incense in their mouths when dealing with the emperor, so that their breath would not offend him.

4 The Chief Minister here is Li Linfu, Yuan Xian's chief patron. "Special pleading" is literally "sweeping the gate," and refers to Wei Bo 魏勃, who was too poor to obtain an audience with the Qi minister Cao Shen 曹參. He then swept the gates of Cao's retainers until they noticed him and brought him to Cao's attention.

10.9

酬郭給事

洞門高閣靄餘輝，
桃李陰陰柳絮飛。
禁裏踈鐘官舍晚，
4 省中啼鳥吏人稀。
晨搖玉佩趨金殿，
夕奉天書拜瑣闈。
強欲從君無那老，
8 將因臥病解朝衣。

10.10

既蒙宥罪旋復拜官伏感聖恩竊書鄙意兼奉簡新除使君等諸公

忽蒙漢詔還冠冕，
始覺殷王解網羅。
日比皇明猶自暗，
4 天齊聖壽未云多。
花迎喜氣皆知笑，
鳥識歡心亦解歌。

10.9

Reply to Supervising Censor Guo

By recessed gate and lofty gallery: gloom, with lingering radiance;
Peach and plum give heavy shade; the willow catkins fly.
Scattered bells within the palace – it's evening in the official lodges;
4 Chirping birds in the ministry – the attendants grow few.
At dawn you shake your jade pendants as you hasten to the gilded hall;
At evening accepting imperial documents, you bow at the chain-patterned gate.[1]
I make an effort to attend on you, but nothing can be done about my age;
8 And because I lie here sick, I'm about to remove my court robes.

10.10

After receiving an imperial pardon and being appointed to a post once more, I am humbly moved by imperial grace as I write my lowly thoughts; I offer the poem on paper to various gentlemen such as the newly appointed prefects and others.

I suddenly received the Han edict returning me to an official post;
For the first time I understand the Yin king undoing the fishing nets.[2]
If I compare the sun to imperial brilliance, it still seems dark;
4 If I equate Heaven's span with that of the Sagely ruler, I cannot say it is longer.
Flowers welcome the aura of joy – all of them know to smile.[3]
Birds recognize a delighted heart – they understand how to sing.

1 See note to 8.8.8.
2 See note to 3.19.8.
3 "Smile" can also mean "blossom."

聞道百城新佩印，
還來雙闕共鳴珂。

10.11

酌酒與裴迪

酌酒與君君自寬，
人情翻覆似波瀾。
白首相知猶按劍，
朱門先達笑彈冠。
草色全經細雨濕，
花枝欲動春風寒。
世事浮雲何足問，
不如高臥且加餐。

10.12

輞川別業

不到東山向一年，
歸來纔及種春田。
雨中草色綠堪染，
水上桃花紅欲然。

I have heard that the prefects have recently tied their waist-pendant seals of office;
They return now to the paired watchtowers with their bridle jades ringing.

10.11

Drinking ale with Pei Di

When I drink ale with you, you are naturally relaxed;
Human nature is changeable, like rolling waves.
Old acquaintances, white-haired, may yet put hands on swords;
Gentry who first achieved eminence laugh at those first taking up office.
Plants in their colors have all passed through a soaking from light rain;
Flowered branches will soon tremble in the chill of the spring breeze.
What use is it to inquire about the floating clouds of worldly affairs?
It is better to recline in reclusion and be sure to eat well.

10.12

My estate at Wangchuan

I have not come to East Mountain for nearly a year;[1]
Now returning, I just arrive in time for planting the spring fields.
In the rain, the color of the plants is a green worthy of dye;
By the water, the peach blossoms are so red, they are about to flame.

1 See note to 2.23.1.

優婁比邱經論學，
傴僂丈人鄉里賢。
披衣倒屣且相見，
8 相歡語笑衡門前。

10.13

早秋山中作

無才不敢累明時，
思向東溪守故籬。
豈厭尚平婚嫁早，
4 却嫌陶令去官遲。
草間蛩響臨秋急，
山裏蟬聲薄暮悲。
寂寞柴門人不到，
8 空林獨與白雲期。

The bhikṣu Uruvilvā Kāśyapa has studied sutras and śastras;[1]
The venerable hunchback is a worthy man of the village.[2]
I throw on a robe, put clogs on backwards as I hurry to see them;[3]
Delighted, we talk and laugh in front of my rustic gate.

10.13

Early autumn, written in the mountains

Without talent, I dare not burden an enlightened age;
I long to head toward the Eastern Stream and keep to my former hedge.
How could I dislike Shang Ziping for marrying off his children early?[4]
But I am disgusted with Magistrate Tao for resigning his post so late.[5]
The echoes of crickets in the grass grows more urgent at the start of autumn;
The sound of cicadas in the hills are grieving at twilight.
All silent by my scrap-wood gate, no one comes to visit;
In the empty woods, alone I keep my appointment with the white clouds.

---

1 A prominent teacher who converted early on in the Buddha's career. Here designates an educated monk that Wang Wei has befriended in the Wangchuan region.

2 *Zhuangzi,* chapter 19: Confucius meets a hunchback who uses the power of spontaneity to catch cicadas successfully.

3 "To put clogs on backwards" is a cliché for hurriedly going to greet a guest.

4 See note to 9.3.6.

5 In one of his poems, Tao Qian speaks of being trapped in the dusty net of the world for thirty years (or thirteen, in a different reading of the text).

10.14

積雨輞川莊

積雨空林烟火遲，
蒸藜炊黍餉東菑。
漠漠水田飛白鷺，
陰陰夏木囀黃鸝。
山中習靜觀朝槿，
松下清齋折露葵。
野老與人爭席罷，
海鷗何事更相疑。

10.15

過乘如禪師蕭居士嵩邱蘭若

無着天親弟與兄，
嵩邱蘭若一峰晴。
食隨鳴磬巢烏下，
行踏空林落葉聲。
迸水定侵香案濕，

1 *Zhuangzi*, chapter 27: After accepting the teaching of Laozi, Yangzi Ju 陽子居 (formerly arrogant in demeanor) projected such a diffident air that others felt no compunction in shoving him off his place on a mat at the inn where he was staying.

10.14

Written on the sustained rainfall at my Wangchuan estate

Sustained rainfall in the empty woods – smoky fires are slow to light.
They steam goosefoot and millet, bring it into the eastern fields.
Over the vast paddies the white egrets fly;
In the gloom of summer trees the yellow orioles trill.
Practicing stillness, I observe the dawn rose of sharon;
Abstaining from meat under the pine trees, I break off a dewy mallow.
A rustic old man, I've given up vying with others for a place on
the mat;[1]
So why should the seagulls be suspicious of me?[2]

10.15

Visiting the *araṇya* of Meditation Master Chengru and Layman Xiao at Mount Song[3]

Vasubandhu and his brother Asaṅga, both without attachments:[4]
In a monastery on Mount Song, where the whole peak is clear.
They eat in accord with the temple chimes, under the roosting crows;
They stroll, treading the empty wood – sounds from the fallen leaves.
Spurting water definitely encroaches and sprays their incense table;

---

2 See note to 5.1.7.

3 See note to 7.28.

4 Wang Wei playfully refers to Chengru and Xiao (evidently his brother) by the names of the two great Buddhist philosophers.

雨花應共石牀平。
深洞長松何所有，
儼然天竺古先生。

10.16

春日與裴迪過新昌里訪呂逸人不遇

桃源一向絕風塵，
柳市南頭訪隱淪。
到門不敢題凡鳥，
看竹何須問主人。
城外青山如屋裏，
東家流水入西鄰。
閉戶著書多歲月，
種松皆老作龍鱗。

1 Both of these images suggest the spiritual powers of Chengru and Xiao. The spurting water may allude to Huiyuan calling forth a stream through his faith when he wanted to found a monastery at Mount Lu. Flowers often rain down from Heaven on buddhas and bodhisattvas teaching the Dharma.

Falling blossoms are probably as deep as their stone meditation seat.[1]
What is there in these deep caverns and tall pine trees?
Two solemn and ancient gentlemen from India.

10.16

On a spring day I went with Pei Di to Xinchang Ward to visit the recluse Lü but he was out

His Peach Blossom Spring all along has been cut off from wind and dust;[2]
At the south edge of Willow Market we visit the recluse.
Arriving at the gate, we did not dare write "common bird";[3]
To view the bamboo it's not necessary to ask the host.[4]
Beyond the city walls the green hills seem to be in the house;
The flowing water from the family to the east enters the western neighbors.
He has shut his gate and written his books for many months and years;
And the pines he planted are already old and grown dragon-scale bark.

2 See note to 2.22a.4.

3 Lü An 呂安 went to visit his friend Xi Kang 嵇康, but met his brother Xi Xi 喜 instead. Rather than stay, Lü took his leave, first writing the word "phoenix" 鳳 on the door. Xi Xi took this as a compliment, but Lü was actually calling him mediocre: the character 鳳 can be read as a combination of 凡 ("ordinary") and 鳥 ("bird").

4 See note to 7.30.4.

10.16a

裴迪：春日與王右丞過新昌里訪呂逸人不遇

恨不逢君出荷蓑，
青松白屋更無他。
陶令五男曾不有，
蔣生三徑任相過。
芙蓉曲沼春流滿，
薜荔成帷晚靄多。
聞說桃源好迷客，
不如高枕盼庭柯。

10.17

送方尊師歸嵩山

仙官欲住九龍潭，
旄節朱旛倚石龕。
山壓天中半天上，
洞穿江底出江南。
瀑布杉松常帶雨，
夕陽彩翠忽成嵐。
借問迎來雙白鶴，
已曾衡嶽送蘇耽。

10.16a

Pei Di: On a spring day I went with Wang Assistant Director of the Right to Xinchang Ward to visit the recluse Lü but he was out

I regret that we could not meet you coming out in your lotus-leaf rain cape;
Just green pines and a white house – nothing more than that.
He has never possessed five sons, as Magistrate Tao did;[1]
Master Jiang's three paths permit us to visit him.[2]
The curving lotus pool fills with the spring current;
Hanging fig vines become curtains – evening mist increases.
I've heard it said that the peach blossom spring has deceived many a traveler;
So it would be better to recline at ease and gaze on the courtyard tree branches.

10.17

Seeing off Revered Master Fang returning to Mount Song

The Transcendent official desires to live by Nine Dragon Pool;[3]
With yak-tail standards and vermilion pennants he leans on a stone shrine.
The mountain draws close to the sky, rises halfway to the sky;
The grotto passes below the Jiang, emerges south of the Jiang.[4]
Firs and pines by waterfalls are always covered in rain;
Bright emerald-green in the twilight sun suddenly turns to mist.
I inquire of the pair of white cranes that have come to greet us;
Have they already seen off Su Dan on the Heng Marchmount?[5]

---

1 Tao Qian wrote a poem criticizing his five sons.

2 See note to 7.30.1.

3 Located on the eastern peak of Mount Song.

4 Many of the grotto-worlds of Daoist belief were said to connect to each other and form a large underground network connecting many mountains.

5 Su Dan 蘇耽 was a Transcendent who left the world and flew off into the sky after being greeted by an entourage of cranes who transformed themselves into young men.

10.18

送楊少府貶郴州

明到衡山與洞庭，
若為秋月聽猿聲。
愁看北渚三湘近，
4 惡說南風五兩輕。
青草瘴時過夏口，
白頭浪裏出湓城。
長沙不久留才子，
8 賈誼何須弔屈平。

10.19

出塞作（時為御史監察塞上作）

居延城外獵天驕，
白草連山野火燒。
暮雲空磧時驅馬，
4 秋日平原好射鵰。
護羌校尉朝乘障，

1 A strong south breeze would take Yang quickly back north and to home, but he is not allowed to return.

2 Wang is predicting that Yang will soon be allowed to return home. To do so he would travel north from Chenzhou in the Xiang River region until he reached Xiakou on the Jiang. He would then travel downriver past Pencheng (Xunyang) until he reached the Grand Canal.

10.18

Seeing off District Defender Yang who has been demoted to a post in Chenzhou

In future days when you arrive at Mount Heng and Lake Dongting,
How will you bear to hear the gibbons' cries under the autumn moon?
You'll grieve to see how near you are to the northern islet and the Three Xiang;
4 You'll hate it when it is said that the south wind buoys the mast wind-vane.[1]
You'll pass Xiakou during the season of spring miasmas,
And on the white-capped waves you'll emerge from Pencheng.[2]
Changsha does not detain talented men for long;
8 Why should you play Jia Yi and mourn Qu Yuan?[3]

10.19

Written going out to the frontier (written while serving as Investigating Censor on the frontier)

Outside Juyan town he hunts down Heaven's brats.[4]
White grasses stretch to the hills; wild fires are burning.
On the empty moraine under twilight clouds, at times he drives his horse;
4 On the level plain under autumn skies, often he goes shooting eagles.
The Defend-Against-Qiang colonel climbs to his ramparts at dawn;[5]

---

3 When the Han scholar Jia Yi 賈誼 was exiled to the Changsha region, he composed a poem mourning the death of the Chu poet Qu Yuan and tossed it into the river where Qu supposedly drowned himself.

4 See note to 9.8.2 and note to 6.6.19.

5 "Qiang" (originally a proto-Tibetan people in ancient times) was applied to Tibetans in the Tang era. "Defend-Against-Qiang Colonel" was an official position in the Han era army.

破虜將軍夜渡遼。
玉靶角弓珠勒馬，
8 漢家將賜霍嫖姚。

10.20

聽百舌鳥

上蘭門外草萋萋，
未央宮中花裏栖。
亦有相隨過御苑，
4 不知若箇向金隄。
入春解作千般語，
拂曙能先百鳥啼。
萬戶千門應覺曉，
8 建章何必聽鳴雞。

The Smashing-Caitff general crosses the Liao at night.[1]
Jade target and horn-tipped bow, horse with jeweled reins;
The Han house is about to award them to Huo Qubing.

10.20

Listening to the gray starlings

Beyond the Shanglan gate the grass grows lush;[2]
Within Weiyang Palace they nest within the flowers.[3]
And sometimes they chase each other past the imperial garden;
I don't know which one is at the Metal Embankments.[4]
As they enter spring, they know how to speak a thousand different phrases;[5]
At daybreak they can anticipate all the various birds.
At a myriad doors, a thousand gates, we should learn that dawn has come;
Why do we need to hear the rooster crow at Jianzhang Palace?[6]

1 A title granted at various times to generals during the Three Kingdoms period. The Liao River is on the northeast frontier.
2 See note to 10.3.2.
3 See note to 9.13.6.
4 Possibly a restricting embankment around the imperial garden.
5 The gray starling was known for its ability to imitate the calls of other birds.
6 See note to 7.1.4.

Textual notes

Abbreviations

1. Pre-modern editions of Wang Wei's works

GKJ: *Tang Wang Youcheng shi ji zhu shuo* 唐王右丞詩集註說. Compiled by Gu Kejiu 顧可久. Preface dated 1560; follows the structure of LCW. Reprinted 1590.

LCW: *Xuxi xiansheng jiao ben Tang Wang Youcheng ji* 須溪先生校本唐王右丞記 Complied by Liu Chenweng 劉辰翁 with critical comments. Yuan edition. Includes only poetry. Evidently based on the Masha edition (SGTB), but collated with something else. Reprinted in 1504.

LMC: *Wang Mojie shi ji* 王摩詰詩集. Compiled by Ling Mengchu 凌濛初. No date; late Ming.

QTS: *Quan Tang shi* 全唐詩. 1707, with later revisions. Poem order and variants suggest sources considerably at odds from other surviving editions.

QTW: *Quan Tang wen* 全唐文. 1814.

QZZ: *Lei jian Tang Wang Youcheng ji* (published by Gu shi Qizizhai) 類箋唐王右丞集（顧氏奇字齋刊）. Compiled by Gu Qijing 顧起經. Preface dated 1555. Earliest suriving edition to collate earlier editions.

SGTB: *Wang Youcheng wen ji* (Qing Qian shi Shugutang yingchao) 王右丞文集（清錢氏述古堂影炒）. This is a facsimile of the Masha 麻沙 Song edition (which only survives in a Japanese collection). Its organization is the same as SSB, but there are enough variant readings to suggest that the Masha edition also incorporated readings from a variant textual line. Includes prose.

SSB: *Wang Mojie wen ji* (Song Shu ben) 王摩詰文集（宋蜀本） Published in Shu, probably Northern Song. Includes prose. Earliest surviving edition.

WMJJ: *Wang Mojie ji* 王摩詰集. 10 juan. No date or name. Includes poetry and prose. Earliest surviving collection to organize texts by metrical genre; order of poems suggests it derives mostly from the Masha textual lineage. Probably printed in first half of sixteenth

https://doi.org/10.1515/9781501516023-011

century. This edition was the basis for various Ming reprints, including compendia of Tang poets.

ZDC: *Wang Youcheng ji jian zhu.* 王右丞集箋注. Compiled by Zhao Diancheng 趙殿成. Preface dated 1737. Zhao notes that he collated from LCW, GKJ, LMC, and QZZ. This is the base edition for this translation.

2. Other sources for Wang Wei texts

GXJ: *Guo xiu ji* 國秀集. Compiled by Rui Tingzhang 芮挺章. C. 740s.

HYYLJ: *Heyue yingling ji* 河嶽英靈集. Compiled by Yin Fan 殷璠. C. 753.

TSJS: *Tang shi ji shi* 唐詩紀事. Compiled by Ji Yougong 計有功. Mid twelfth century.

TSPH *Tang shi pin hui* 唐詩品彙. Compiled by Gao Bing 高㯳. Late 1300s.

TWC: *Tang wen cui* 唐文粹. Compiled by Yao Xuan 姚鉉. Completed in 1011, printed in 1039.

WSTR: *Wan shou Tang ren jueju* 萬首唐人絕句. Compiled by Hong Mai 洪邁. Presented to throne 1192.

WYYH: *Wenyuan yinghua* 文苑英華. Finished 987, with later supplements and corrections.

YFSJ: *Yuefu shi ji*. Compiled by Guo Maoqian 郭茂倩. Twelfth century.

YKLS: *Yingkui lüsui* 瀛奎律髓. Compiled by Fang Hui 方回. 1282.

1.1.11: QTS has 降 for 獻.

1.7.10: 神之來兮不來: HYYLJ, YFSJ have 不知神之來不來.

1.7.11: HYYLJ reads 使我心苦.

1.8.1: 拜: YFSJ and QTS read 舞.

1.8.6: 靈: HYYLJ and QTS read 神.

1.9.9: 瀨: WMJJ, QZZ and others have 湫.

1.10: title:官出: SSB and QTS have 官未出.

1.10.10: 負: SSB has 魚, QZZ and LMC have 漁.

1.10.20: SSB and WMJJ have 折枝作花.

1.10.21: Supplying 靜 from QTS for ZDC 淨.

2.3.4: 樓: YFSJ has 筵.

2.6.3: 悲: WYYH has 應, YFSJ has 鳴.
2.6.6: 戰聲: WYYH has 力戰.
2.6.7: 名王: WYYH has 番王.
2.6.8: 報: WYYH, SSB, WMJJ, QTS have 獻, LMC has 見.

2.8.3: 女: SSB has 柳.

2.10.12: 搖: QZZ and LMC have 播.
2.10.18: 聞: SGTB and LCW have 間.
2.10.19: Supplying 囀 from QTS for 轉.

2.11.35: 已: QTS has 己.

2.13: title: 淅: SSB, SGTB, WMJJ have 浙

2.14.10: 林: SSB has 陵.

2.15.3: 陂: SGTB, LCW have 波.

2.16.11: 皓: QTS has 浩.

2.19.2: 柴: HYYLJ, TWC, and QTS have 荊.

2.20.13: 踈: LMC has 散.
2.20.15: 向: QTS has 尚.

2.21.5: 館: LMC has 閣.

2.23–25: title: WMJJ and GKJ lack 戲. 東園: SGTB has 東閣.
2.23.5: 領: TSPH has 頭.
2.23.7: Supplying 與 from SSB, LCW and WMJJ for ZDC 興.
2.23.13: Supplying 慮 from LMC, TSPH for ZDC 象.

2.24.7: Supplying 野人野 from SSB and QTS for ZDC 野人也.
2.24.8: Supplying 漁父漁 from SSB and QTS for ZDC 漁夫魚.
2.24.9: 日: QTS has 自.

2.25.5: 靜: QTS has 淨.

2.27.5: 翮: SSB, SGTB, QZZ have 翰.

2.28.7: WYYH has 曖曖閨日暖.
2.28.12: 其: QZZ, LMC and QTS have 芳.

2.29.2: 翠: QTS has 雪.
2.29.3: Supplying 凝 from SSB and QTS for ZDC 疑.

2.29.7: 閑: WYYH has 開.
2.29.8: 造: SSB, WYYH have 變.
2.29.9: 止: SSB, SGTB, WYYH have 山.
2.29.13: 峙嶽: WYYH has 嶽峙.

3.2: In SGTB and LCW, the following note follows the title: 梵志體, "In the Fanzhi style."

3.4.3: 玩: QTS has 探.
3.4.4: 緣: TSJS has 尋.
3.4.6: 疑: WYYH has 言.
3.4.16: 問: WYYH has 聞.

3.5: title: WYYH has 過青谿水作.

3.7: title: HYYLJ, WYYH, and TRC have 入山寄城中故人. GXJ has 初至山中.
3.7.4: 空: GXJ has 祗.
3.7.7: 值: GXJ has 見.

3.8: title: 李: WMJJ, QZZ have 石.
3.8.4: 林: LCW has 城.
3.8.5: 未: SGTB has 木.

3.9.10: 故: SSB, LMC, QTS have 胡.
3.9.12: 馬: SSB has 騎.

3.10.5: 鄰: SSB has 陽.
3.10.8: 婦: SSB, QTS have 妾.

3.11: title: 川: WYYH has 水.
3.11.1: 光: WYYH, QTS have 陽.
3.11.2: 窮: TWC has 深.
3.11.7: Supplying 至 from SSB, WMJJ, WYYH, TWC for ZDC 立.
3.11.9: TWC has 羨此良閒逸.
3.11.10: 歌: SSB, WMJJ, QTS have 吟.

3.12: title: 中: LMC has 日。The SSB includes a second poem here under this title, 淇上即事田園 (7.26, a regulated verse).
3.12.5: 歸: SGTB has 新. 故: SSB, SGTB, WYYH have 舊.
3.12.8: 遠行: WYYH has 思遠.

3.13: title: 揖: QTS has 楫.
3.13.1: 閒: LCW, QZZ have 閑.
3.13.4: 林: TSPH has 籬.

3.14.1: 淨: SSB has 靜.
3.14.11: 已: SGTB, LCW, QTS have 一.

3.15: Preface: 無得: QZZ, LMC, QTS have 無礙.

3.16.1: 氏: WYYH has 兄.
3.16.7: Supplying 臥 from SGTB for ZDC 樹.
3.16.10: Supplying 洛 from SSB, WMJJ, and QTS for ZDC 路.
3.16.16: 宮: WYYH has 都.

3.17.10: 來: QTS has 勞.

3.18.4: 隸: SSB, WMJJ, QTS have 除.
3.18.16: 嗟: SSB has 詰.
3.18.18: 南山: SSB has 商山.

3.20: title: 校: SSB, QTS have 祕.
3.20.8: 澄: QZZB, LMC have 九.
3.20.14: 日: SSB, QZZ, LMC have 白.

3.21: title: SSB, QTS add 奉 to the beginning of the title.

3.22: title: taken from QTS

4.1.6: 掃: LCW, WMJJ have 歸.

4.2: title: Supplied from HYYLJ, WYYH, TWC, TSJI for ZDC 齊州送祖三. GSJ has 河上送趙仙舟.
4.2.3: 帳: HYYLJ, GXJ have 席. 已: TSJS has 忽.
4.2.8: 猶: GSJ, WYYH, TWC have 空.

4.3.1: Supplying 主 from WMJJ, QZZ and QTS for ZDC 王.

4.4: title: 文苑英華 has 送從叔游淮南座上成.
4.4.5: 自: WYYH has 為.

4.6.2: Substituting 拓 from SGTB and LCW for ZDC 魄.

4.7: title: Supplying title from HYYLJ, WYYH, TWC and XTS for ZDC title 送別.
4.7.5: 君: SSB, QZZ, GKJ, LMC have 金.

4.7.8: 京洛: HYYLJ, TWC have 京兆.
4.7.9: 臨長道: WMJJ, QZZ have 長安道. TWC has 長亭送.
4.7.14: 城: HYYLJ, TWC, QTS have 村.

4.9.8: 宸: SGTB, LCW have 衣.
4.9.10: 遂: QZZ, LMC have 逐.
4.9.12: Supplying 澹 from SGTB and GKJ for ZDC 瞻.
4.9.15: Supplying 質 from SSB, WMJJ, and QZZ for ZDC 資.
4.9.29: Supplying 壯心 from SSB and QTS for ZDC 功名.

4.10.4: 此: WYYH has 正.

4.11.10: 歇: SSB, WMJJ, QTS have 渴.
4.11.11: 少狎隱: QZZ has 狎小隱. QTS has 小狎隱.
4.11.16: 拂: WMJJ, QZZ, QTS have 歇.

4.12.9: 帳: WMJJ, GKJ have 悵. 畢: LMC has 別.
4.12.14: 時時: SSB, WMJJ, QTS have 時見.

4.16.3: 看: SSB, WMJJ, QTS have 刊.
4.16.5: Supplying 輕微祿 from WYYH for ZDC 偶輕人. SSB has 輕偶人. SGTB has 輕黴人.

4.17: title: Supplying 野 from SSB and QTS for ZDC 晚.

4.18.4: 驂: SGTB, LCW, WYYH have 弁. X: SGTB, LCW have 託.
4.18.5: 極: SSB, WMJJ, QTS have 平.
4.18.7: 竟: SGTB, LCW have 共. 北: SGTB, LCW have 曲.
4.18.10: 家臣: SSB, WMJJ, QTS have 佳辰.

4.19.3: 人里: QZZ, LMC, QTS have 仁里.
4.19.11: WYYH and SGTB for this line read 歸轍繼微官. LCW, GKJ read 車轍紬微官.

4.20.1: 中: WYYH has 日.
4.20.3: 暢: SSB has 揚.
4.20.4: Supplying 多秀 from WYYH and QTS for ZDC 好天.
4.20.5: Supplying 晨炊 from SSB, QZZ and QTS for ZDC 豐酌.
4.20.6: Supplying 後 from SSB, WMJJ, and QZZ for ZDC 雲.

4.21.2: 望: SSB, WMJJ, QTS have 然.

4.23.7: 溪: WYYH has 林.

4.23.10: 日: SSB, QZZ, QTS have 露.

4.24: title: 假: LMC, TSPH have 暇.
4.24.4: 柴: WYYH, TSJS, SSB, SGTB have 衡.
4.24.5: 時輩: TSJS has 儔類. 皆: WYYH has 今.
4.24.7: 嘉: LMC has 顧.
4.24.8: 齒: TSJS, TSPH have 過.
4.24.10: 目: WYYH, TSPH have 自.
4.24.16: 休: WYYH has 歸.
4.24.17: 飯: SSB has 飲.

4.25.7: Supplying 野 from SSB, WYYH, and QTS for ZDC 晚. SGTB and WMJJ have 田. 田: SGTB, WMJJ have 晚.

4.26.1: 人: LMC has 地.
4.26.10: 遶: SGTB has 充.
4.26.11: 思: WYYH has 鳴. 鳴: SSB, WMJJ, QTS have 悲; WYYH has 休.
4.26.15: 言: SYYH has 之.
4.26.16: 徇: SSB has 食.

5.1.5: 世: WYYH has 跡.

5.2.6: 心: WYYH has 交.
5.2.7: 志: WYYH, QTS have 意.

5.3: title: HYYLJ, WYYH have 寄崔鄭二山人.
5.3.1: 繁: HYYLJ has 京.
5.3.2: 出: WYYH has 事.
5.3.4: 早蒙: HYYLJ has 思逢; WYYH has 早逢.
5.3.7: 乏: HYYLJ has 知.
5.3.10: 霍: HYYLJ has 崔.
5.3.12: 盈: HYYLJ has 仍.

5.4.7: 未嘗肯: SSB has 未能皆.

5.5.12: Supplying 君 from SSB and LCW for ZDC 天.
5.5.17: 放: SSB has 忘.

5.7.2: 頗耽酒: HYYLJ has 耽嗜酒.
5.7.9–10: For this couplet, HYYLJ reads 白衣攜觴來，果不違老叟.

5.9.3: 宿世: TSJS has 當代.

5.9.7: Supplying 習離 from SGTB for ZDC 皆是.
5.9.8: 心: SSB, SGTB have 知.

5.10: title: 詠: HYYLJ, TWC, TSJS have 篇.
5.10.3: 為: HYYLJ, TSJS, QTS have 仍.
5.10.7: For this line, HYYLJ has 要人傳香粉; QTS has 邀人傳香粉.
5.10.13: 持謝: HYYLJ has 寄謝, TSJS has 寄言. 子: HYYLJ has 女.

5.11.5: 上: SGTB has 門.

5.12: title: Supplying 詠 from SSB.
5.12.19: 多: SSB has 苦.

5.15: title: SSB, SGTB, LCW have 早朝二首. The second poem of the group is the regulated verse 早朝 (9.14).
5.15.3: Supplying 鬱 from SGTB, LCW, and WYYH for ZDC 暗.
5.15.8: 金: WYYH has 重.

5.18.2: 城: LMC, QTS have 陽.
5.18.5: Supplying 椀 from SSB for ZDC 腕.

5.19.2: 水: WYYH has 中.

5.20.7: 決漭: WYYH has 訣別.
5.20.11: 何: TSJS has 同.

5.21: title: SSB, SGTB, LCW have 歎白髮二首. The second poem of the group is the quatrain 14.29.

6.4.1: Supplying 長安 from HYYLJ, YFSJ, and QTS for ZDC 長城.
6.4.6: 駐: CDJ has 驅.

6.5.13: Accepting the ZDC suggested emendation of 雀 for 箭.
6.5.17: Supplying 蒼茫 from WYYH and QTS for ZDC 茫茫.
6.5.27: 大: SSB, LCW, QTS have 天.

6.6.1: 天: QZZ has 大.
6.6.24: 先伐謀: TWC, WFSJ have 伐謀猷.

6.7.2: 去: TWC, YFSJ have 古.
6.7.4: 不見: WYYH, TWC, YFSJ have 忽值.
6.7.15: 驚: WYYH has 忽.
6.7.20: Supplying 及至 from WYYH, TWC, and QTS for ZDC 更聞. SSB SGTB, LCW have 更問. 遂: WYYH, TWC have 去.

6.15.8: 輕: LMC has 驚.

6.18: title: SSB and QTS have 李楫; SGTB, LCW have 季揖.

6.19.11: 霧: SSB has 露.
6.19.13: 幾: QTS has 紀.
6.19.15: 筆: SSB, SGTB have 草.

6.20.10: 遲遲: QZZ has 遙遙.

6.21.4: 半: SSB, SGTB, WMJJ have 共.

7.2: The first four lines occur in the YFSJ and other places as a song lyric, 崑崙子.
7.2.1: 所: WYYH has 處, YFSJ, WSTR have 去.

7.3.5: 暗: WYYH has 透.

7.5.6: 消: WYYH has 開.

7.7.6: Supplying 犬繞 from SSB for ZDC 火燒.
7.7.8: Supplying 間 from LCW for ZDC 聞.

7.8: title: 臺: WYYH, LMC have 堂.
7.8.4: 樹: QZZ, LMC have 徑.

7.10.8: 特: SSB, QTS have 持.

7.11: title: Supplying 慕容十一 from SSB, QTS for ZDC 慕容上.
7.11.5: 老年: SSB has 若思.
7.11.8: Accepting ZDC emendation of 姓 to 住.

7.14.4: 齊: LMC has 高.

7.15.7: 飛: SSB, QZZ, LMC have 無. 鳥: WMJJ, QTS have 雁.

7.16.1: 轉: GKJ has 積.

7.19.1: 清: WYYH has 晴.
7.19.4: 禽: WYYH has 雲.
7.19.7: 高: WYYH has 山.

7.22.5: 嫩: SSB, WMJJ, QTS have 綠.

7.23: title: SSB has 終南山行; WYYH has 終山行.
7.23.8: 水: WYYH, YFSJ have 浦.

7.24.5: 映: SSB has 披; QTS has 拔.

7.26.3: 日隱: SGTB has 白日.
7.26.6: 獵: SGTB, LCW have 田.

7.27.1: 愛: LMC has 對.
7.27.8: 達: LMC has 適.

7.28.1: 轉: SGTB, LCW have 傳; WYYH has 帶. 微: WYYH has 松.
7.28.4: 跪: LMC has 跽.

7.31.7: 林: LCW, WMJJ have 村.

7.31a: title: Taken from QTS.

7.32a: title: Taken from QTS.

7.33: title: 相: LMC has 見.
7.33.1: 麗: SGTB, LCW have 斜.
7.33.3: 前: QZZ, LMC have 頭.
7.33.4: 林裹: WMJJ, QTS have 樹下; LMC has 花下.
7.33.8: 當恕: WYYH has 常恐.

7.34.4: 深: WYYH has 空.

7.36: title: Supplying 東江 from QTS for ZDC 江東.

8.1.6: 攢: SSB has 藏.

8.2.1: 為: WYYH has 真.

8.4.6: 槿: SSB, SGTB have 堇.

8.5.2: 毛: SSB, SGTB, LCW have 茅.
8.5.5: 若剩住: WYYH has 數剩住; WMJJ has 苦難住; QZZ, LMC have 苦難剩.

8.6: title: Supplying QTS 同崔興宗送衡岳瑗公南歸 for ZDC 同崔興宗送瑗公.

8.6a: title: Taken from QTS.

8.7.8: 得: SSB, QTS have 是.

8.8: Title here is taken from the Qian Qi collection, replacing ZDC 留別錢起.

8.10.6: 經: LMC has 看. 春: LMC has 城.
8.10.7: 御: SSB, SGTB, LCW have 高.

8.11.8: Supplying 歲 from SSB, SGTB, and TSJS for ZDC 處.

8.12.5: Supplying 迴 from SSB, WMJJ, and QTS for ZDC 闊. 山: LMC has 江. 淨: SSB has 靜.

8.13.5: Supplying 到 from SSB, WMJJ, and WYYH for ZDC 別.

8.14.3: 枕: SGTB has 椀.
8.14.5: Supplying 沽 from WYYH and TSJS for ZDC 無.
8.14.7: 厭: WYYH has 怨.

8.15.2: Supplying 沙 from SSB, SGTB, and WYYH for ZDC 煙.

8.16.2: 地: SSB has 沚; WMJJ, QTS have 上.
8.16.8: 老: SGTB has 著, LCW has 着.

8.19.2: WYYH has 鄉音聽杜鵑 for this line.
8.19.3: 半: WMJJ, QZZ, GKJ, LMC, QTS have 夜.

8.20.6: Supplying 萋萋 from QTS for ZDC 淒淒.
8.20.7: 蘭陵: SGTB has 南陵.

8.21.2: 亦稀: WYYH has 欲飛.
8.21.6: 米: SSB has 菜.

8.25.1: 吹: WYYH has 笛.

8.26.1: WYYH has 郭外誰將送 for this line.
8.26.6: 起: WYYH has 薄.

8.27.4: Supplying 解 from WYYH for ZDC 念.

8.28.5: 宅: WYYH has 地.
8.28.7: 禰: SGTB has 你; SSB, WMJJ have 爾.
8.28.8: 為: TSJS, QZZ, QTS have 稱; WYYH has 看.

8.30.3: 盡: WYYH has 靜.

8.32: title: TSJS has 獵騎.

9.1.6: 梨花: SSB, YKLS have 花明.
9.1.8: 坐: YKLS has 步.

9.2.2: 間: WYYH has 寰.
9.2.3: 暢: SSB has 揚.
9.2.5: 澄波: SSB has 登陂.

9.3.2: 狂: WYYH has 往. 或: QTS has 止.
9.3.4: 林: WYYH has 陰.

9.4.7: 暮: LMC has 外.

9.6: title: HYYLJ, QTS have 初出濟州別城中故人.
9.6.2: 川: SSB, SGTB have 州.
9.6.8: 多: SGTB, WMJJ, QTS have 各.

9.8.1–2: WYYH has 銜命辭天闕，單車欲問邊.

9.9: title: HYYLJ has 春閨, QTS has 晚春歸思.
9.9.2: 羅: HYYLJ has 簾.
9.9.3: 鑪: HYYLJ has 淑.

9.10.5: 穿: QZZ, LMC have 藏.

9.12.5: Supplying 晚 from SSB, SGTB, LCW, and WMJJ for ZDC 曉.

9.13.2: Supplying 宮 from SSB, WYYH, and QTS for ZDC 春. 囀曙光: WYYH has 次第翔.
9.13.3: 欲: SSB, SGTB, QTS have 忽.
9.13.4: Supplying 哢 from LCW for ZDC 弄.
9.13.6: Supplying 排 from SGTB, LCW for ZDC 攀.
9.13.8: 思故鄉: WYYH has 始思鄉.

9.14.3: 烏: WYYH has 鵶.
9.14.5: 侍: WYYH has 召.

9.16.1: 吾: SGTB, LCW, GKJ have 愚.

9.17.8: 歸臨: SSB has 窺林.

9.18.2: Supplying 新 from SSB, SGTB, and QTS for ZDC 初.

9.19: title: 秦皇: SSB, WYYH have 始皇, SGTB has 秦始皇. 。十五: WYYH has 二十.

9.20.7: 常: SSB has 嘗.

9.21.2: 贊: QTS has 戴. 乘: WYYH, QTS have 宸.
9.21.8: 頃: WYYH has 畝.

9.22.2: 辰: SGTB, LCW have 晨.
9.22.5: Supplying 首 from SSB, SGTB, LCW, and WYYH for ZDC 闕.

9.24.5: 苦: WYYH, SGTB, LCW have 善.

9.25.2: Supplying 妻 from QTS for ZDC 棲.

9.27.1: Supplying 苐 from SSB, WMJJ, and QTS for ZDC 黻.

9.29: title: 吏部 added from WYYH.
9.29.4: 勸: WYYH has 助.

9.30.3: 占: WYYH has 瞻.

9.33.3: Supplying 禮 from LCW for ZDC 愷.

10.1.1: 塞: WYYH has 旬.
10.1.3: 仙: QTS has 千.
10.1.4: 迴: WYYH has 遙.
10.1.8: 重: QZZ, LMC, QTS have 玩.

10.2.2: 遙: LMC has 還.
10.2.3: 如: QZZ, QTS have 知.

10.3.3: Supplying 纔 from SSB, WYYH, and QTS for ZDC 總.

10.3a: title: Taken from QTS.

10.5.3: 天: WYYH has 重.
10.5.5: 色: YKLS has 影.
10.5.8: 向: LMC, YKLS have 到.

10.5b, 5c: titles: Taken from QTS.

10.7a: title: Taken from QTS.

10.8: preface: 類: LMC has 意.

10.9.3: 官: LMC has 客.
10.9.6: 天: LMC has 丹.

10.10.5: 皆知: SGTB, LCW have 猶能.

10.12.4. 欲: SGTB has 亦.

10.13: title: 中: GKJ has 居.
10.13.3: Supplying 豈 from SSB, WMJJ, and QZZ for ZDC 不.
10.13.5: Supplying 閑 from SGTB, LCW, and WMJJ for ZDC 堂. 蛩: WYYH has 蟲.
10.13.6: 聲: WYYH has 鳴.

10.14 title: 積雨: SSB, WYYH have 秋雨.

10.15.5: 迸: SSB has 晻。
10.15.6: 牀: SSB has 林。

10.16.1: 一向: QZZ, LMC have 四面.
10.16.5: 外: QTS has 上.
10.16.7: 著: WYYH has 看.
10.16.8: 老作: SSB, SGTB, QZZ have 作老.

10.16a: title: Taken from QTS.

10.17.1: Supplying 住 from SSB, WYYH for ZDC 往.
10.17.2: 旄: SSB, WMJJ, QZZ have 毛.
10.17.6: 彩: QTS has 蒼.

10.18.3: 看: SGTB has 君. 近: SBTB, LCW, WMJJ have 客. QTS has 遠.

10.20.3: 有: QZZ, LMC have 自.

Selected Bibliography on Wang Wei's works

Chen Tiemin 陳鐵民. *Wang Wei ji jiao zhu* 王維集校注. Beijing: Zhonghua shuju, 1997.

———. *Wang Wei lun gao* 王維論稿. Beijing: Renmin wenxue chubanshe, 2006.

———. *Wang Wei xin lun*. 王維新論. Beijing: Beijing shifan xueyuan chubanshe, 1990.

Chou, Shan. "Beginning with Images in the Nature Poetry of Wang Wei." *HJAS* 42.1 (1982): 117–37.

Hsieh, Daniel. "'The Nine Songs,' and the Structure of the 'Wang River Collection.'" *Chinese Literature: Essays, Articles, Reviews* 35 (2013): 1–30.

Iritani Sensuke 入谷仙介. *Ō I kenkyū* 王維研究. Sōbunsha, 1976.

Li Liangwei 李亮偉. *Han yong da ya: Wang Wei yu zhongguo wenhua* 涵泳大雅：王維與中國文化. Beijing: Zhonghua shuju, 2003.

Liu Shengjun 柳晟俊. *Wang Wei shi yanjiu* 王維詩研究. Taipei: Liming wenhua shiye gongsi, 1987.

Liu Weichong 劉維崇. *Wang Wei ping zhuan* 王維評傳. Taibei: Zhengzhong shuju, 1972.

Owen, Stephen. "The Formation of the Tang Estate Poem." *HJAS* 55:1 (1995): 39–59.

———. *The Great Age of Chinese Poetry: The High T'ang*. New Haven: Yale University Press, 1981.

Pi Shumin 皮述民. *Wang Wei tan lun* 王維探論. Taibei: Lianjing chuban shiye gongsi, 1999.

Tan Zhaoyan 譚朝炎. *Hong chen fo dao mi wangchuan: Wang Wei de zhutixing quanshi* 紅塵佛道覓輞川：王維的主體性詮釋. Beijing: Zhongguo shehui kexue chubanshe, 2004.

Tsuru Haruo 都留春雄, Yoshikawa Kōjirō 吉川幸次郎, Ogawa Tamaki 小川環樹, et al. *Ō I* 王維. Iwanami Shoten, 1958.

Wagner, Marsha L. *Wang Wei*. Boston: Twayne Publishers, 1981.

Wang Congren 王從仁. *Wang Wei he Meng Haoran* 王維和孟浩然. Shanghai: Shanghai guji chubanshe, 1983.

Wang Wei yanjiu 王維研究. Beijing: Zhongguo gongren chubanshe, 1992.

https://doi.org/10.1515/9781501516023-012

Warner, Ding Xiang. "The Two Voices of *Wangchuan Ji*: Poetic Exchange between Wang Wei and Pei Di." *Early Medieval China* 10–11.2 (2005): 57–72.

Yang Jingqing. *The Chan Interpretation of Wang Wei's Poetry: A Critical Review.* Hong Kong: The Chinese University Press, 2007.

Yang Wenxiong 楊文雄. *Shifo Wang Wei yanjiu* 詩佛王維研究. Taipei: Wen shi zhe chubanshe 1988.

Yu, Pauline. *The Poetry of Wang Wei: New Translations and Commentary.* Bloomington: Indiana University Press, 1980.

Zhang Qinghua 張清華. *Wang Wei nianpu* 王維年譜. Shanghai: Xuelin chubanshe, 1989.

Zhuang Shen 莊申. *Wang Wei yanjiu* 王維研究. Hong Kong: Wanyou tushu gongsi, 1971.

www.ingramcontent.com/pod-product-compliance
Lightning Source LLC
Chambersburg PA
CBHW021149160426
42812CB00078B/285